Droid™ 3

FOR

DUMMIES®

Droid™ 3
FOR
DUMMIES®

by Dan Gookin

WILEY

John Wiley & Sons, Inc.

Droid™ 3 For Dummies®

Published by
John Wiley & Sons, Inc.
111 River Street
Hoboken, NJ 07030-5774

www.wiley.com

Copyright © 2012 by John Wiley & Sons, Inc., Indianapolis, Indiana

Published by John Wiley & Sons, Inc., Indianapolis, Indiana

Published simultaneously in Canada

For general information on our other products and services, please contact our Customer Care Department within the U.S. at 877-762-2974, outside the U.S. at 317-572-3993, or fax 317-572-4002.

For technical support, please visit www.wiley.com/techsupport.

Wiley also publishes its books in a variety of electronic formats and by print-on-demand. Not all content that is available in standard print versions of this book may appear or be packaged in all book formats. If you have purchased a version of this book that did not include media that is referenced by or accompanies a standard print version, you may request this media by visiting http://booksupport.wiley.com. For more information about Wiley products, visit us www.wiley.com.

Library of Congress Control Number: 2011939650

ISBN 978-1-118-15721-3 (pbk); ISBN 978-1-118-19858-2 (ebk); ISBN 978-1-118-19857-5 (ebk); ISBN 978-1-118-19856-8 (ebk)

Manufactured in the United States of America

10 9 8 7 6 5 4 3 2 1

WILEY

About the Author

Dan Gookin has been writing about technology for over 20 years. He combines his love of writing with his gizmo fascination to create books that are informative and entertaining and not boring. Having written more than 120 titles with 12 million copies in print translated into over 30 languages, Dan can attest that his method of crafting computer tomes seems to work.

Perhaps his most famous title is the original *DOS For Dummies,* published in 1991. It became the world's fastest-selling computer book, at one time moving more copies per week than *The New York Times* number-one best seller (though, as a reference, it could not be listed on the paper's Best Sellers list). That book spawned the entire line of *For Dummies* books, which remains a publishing phenomenon to this day.

Dan's most popular titles include *PCs For Dummies, Word For Dummies, Laptops For Dummies*, and *Droid X For Dummies.* He also maintains the vast and helpful website www.wambooli.com.

Dan holds a degree in communications/visual arts from the University of California, San Diego. He lives in the Pacific Northwest, where he enjoys spending time playing video games indoors with his sons while they watch the gentle woods of Idaho.

Publisher's Acknowledgments

We're proud of this book; please send us your comments at http://dummies.custhelp.com. For other comments, please contact our Customer Care Department within the U.S. at 877-762-2974, outside the U.S. at 317-572-3993, or fax 317-572-4002.

Some of the people who helped bring this book to market include the following:

Acquisitions and Editorial

Senior Project Editor: Mark Enochs

Acquisitions Editor: Katie Mohr

Copy Editor: Rebecca Whitney

Editorial Manager: Leah Cameron

Editorial Assistant: Amanda Graham

Sr. Editorial Assistant: Cherie Case

Cover Photos: © iStockphoto.com / yewkeo;
© iStockphoto.com / higyou

Cartoons: Rich Tennant (www.the5thwave.com)

Composition Services

Project Coordinator: Nikki Gee

Layout and Graphics: Timothy C. Detrick
Sennett Vaughan Johnson, Lavonne Roberts,
Corrie Socolovitch

Proofreader: Kathy Simpson

Indexer: WordCo Indexing Services

Publishing and Editorial for Technology Dummies

Richard Swadley, Vice President and Executive Group Publisher

Andy Cummings, Vice President and Publisher

Mary Bednarek, Executive Acquisitions Director

Mary C. Corder, Editorial Director

Publishing for Consumer Dummies

Kathy Nebenhaus, Vice President and Executive Publisher

Composition Services

Debbie Stailey, Director of Composition Services

Contents at a Glance

Introduction *1*

Part 1: Droid, Droid, Droid *7*

Chapter 1: Thrice the Droid, Thrice the Fun 9
Chapter 2: Setup and Configuration 21
Chapter 3: The Droid 3 Tour 33
Chapter 4: The Keyboard-and-Text Chapter 49

Part 11: Basic Phone *65*

Chapter 5: Yes, It Can Make Phone Calls 67
Chapter 6: Advanced Phone Duties 81
Chapter 7: At the Sound of the Tone 91
Chapter 8: Your Address Book 99

Part 111: Nonverbal Communications *115*

Chapter 9: Don't Say It — Text It 117
Chapter 10: Mail of the Electronic Kind 127
Chapter 11: Fun on the Web 143
Chapter 12: Friends and Followers 155

Part 1V: Magical and Nontraditional Activities *165*

Chapter 13: There's a Map for That 167
Chapter 14: Picture This, Video That 181
Chapter 15: Your Digital Photo Album 193
Chapter 16: Music, Music, Music 205
Chapter 17: Even More Apps 217
Chapter 18: Behold the Android Market 233

Part V: Nuts and Bolts *245*

Chapter 19: No Wires Ever! 247
Chapter 20: Connect, Store, Share 259
Chapter 21: On the Road Again 271
Chapter 22: Personalize Your Droid 3 281
Chapter 23: Maintenance and Troubleshooting 295

Part VI: The Part of Tens 309

Chapter 24: Ten Tips, Tricks, and Shortcuts 311
Chapter 25: Ten Things to Remember 319
Chapter 26: Ten Worthy Apps...325

Index 331

Table of Contents

Introduction *1*

About This Book...1
How to Use This Book..2
Foolish Assumptions..3
How This Book Is Organized 4
    Part I: Droid, Droid, Droid..4
    Part II: Basic Phone...4
    Part III: Nonverbal Communications 4
    Part IV: Magical and Nontraditional Activities.................4
    Part V: Nuts and Bolts 5
    Part VI: The Part of Tens..5
Icons Used in This Book 5
Where to Go from Here...5

Part 1: Droid, Droid, Droid *7*

Chapter 1: Thrice the Droid, Thrice the Fun. 9

Droid 3 Liberation and Setup...9
    Looking in the box 10
    Obtaining and installing a MicroSD card 11
    Installing the phone's battery 12
    Charging the battery...13
A Look Around the Droid 3...14
    Knowing what's what on your phone...........................14
    Listening with earphones 17
    Using other, fashionable accessories..........................18
A Home for Your Phone...19
    Carrying the Droid 3 19
    Storing the Droid 3...20

Chapter 2: Setup and Configuration 21

Greetings, Human 21
    Turning on the Droid 3 for the first time 22
    Turning on the phone..23
    Waking the phone 26

Get Thee a Google Account!...27
   Creating your own Google account 27
   Setting up a Google account on your phone 28
Goodbye, Phone...29
   Snoozing the phone 29
   Controlling snooze options 30
   Hibernating the phone 30
   Turning off the phone..31

Chapter 3: The Droid 3 Tour 33

Basic Droid 3 Operations...34
   Using the soft buttons 34
   Manipulating the touchscreen 35
   Setting the volume 36
   "Silence your phone!"...36
   Going horizontal..37
There's No Screen Like Home..38
   Looking at the Home screen..38
   Viewing all Home screen panels 40
   Using Car Home..41
I've Been Working on the Home Screen..42
   Reviewing notifications...42
   Starting an application 44
   Using a widget 45
The App Menu...45
   Starting an app from the App menu 45
   Reviewing your most recently used apps...................................47

Chapter 4: The Keyboard-and-Text Chapter .49

Keyboard Mania...50
   Typing on the Multi-Touch keyboard...51
   Sliding out the sliding keyboard 53
Droid 3 Hunt-and-Peck 54
   Typing on your Droid 3 54
   Accessing special characters 56
   Choosing a word as you type 58
Text Editing 58
   Moving the cursor..58
   Selecting text 59
   Cutting, copying, and pasting text...61
Voice Input 62
   Dictating to your phone...62
   Controlling the Droid 3 with voice commands 63
   Uttering f**** words 64

Part II: Basic Phone **65**

Chapter 5: Yes, It Can Make Phone Calls. **67**

Reach Out and Touch Someone 67

Placing a phone call.. 68

Dialing a contact 72

Phoning someone you call often................................... 73

Someone's Calling!... 74

Receiving a call... 74

Using text message reply 76

Setting the incoming call signal volume 77

Who's Calling Who When?... 78

Dealing with a missed call 78

Reviewing recent calls... 79

Chapter 6: Advanced Phone Duties. **81**

Speed Dial.. 82

Multiple Call Mania.. 83

Receiving a new call when you're on the phone........... 83

Juggling two calls.. 84

Making a conference call 84

Send a Call Elsewhere 85

Forwarding phone calls... 85

Sending a contact directly to voice mail...................... 86

Fun with Ringtones... 87

Choosing the phone's ringtone 87

Setting a contact's ringtone... 88

Using music as a ringtone... 88

Creating your own ringtones....................................... 89

Chapter 7: At the Sound of the Tone **91**

Boring Ol' Carrier Voice Mail 91

Setting up carrier voice mail 92

Retrieving your messages.. 92

Visual Voice Mail 93

Setting up Visual Voice Mail 94

Accessing Visual Voice Mail 94

The Wonders of Google Voice 94

Setting up a Google Voice account.............................. 95

Adding your phone to Google Voice 95

Retrieving your Google Voice messages...................... 96

Chapter 8: Your Address Book **99**

Folks You Know 100
Presenting the Contacts app 100
Sorting the Contacts list 102
Searching contacts 103
A New Contact Is Born 103
Adding a new contact from the Recent Calls list 103
Creating a new contact from scratch 104
Importing contacts from your computer 105
Creating a new contact from a Maps location 106
Organize and Manage Your Peeps 107
Making basic changes 107
Adding an image for a contact 108
Setting the default phone number and e-mail address 109
Making a favorite 110
Creating a contact group 111
Sharing a contact 112
Removing a contact 112

Part III: Nonverbal Communications *115*

Chapter 9: Don't Say It — Text It **117**

Message for You! 117
Composing a new text message to a contact 118
Sending a text message when you know only
the phone number 121
Receiving a text message 121
Forwarding a text message 121
Multimedia Messages 122
Composing a multimedia message 123
Receiving a multimedia message 125
Message Management 125

Chapter 10: Mail of the Electronic Kind **127**

Mail Call! 128
Setting up a web-based e-mail account 128
Setting up an ISP e-mail account 129
You've Got Email 131
Getting a new message 131
Checking the Gmail inbox 131
Visiting the universal inbox 132
Reading an e-mail message 133
Make Your Own Mail 135
Composing a new electronic message 135
Starting a new message from a contact 137

Message Attachments 138
E-Mail Configuration... 139
   Creating a signature.. 139
   Configuring the manual delete option........................... 140
   Setting the default e-mail account 141

Chapter 11: Fun on the Web **143**
Behold the Web Page 144
   Viewing the web 144
   Visiting a web page 144
   Browsing back and forth.. 146
   Using bookmarks 146
   Managing multiple web page windows 148
   Searching the web... 148
   Sharing a page 149
The Perils and Joys of Downloading 150
   Grabbing an image from a web page 151
   Downloading a file.. 151
   Reviewing your downloads 152
Browser Controls and Settings 152
   Setting a home page 152
   Changing the way the web looks 153
   Setting privacy and security options 153

Chapter 12: Friends and Followers **155**
Droid 3 Social Networking... 155
   Adding a social networking account 156
   Managing your social networking accounts..................... 157
Your Digital Social Life.. 157
   Finding out what's going on 158
   Setting your status.. 159
   Uploading a picture 160
Various Social Networking Apps 161
   Using the Facebook app... 161
   Tweeting to other twits.. 162
   Exploring other social networking opportunities.............. 163

Part IV: Magical and Nontraditional Activities *165*

Chapter 13: There's a Map for That. **167**
Basic Map 167
   Using the Maps app 168
   Adding layers... 169
Where You At? 171
   Finding out where you are 171
   Sending your location to a friend 173

Find Things 174
    Looking for a specific addresses 174
    Finding a business, restaurant, or point of interest 174
    Searching for interesting places 175
    Locating a contact 176
The Droid 3 Is Your Copilot 176
    Getting directions 176
    Navigating to your destination 177
    Adding a navigation shortcut to the Home screen 178

Chapter 14: Picture This, Video That. 181
The Droid 3 Has a Camera 181
    Taking a picture 182
    Deleting an image immediately after you take it 183
    Setting the flash 184
    Changing the resolution 184
    Doing a self-portrait 185
    Shooting a panorama 185
    Setting the image's location 186
    Adjusting the camera 187
You Ought to Be on Video 187
    Recording video 187
    Setting video quality 189
    Taping a confession 190
    Making a video message 190
    Turning on the light 191

Chapter 15: Your Digital Photo Album 193
The Droid 3 Gallery 194
Image Organization 195
    Viewing albums in the library 195
    Creating a new album 196
About Those Thousand Words 197
    Tagging an image 197
    Finding an image location on a map 199
    Printing a picture 200
Picture Editing 200
    Cropping an image 200
    Rotating your pics 200
    Setting an image for a contact or as wallpaper 201
    Deleting an image 202
Share Your Pics and Vids with the World 202
    Using the Share button 202
    Uploading a video to YouTube 204

Chapter 16: Music, Music, Music **205**

The Hits Keep On Coming 205
    Browsing your music library 206
    Playing a tune 207
More Music for Your Phone 209
    Stealing music from your computer 209
    Buying music at the Amazon MP3 store 211
Organize Your Music 213
    Reviewing your playlists 213
    Creating a playlist 214
    Deleting music 215
Your Phone Is a Radio 215

Chapter 17: Even More Apps **217**

An Appointment to Remember 217
    Understanding the Calendar 218
    Browsing dates 218
    Reviewing your schedule 220
    Making a new event 221
Your Phone, the Calculator 223
No Need to Alarm You 224
Something to Read 225
    Reading with Google Books 226
    Using the Amazon Kindle app 227
Movies in the Palm of Your Hand 228
    Viewing vids on YouTube 228
    Renting movies 230
The Droid 3 Does Games 231

Chapter 18: Behold the Android Market **233**

Shop at the Android Market 233
    Visiting the Market 234
    Finding apps at the Market 235
    Getting a free app 236
    Buying an app 237
Manage Your Apps 238
    Reviewing your downloaded apps 238
    Sharing an app 239
    Updating an app 240
    Removing downloaded apps 240

Part V: Nuts and Bolts *245*

Chapter 19: No Wires Ever! .... .247
Wireless Network Access 248
Understanding the digital network................................ 248
Understanding Wi-Fi 248
Activating Wi-Fi 249
Accessing a Wi-Fi network 250
Share the Connection... 251
Creating a mobile hotspot 252
Tethering the Internet connection 253
Bluetooth Gizmos 253
Activating Bluetooth... 254
Using a Bluetooth headset.. 254
Fun with Wireless Printing 255
Printing to a Bluetooth printer...................................... 256
Using MOTOPRINT 257
Sharing with the Print to Retail option 258

Chapter 20: Connect, Store, Share. .... .259
The USB Connection 259
Connecting the phone to a computer 260
Configuring the USB connection 260
Disconnecting the phone from the computer............... 262
That Syncing Feeling 262
Synchronizing with doubleTwist 263
Doing a manual sync.. 264
Phone Storage Fun.. 266
Viewing Your Media Elsewhere 267
Making the HDMI connection 267
Doing the DLNA thing.. 268

Chapter 21: On the Road Again .... .271
Where the Phone Roams 271
Airplane Mode... 273
International Calling.. 275
Dialing an international number 275
Making international calls with Skype Mobile 276
Taking your Droid 3 abroad 278

Chapter 22: Personalize Your Droid 3 . . . .**281**

It's Your Home Screen 282
  Changing wallpaper 282
  Adding apps to the Home screen.. 284
  Adding an app to the Dock 284
  Slapping down widgets 285
  Creating shortcuts 285
  Rearranging and removing icons and widgets............................... 286
Droid 3 Security 287
  Finding the screen locks 287
  Removing the lock 288
  Creating an unlock pattern 288
  Setting a PIN.. 290
  Assigning your Droid 3 a password.. 290
Various Phone Adjustments.. 291
  Stopping the noise! 291
  Performing automatic phone tricks... 291
  Changing various settings... 292
  Setting the Double Tap Home
    Launch soft button function 293
  Using accessibility settings 294

Chapter 23: Maintenance and Troubleshooting **295**

Battery Care and Feeding 295
  Monitoring the battery.. 296
  Determining what is sucking up power.. 297
  Managing battery performance... 298
  Saving battery life 299
Regular Phone Maintenance 302
  Keeping it clean... 302
  Backing it up.. 302
  Updating the system... 303
Help and Troubleshooting... 304
  Getting help 304
  Fixing random and annoying problems 305
  Getting support 307
Droid 3 Q&A 307
  "The touchscreen doesn't work!" 307
  "The battery doesn't charge" 308
  "The phone gets so hot that it turns itself off!"............................... 308
  "The phone doesn't do Landscape mode!"..................................... 308

Part VI: The Part of Tens *309*

Chapter 24: Ten Tips, Tricks, and Shortcuts 311
    Quick Launch 311
    Sliding-Keyboard Menu Shortcuts.............................312
    In-Pocket Detection 313
    Contact Quick Actions 314
    Add Spice to Dictation 315
    Add a Word to the Dictionary...................................315
    Create a Direct-Dial Shortcut 316
    Create a Direct Text-Message Shortcut 316
    Find Your Lost Cell Phone..317
    The Task Manager 317

Chapter 25: Ten Things to Remember 319
    Lock the Phone on a Call 319
    Landscape Orientation 320
    Use the Arrow Keys...320
    Use the Keyboard Suggestions 320
    Things That Consume Lots of Battery Juice 321
    Check for Roaming 321
    Use + When Dialing Internationally 322
    Properly Access Phone Storage.................................322
    Snap a Pic of That Contact 322
    The Search Command 323

Chapter 26: Ten Worthy Apps 325
    AK Notepad 326
    CardStar 326
    Dolphin Browser...327
    Gesture Search 327
    Google Finance...327
    Google Sky Map..328
    Movies 328
    SportsTap 328
    Voice Recorder 329
    Zedge..329

Index *331*

Introduction

*D*on't be fooled: Just because the Droid 3 is a *smartphone* doesn't mean that it's harboring some form of insidious intelligence. There's no alien brain in the device. It isn't going to take over the world, though it can intimidate you — that is, until you understand and accept that it's *your* phone. The Droid 3 is a gizmo that helps make your life a heck of a lot easier.

This book, *Droid 3 For Dummies,* is your key to unlocking the potential of a device that may intimidate and frighten you. Don't worry: The advice here is friendly, formative, relaxed, and often irrelevant. The goal is to get you and your phone on speaking terms so that the two of you can better reach your full potential.

Now that I've written all that, this is the book's introduction, which few people read. (I honestly don't know why I'm still writing.) I know that because there's some good info in here and because every so often I read an e-mail where someone (not you, of course), says, "I couldn't find *blah-blah* in your book." Well, I write back, it's in the introduction. And they say, "But I didn't read the introduction." And I reply that they should. Because you're still reading, I know that person won't be you, so I'll stop writing about him, and instead I'll write:

About This Book

This book is a reference. I don't intend for you to read it from cover to cover. In fact, I forbid you to do so.

Though you're forbidden to read the book cover to cover, I remain steadfast in my admiration of your continued perusal of the introduction. Thanks.

Every chapter in this book is written as its own, self-contained unit, covering a specific topic about using the Droid 3 phone. The chapters are further divided into sections representing tasks you perform with the phone or explaining how to get something done. Sample sections in this book include

- Typing on your Droid 3
- Phoning someone you call often
- Setting up a Google Voice account
- Uploading a picture
- Creating a mobile hotspot

 ✔ Stealing music from your computer

 ✔ Dialing an international number

 ✔ Saving battery life

Every section explains a topic as though it's the first one you read in this book. Nothing is assumed, and everything is cross-referenced. Technical terms and topics, when they come up, are neatly shoved to the side, where they're easily avoided. The idea here isn't to learn anything. This book's philosophy is to help you look it up, figure it out, and get back to your life.

I'm serious: Get back to your life after you read a solution in this book. It's unhealthy to sit and read all the time. Play video games or complain about politics on a blog instead. These things are far more recreational than reading.

How to Use This Book

This book follows a few conventions for using your phone, so pay attention!

The main way you interact with your phone is by using its touchscreen, which is the glassy part of the phone as it's facing you. Buttons also adorn the Droid 3, all of which are explained in Part I of this book.

There are various ways to touch the screen, which are described in Chapter 3.

Chapter 4 discusses text input on the Droid 3, which involves using either the onscreen keyboard or the sliding keyboard. The Droid 3 also features the Swype onscreen keyboard for superfast text entry. And, when you tire of typing, you can always input text on your Droid 3 by dictation.

This book directs you to do things on your phone by following numbered steps. Every step involves a specific activity, such as touching something on the screen, as shown in this example:

3. Choose Downloads.

This step directs you to touch the text or item on the screen labeled Downloads. You might also be told to do this:

3. Touch Downloads.

Some phone options can be turned off or on, as indicated by a gray box with a green check mark in it, as shown in the margin. By touching the box on the screen, you add or remove the green check mark. When the green check mark appears, the option is on; otherwise, it's off.

The bar codes in the margins are there to help you install recommended apps. To install the app, scan the bar code using special software you install on the Droid 3. Chapter 18 discusses how to add software to your phone, and in Chapter 26 I discuss how to use the Barcode Scanner app to read bar codes.

Foolish Assumptions

Even though this book is written with the gentle handholding required by anyone who is just starting out or who is easily intimidated, I have made a few assumptions.

Number one: I'm assuming that you're still reading the introduction. That's great. It's much better than getting a snack right now or checking to ensure that you haven't left the iron turned on. And I congratulate you for not checking the TV to see which movie AMC is playing over and over again this month. You're a hero.

My biggest assumption: You have a Droid 3 phone by Motorola. Though you can use this book generically with any Android phone, it's specific to the things the Droid 3 can do.

In the United States, cellular service for the Droid 3 is provided by Verizon. Many things that the Droid 3 can do are based on the services Verizon offers, such as Visual Voice Mail or Backup Assistant, even though I don't have much to say about those features in this book.

I also assume that you have a computer, either a desktop or laptop. The computer can be a PC or Windows computer or a Macintosh. Oh, I suppose it could also be a Linux computer. In any event, I refer to your computer as "your computer" throughout this book. When directions are specific to a PC or Mac, the book says so.

The Droid 3 doesn't come with a MicroSD (memory storage) card installed. I highly recommend that you get one. In fact, get a high-capacity card, such as one that stores 16GB (gigabytes) or even 32GB of data. This book assumes in several chapters that you have and use the MicroSD card. And, the phone works better with a MicroSD card installed.

Programs that run on the Droid 3 are *apps,* which is short for *applications.* A single program is an app.

Finally, this book assumes that you have a Google account, but if you don't, Chapter 2 explains how to configure one. Do so. Having a Google account opens up a slew of useful features, information, and programs that make using your Droid 3 phone more productive.

Still reading? Good.

How This Book Is Organized

This book has been sliced into six parts, each of which describes a certain aspect of the Droid 3 or how it's used.

Part I: Droid, Droid, Droid

This part of the book serves as your introduction to the Droid 3. Chapters cover setup and orientation and familiarize you with how the phone works. Part I is a good place to start — plus, you discover things in this part that aren't obvious from just guessing how the phone works.

Part II: Basic Phone

Nothing is more basic for a phone to do than make calls, which is the topic of the chapters in this part of the book. The Droid 3 can make calls, receive calls, and serve as an answering service for calls you miss. It also manages the names of all the people you know and even those you don't want to know but have to know anyway.

Part III: Nonverbal Communications

The Droid 3 is about more than just telephone communications. Part III of this book explores other ways you can use your phone to stay in touch with people, browse the Internet, check your e-mail, do your social networking, exchange text messages, and more.

Part IV: Magical and Nontraditional Activities

This part of the book explores the nonphone things your phone can do. For example, your phone can find locations on a map, give you verbal driving directions, take pictures, shoot videos, play music, play games, and do all sorts of wonderful things that no one would ever think a phone can do. The chapters in this part of the book get you up to speed on those activities.

Part V: Nuts and Bolts

The chapters in this part of the book discuss a slate of interesting topics, from connecting the phone to a computer, using Wi-Fi and Bluetooth networking, and taking the phone overseas and making international calls to customizing and personalizing your Droid 3 and the necessary chores of maintenance and troubleshooting.

Part VI: The Part of Tens

Finally, this book ends with the traditional *For Dummies* The Part of Tens, where every chapter lists ten items or topics. For the Droid 3, the chapters include tips, tricks, shortcuts, and things to remember, plus a list of some of my favorite Droid 3 phone apps.

Icons Used in This Book

This icon flags useful, helpful tips or shortcuts.

This icon marks a friendly reminder to do something.

This icon marks a friendly reminder *not* to do something.

This icon alerts you to overly nerdy information and technical discussions of the topic at hand. Reading the information is optional, though it may win you a pie slice in *Trivial Pursuit*.

Where to Go from Here

Thank you for reading the introduction. I can offer you no prize other than the knowledge that you're one of the few humans on the planet to do so.

Follow these instructions now: Start reading the rest of the book, but not the whole thing, and especially not in order. Observe the table of contents and find something that interests you. Or look up your puzzle in the index. When these suggestions don't cut it, just start reading Chapter 1.

My e-mail address is dgookin@wambooli.com. Yes, that's my real address. I reply to all e-mail I receive, and you get a quick reply if you keep your question short and specific to this book. Although I enjoy saying Hi, I cannot answer technical support questions, resolve billing issues, or help you troubleshoot your phone. Thanks for understanding.

 You can also visit my web page for more information or as a diversion: www.wambooli.com.

Enjoy this book and your Droid 3!

Part I
Droid, Droid, Droid

The 5th Wave   By Rich Tennant

©RICHTENNANT

"You can do a lot with a Droid 3, and I guess dressing one up in G.I. Joe clothes and calling it your little desk commander is okay, too."

Text Messaging Market Accounts & sync settin... My Accounts

Settings Calendar Google Search Music

Browser Voice Search Contacts Gmail

In this part . . .

In Hollywood, the second movie is a *sequel*. Clever wags refer to the third film in a trilogy as a *threequel*, but usually by then the film gets a clever name or, at minimum, the *III* suffix. If history is any judge, generally the third film isn't the greatest thing. Fortunately, this rule doesn't apply to cell phones.

First came the Droid. Then came the Droid 2, which was really the Droid^2. (I pronounced it "Droid squared," but the Verizon Phone Store people didn't understand me.) Now there's the Droid^3, which is the Droid *three*, but it's also the Droid *cubed*, or Droid × Droid × Droid. Rather than dwell on frustrating mathematical concepts and strange Hollywood marketing, I decided to write this part of the book to help you get oriented to the Droid 3, a useful yet potentially intimidating device.

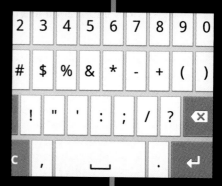

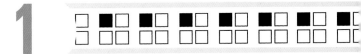

Thrice the Droid, Thrice the Fun

In This Chapter

▶ Freeing the phone from its box

▶ Installing the MicroSD card

▶ Charging the battery

▶ Familiarizing yourself with the Droid 3

▶ Obtaining optional accessories

▶ Taking the phone with you

▶ Keeping the phone in one place

*T*here's *once* for the first time and *twice* for the second time. The third time is *thrice,* which isn't as popular as *once* or *twice,* but it's still a legitimate word. *Fourse* isn't a word — yet. If it were, it would mean "the fourth time," but that's not important because the Droid 3 is merely the third phone in the Droid lineage.

Your Droid 3 cell phone adventure begins with a specific ritual: First is the out-of-the-box experience, followed perhaps by some initial assembly and then the gawking phase, where you physically examine the phone and ponder, "What exactly have I gotten myself into?" This chapter covers all this important information in a cheerful, friendly manner.

Droid 3 Liberation and Setup

Any electronic gizmo works better when you take it out of the box. Then there's perhaps some assembly involved, maybe some plastic cling sheets to remove, and then other setup activities. It all ends with a delightful, powerful, and intimidating device you can behold. I'll deal with the intimidating part later — for now, the topic is the liberation and physical setup of your new phone.

Looking in the box

You find several items inside the Droid 3 box, most of which are potentially useful. Even if you've already opened the box and strewn its contents across the table, take a few moments to locate and identify each of the following goodies:

- The Droid 3 phone
- Papers, instructions, warranty, and perhaps the booklet titled *Master Your Device* or even *Domina Tu Aparato*
- The phone's battery, which might already be inside the phone
- The phone's back (battery) cover, which also might already be on the phone
- The charger/data cable, which is basically a USB cable
- The charger head, which is a wall adapter for the charger/data cable

The Droid 3 may ship with a clingy, static plastic cover over its screen. Another plastic clingy thing might be on the back of the phone's screen — plus, a tiny plastic circle over the Motorola logo is stuck on the device's battery cover. The plastic thingies tell you where various features are located or how to install the battery. You can remove all the plastic clingy sheets at this time.

To remove the plastic from the back of the screen area of the phone, slide out the keyboard and then flip over the phone. Use the plastic tab to remove the plastic.

In addition to the items described in the preceding list, you might have been given a bonus package of goodies from whoever sold you the phone. If the outfit is classy, you have a handy little tote bag with perhaps the Verizon logo on it. Inside the bag, you might find these items:

- A smart-looking, leatherette belt-clip phone holster
- A micro-USB car charger
- A car windshield mount
- Headphones
- Even more random pieces of paper

The most important doodad is the phone itself, which might require some assembly before you can use it; refer to the next section for assembly directions.

You can safely set aside all this stuff until you put together the phone. I recommend keeping the instructions and other information as long as you own the phone: The phone's box makes an excellent storage place for that stuff and for anything else you don't plan to use right away.

If anything is missing or appears to be damaged, contact the folks who sold you the phone.

Obtaining and installing a MicroSD card

To complete your Droid 3 purchase, get some removable storage. It's provided in the form of a MicroSD media card — a tiny memory chip that you install in the phone. You need to install it because, unlike other popular phones, the Droid 3 doesn't come with a MicroSD card.

If the folks who sold you the phone didn't sell you a MicroSD card, run — don't walk — to a computer or office supply store and buy one. After you have the card, install it in the phone by following these steps:

1. **If necessary, remove the phone's back cover.**

   The phone may ship with its cover off. If not, flip over the phone and locate the thumbnail hole, by the Power Lock button at the top of the phone. Insert a fingernail into the hole and then pry the back cover from the phone. It takes effort, and the cover makes a horrid popping noise as it's peeled away and freed. That's normal.

2. **Insert the MicroSD card into the slot.**

   Use Figure 1-1 as your guide: The card inserts only one way; use the icon inside the phone to ensure that the MicroSD card is oriented properly.

   Unlike with other phones, you don't have to remove the battery to insert the MicroSD card.

3. **If you haven't yet installed the phone's battery, do so now: Skip to the next section.**

4. **Replace the phone's back cover.**

   Insert the bottom of the back cover into the lower part of the phone, as illustrated in Figure 1-1, to ensure that everything is lined up. Then close the back cover, from top to bottom. Press down the cover so that it makes an ugly crunching noise as it snaps into place.

Reattach back cover by
inserting this edge first.

Lift here to remove battery.

SIM card

Battery

MicroSD card

Battery contacts

Figure 1-1: Stuff inside your phone.

MicroSD cards come in a variety of capacities, measured in gigabytes (GB). The Droid 3 can use MicroSD cards in capacities of 8GB, 16GB, and 32GB. Yes, you pay more for the 32GB card, but if you plan to store lots of music, pictures, and video, the price is worth it.

✔ You don't need a MicroSD card to use your Droid 3, but the phone works better with one installed. This book assumes that you have a MicroSD card in your phone.

✔ Figure 1-1 also illustrates other items found inside the Droid 3: The SIM card and the battery are the most interesting.

✔ The Droid 3 uses its SIM card to access the cellular network. See the nearby sidebar "SIM card nonsense" for more information on this SIM card nonsense.

✔ If you're upgrading to the Droid 3 from another Android phone, simply remove the MicroSD card from that phone and install it on the Droid 3. By doing so, you save yourself a few bucks — plus, you instantly transfer your pictures, music, and videos from the old phone to the new one.

Installing the phone's battery

The Droid 3 comes disassembled inside the box. If the nice people who sold you the phone haven't already installed the battery, that chore befalls to you. Otherwise, remove the back cover and insert the battery; refer to the preceding section for directions.

SIM card nonsense

The Droid 3 features a SIM card, which sets the phone's identity. The SIM, which stands for Subscriber Identity Module, contains a special serial number used by your cellular provider to help identify your phone and keep track of the calls you make. Additionally, the SIM can be used to store information, such as electronic messages and names and addresses, though you probably won't use this feature on your Droid 3.

A typical way to use a SIM is to replace a broken phone with a new one: You plug the SIM from the old phone into the new phone, and instantly the phone is recognized as your own. Of course, the two phones need to use similar cellular networks for the transplant operation to be successful.

Install the battery by inserting it into the phone: Orient the battery as illustrated in Figure 1-1. Ensure that the battery's contacts are just above the spot where you insert the MicroSD card, as illustrated in the figure.

Insert the contacts edge of the battery first. Then lower the top part of the battery like you're closing the lid on a tiny box. Properly inserted, the battery is flush with the back of the phone.

After the battery is installed, replace the back cover: Insert the lower edge of the back cover first to line things up. Then press the back cover to shut it, enjoying the horrid crunchy sound it makes as it reattaches itself.

After the battery is installed, your next step is to charge it. Continue reading in the next section.

Charging the battery

The Droid 3 battery may have enough oomph in it to run setup at the Phone Store. If so, count yourself lucky. Otherwise, you need to charge the phone's battery. Don't worry about flying a kite and waiting for a lightning storm. Instead, follow these steps:

1. **Connect the charger head (the plug thing) to the USB cable that comes with the phone.**

   They connect in only one way.

2. **Plug the charger head and cable into a wall socket.**

3. **Plug the phone into the USB cable.**

   The charger cord plugs into the micro-USB connector, found at the phone's left side. The connector plugs in only one way.

As the phone charges, the notification light on the phone's front side may glow. When the light is orange-yellow, the phone is charging. When the light is green, the phone is fully charged.

The phone may turn on when you plug it in for a charge. That's okay, but read Chapter 2 to find out what to do the first time the Droid 3 turns on. You also may need to phone your cell provider for additional setup instructions before you turn on the phone.

> ✒ Wait until the notification light turns green before unplugging the phone from its power cable, especially the first time you charge the phone.

> ✒ The notification light uses three colors: amber for charging, green for fully charged, and red for warning that the battery is low.

> ✒ You can use the phone while it's charging.

> ✒ You can charge the Droid 3 in your car, using what was once called a cigarette lighter. Simply ensure that your car cell phone charger features a micro-USB connector and that it's designed for use with the Droid 3.

> ✒ The phone also charges itself when it's plugged into a computer by way of a USB cable. The computer must be on for charging to work.

> ✒ The Droid 3 charges more quickly when it's plugged into the wall as opposed to a computer's USB port or a car adapter.

> ✒ A micro-USB connector has a flat, trapezoid shape, which makes it different from the mini-USB connector, which is squat and slightly larger and used primarily on evil cell phones.

A Look Around the Droid 3

You don't have a second chance at a first impression, and the Droid 3's first impression is often intimidating. That's because it probably looks unlike any other phone you've ever owned or used. So take a few seconds to look around your new gizmo, using the helpful, non-intimidating advice found in this section.

Knowing what's what on your phone

Rather than call everything on the Droid 3 a *doodad,* consider poring over Figures 1-2 and 1-3. Figure 1-2 illustrates the names of all the useful things you find on the front of your new phone; Figure 1-3 does the same for the phone's rump.

The terms referenced in Figures 1-2 and 1-3 are the same as the terms used elsewhere in this book and in whatever pitiful Droid 3 documentation exists.

Power/Lock button   Speaker   Headphone jack

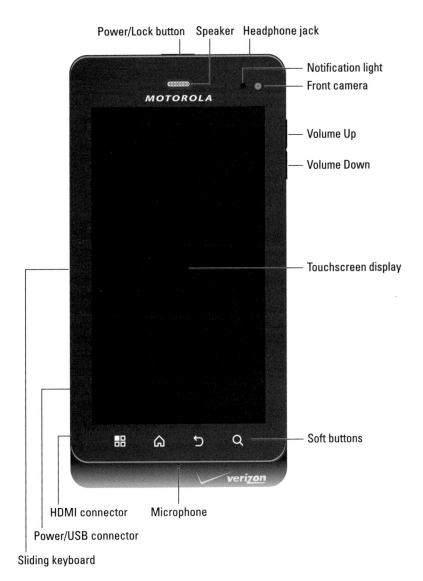

Notification light

Front camera

Volume Up

Volume Down

Touchscreen display

Soft buttons

HDMI connector   Microphone

Power/USB connector

Sliding keyboard

Figure 1-2: Your phone's face.

In addition to a front and back, your phone has a middle part, which slides out, as illustrated in Figure 1-4. It's a teensy keyboard that was added to the Droid 3 because of a shipping error from Lilliput. You slide the keyboard out to the left when facing the phone vertically or down when you orient the phone horizontally.

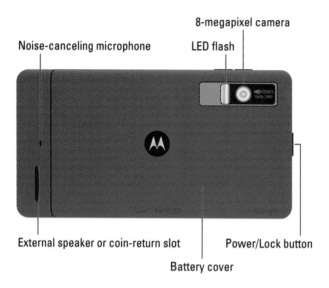

Noise-canceling microphone

8-megapixel camera

LED flash

External speaker or coin-return slot

Power/Lock button

Battery cover

Figure 1-3: Your phone's rump.

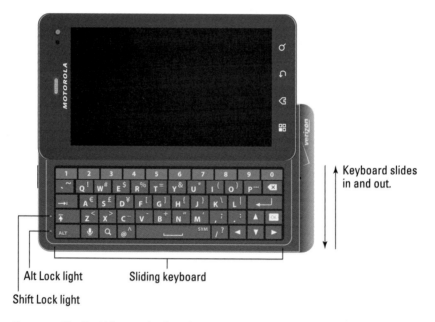

Keyboard slides in and out.

Alt Lock light

Sliding keyboard

Shift Lock light

Figure 1-4: The Droid 3 secret keyboard.

When you're done using the keyboard, you can slide it back into the phone, as shown in Figure 1-4.

- ✔ The phone's Power Lock button, which turns the phone off or on, is found atop the phone, as shown in Figures 1-2 and 1-3.

- ✔ The main part of the phone is the *touchscreen* display. You use the touchscreen with one or more of your fingers to control the phone, which is where it gets the name *touch*screen.

- ✔ The *soft buttons* appear below the touchscreen, as shown earlier, in Figure 1-2. They have no function unless the phone is turned on.

- ✔ Yes, the main microphone is on the bottom of the phone. Even so, it picks up your voice loud and clear. There's no need to hold the phone at an angle for the microphone to work.

- ✔ The phone's volume is adjusted by using the Volume buttons on the phone's right side (refer to Figure 1-2).

- ✔ The Volume button can also be used as a zoom function when using the Droid 3 as a camera. See Chapter 14 for more information.

- ✔ Sliding out the keyboard wakes up the phone when it has been sleeping. Refer to Chapter 2 for more information on why the phone gets tired and falls asleep.

- ✔ Officially, the keyboard is the *sliding keyboard.* Chapter 4 covers using the sliding keyboard.

- ✔ When the keyboard is out, the phone's touchscreen display switches to landscape orientation. You can read more about the phone's ability to orient the display into Landscape and Portrait modes in Chapter 3.

Listening with earphones

The Droid 3 most likely didn't come with earphones. That's not a reason to give up on the concept. In fact, the nice people who sold you the Droid 3 might have tossed in a set of earbud-style earphones for you to use. If not, well then, they weren't that nice, were they?

You're probably familiar with earbud-style earphones: The buds are set into your ears. The sharp, pointy end of the earphones, which you don't want to stick into your ear, plugs into the top of the phone.

Between the earbuds and the sharp, pointy thing is often found a doodle on which a button sits. The button can be used to mute the phone or to start or stop the playback of music when the Droid 3 is in its music-playing mode.

You can also use the doodle button to answer the phone when it rings.

A teensy hole that's usually on the back side of the doodle serves as the phone's microphone. You can use the earphones as a hands-free headset with the Droid 3. Because I'm half Italian, I love this option.

✔ You can purchase any standard cell phone headset for use with the Droid 3. Ensure that the headset features a microphone; you need to talk and listen on a phone.

✔ Some headsets feature extra Doodle buttons. These headsets work fine with the Droid 3, though the extra buttons may not do anything specifically.

✔ The earbuds are labeled R for right and L for left.

✔ You don't use the earphone's doodle to set the phone's volume, either in a call or while you're listening to music. Instead, the volume is set by using the volume-control buttons, found on the side of the phone, as illustrated in Figure 1-2.

✔ See Chapter 16 for more information on using your Droid 3 as a portable music player.

✔ Be sure to fully insert the earphone connector into the phone. The person you're talking with can't hear you well when the earphones are plugged in only part of the way.

✔ You can also use a Bluetooth headset with your phone, to listen to a call or some music. See Chapter 19 for more information on Bluetooth attachments for the Droid 3.

✔ Fold the earphones when you don't need them, as opposed to wrapping them in a loop: Put the earbuds and connector in one hand and then pull the wire straight out with the other hand. Fold the wire in half and then in half again. You can then put the earphones in your pocket or on a tabletop. By folding the wires, you avoid creating one of those Christmas-tree-light wire balls that would otherwise happen.

Using other, fashionable accessories

Beyond earphones, you should consider obtaining two other items to enhance your mobile communications experience. These items can be obtained at the Phone Store or online at www.verizonwireless.com in the United States.

The Multimedia Station

The *Multimedia Station* is a heavy base into which you can set your phone. The station features both USB and HDMI connections so that the phone can recharge inside the Multimedia Station, communicate with a computer, and use an external monitor or a TV.

The Multimedia Station makes a great home for the phone (see the next section) and can be used as a bedside alarm or as a helpful way to access the phone when it's deskbound.

The window mount

The *window mount* provides a cradle for the phone while you're in your car, though I assume it works on noncar windows as well. A suction cup attaches the cradle to the glass, which keeps the phone handy and visible while you perilously navigate the roads in your auto.

You'll probably want to buy the car charger adapter in addition to the window mount, especially if you plan to use the Droid 3 as your map/navigator on the road. See Chapter 13 for details.

Also see Chapter 3 for information on the Car Home screen, which appears whenever the Droid 3 is nestled inside the window mount.

An HDMI cable

Your Droid 3 can throw its sound and image onto a computer monitor or TV screen, but only if you obtain an HDMI cable. The cable plugs into the phone's HDMI hole (refer to Figure 1-2) and then into the monitor or TV. After choosing the proper HDMI input on the monitor or TV, you see the same image from the Droid 3 touchscreen displayed on the monitor or TV.

Chapter 20 offers more information on making the HDMI connection with your Droid 3.

A Home for Your Phone

There was no point in finding a home for your phone back when the Telephone Company bolted the thing to the wall. I remember hunting all over the house for our family's first cordless phone. That task was a pain when the batteries were dead and the phone's locator-ring trick didn't work. It was even more of a pain when you just *knew* that the phone was lost in the sofa cushions and Uncle Leroy was pulling some zzz's on the couch.

As portable as the Droid 3 is, I still recommend that you find it a permanent spot. Make a place for it when you carry it around, and have a spot where you keep the phone when it's not on your belt, in your pocket, or tumbling around in your purse.

Carrying the Droid 3

The compact design of the Droid 3 is perfect for a pocket or even the teensiest party purse. It's well designed so that you can carry your phone in your pocket or handbag without fearing that something will accidentally turn it on, dial Sri Lanka, or run up a heck of a cell phone bill.

Because the Droid 3 features a proximity sensor, you can even keep the phone in your pocket while you're on a call. The proximity sensor disables the touchscreen, which ensures that nothing accidentally gets touched when you don't want it to be touched.

- Though it's okay to place the phone somewhere when you're making a call, be careful not to touch the phone's Power Lock button (refer to Figure 1-2). Doing so may temporarily enable the touchscreen, which can hang up a call, mute the phone, or do any of a number of undesirable things.

- You can always store the Droid 3 in one of a variety of handsome carrying case accessories, some of which come in fine Naugahyde or leatherette.

- Don't forget that the phone is in your pocket, especially in your coat or jacket. You might accidentally sit on the phone, or it can fly out when you take off your coat. The worst fate for the Droid 3, or any cell phone, is to take a trip through the wash. I'm sure the phone has nightmares about it.

Storing the Droid 3

I recommend that you find a place for your phone when you're not taking it with you. Make the spot consistent: on top of your desk or workstation, in the kitchen, on the nightstand — you get the idea. Phones are as prone to being misplaced as are your car keys and glasses. Consistency is the key to finding your phone.

Then again, your phone rings, so when you lose it, you can always have someone else call your cell phone to help you locate it.

- The Multimedia Station makes a handsome permanent location for your Droid 3.

- I keep my Droid 3 on my desk, next to my computer. Conveniently, I have the charger plugged into the computer so that I keep the phone plugged in, connected, and charging when I'm not using it.

- Phones on coffee tables get buried under magazines and are often squished when rude people put their feet on the furniture.

- Avoid putting the Droid 3 in direct sunlight; heat is a bad thing for any electronic gizmo.

- Do not put your phone in the laundry (see the preceding section). See Chapter 23 for information on properly cleaning the phone.

2

Setup and Configuration

In This Chapter

▶ Setting up the Droid 3

▶ Turning on the phone

▶ Setting up a Google account

▶ Snoozing the Droid 3

▶ Hibernating the Droid 3

▶ Turning off your phone

*I*n the book *Going to the Moon For Dummies,* the chapter on the setup of the Saturn V rocket booster is quite brief. That's because only one configuration is possible: vertical. *Brain Surgery For Dummies* has no chapter on synchronizing brains or adding a new brain account. And, *Surviving a Shark Attack For Dummies* offers no information on Sleep mode. For this book on the Droid 3, that type of information is more important.

> Draw pattern to unloc

From the moment you first turn on your phone, it nags you with setup and configuration questions — that is, *if* you know how to turn it on. So first things first: This chapter covers how to turn on the phone and then how to set up and configure accounts. Also covered here are how to off the Droid 3 and the whole topic of Sleep mode.

Greetings, Human

One of the most basic operations for any electronic gizmo is turning it on. Don't bother looking for an on-off switch: The Droid 3 doesn't have one. Instead, it has the *Power Lock* button. This button can be used in several ways, which is why it's named Power Lock and why I had to write this section to explain things.

The Droid 3 doesn't turn on unless its battery is installed and fully charged. Sure, you can try turning on the phone without a battery, but it takes forever. See Chapter 1.

Turning on the Droid 3 for the first time

To turn on the Droid 3 for the first time, press the Power Lock button. You see the Motorola logo, the word *Droid,* and some fancy graphics and animation. After a moment, you hear the phone say, robotically: "Droid!" Don't be alarmed — it isn't the Robot Apocalypse. Not yet, at least.

The first thing the Droid 3 prompts you to do is to activate the phone for use on the cellular network. Odds are good that the fine folks at the Phone Store completed the activation for you. If not, follow the directions on the screen: Touch the Activate button to activate the phone on the Verizon network.

Touch the speaker button to hear the cheerful Verizon robot and look at the phone's dialpad at the same time. You use the dialpad to complete activation; follow the directions given to you by the cheerful Verizon robot.

If you're prompted to agree to the Motorola Terms of Service agreement, touch the check box on the screen. Touch the Next button.

The final step in the first-time setup process is to coordinate the phone with your Google account. By doing so, you share with the Droid 3 whatever information you have on the Internet for your e-mail and contacts on Gmail, appointments on the Google Calendar, and information and data from other Google Internet applications.

Generally speaking, fill in all requested information. Touch the Next button to continue.

Here are some hints to help you complete the setup process:

✔ See the later section "Creating your own Google account," if you don't yet have one.

✔ Use information from the later section "Setting up a Google account on your phone" if you skipped account setup when you first turned on the Droid 3.

✔ Touch a text field to summon the onscreen keyboard. Or, you can use the sliding keyboard to fill in the blanks. Chapter 4 covers using the keyboard if you need some tips or suggestions.

- Text typed into a password field appears briefly but is then replaced by black dots. The dots prevent prying eyes from stealing your password.

- If you're using the onscreen keyboard, touch the Done key when you finish typing. Then you can see the Sign In button, which is obscured by the onscreen keyboard.

- I recommend skipping the Backup Assistant: Touch the second Skip button again to confirm.

- Ensure that you activate all three of the services on the Location Consent screen: Touch the check box by each one and then touch the Agree button on the screen that appears. You need the location services to best use the phone's mapping and location abilities.

- Optionally, take the guided tour or just touch the Finish button.

- If you find any option that perplexes you, use this book's index to look up the item and glean more information.

- After the initial setup, you're taken to the Home screen. Chapter 3 offers more Home screen information, which you should probably read right away, before the temptation to play with the Droid 3 becomes unbearable.

Turning on the phone

Unlike turning on the phone for the first time, turning it on at any other time isn't that involved. In fact, under normal circumstances, you probably won't turn off the Droid 3 that much.

To turn on the Droid 3, press and hold the Power Lock button for a moment. You see the Droid 3 logo and animation, and the phone may scream "Droid!" at you. Eventually, you're plopped into an unlocking screen.

The primary unlocking screen is shown in Figure 2-1. To access your phone, use your finger to slide the Padlock icon to the right.

If you choose to add more security, you see one of three additional unlocking screens: pattern lock, PIN lock, or password lock.

The pattern lock is shown in Figure 2-2. Drag your finger over the dots on the screen, duplicating a preset pattern. Only after you drag over the dots in the proper sequence does the phone unlock.

Slide to the right to
unlock the phone.

Slide to the left to
silence the phone.

Phone Silenced icon

Figure 2-1: Unlocking the phone.

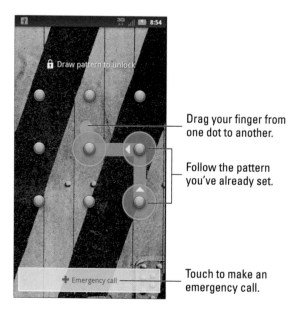

Drag your finger from
one dot to another.

Follow the pattern
you've already set.

Touch to make an
emergency call.

Figure 2-2: Tracing the phone's security pattern.

Another type of unlocking screen uses a *PIN,* or secret number, which must be typed before you're allowed access to the phone. Use the keypad, shown in Figure 2-3, to type the number. Touch the Enter key to accept.

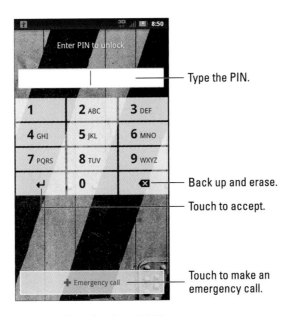

Figure 2-3: Type the phone's PIN.

You may also see a password unlock screen, where you use the onscreen keyboard to type a password, just as you type a password to get into your computer or log in to a website.

Eventually, you see the Home screen, which is where you control the phone, run applications, and do all sorts of other interesting things. The Home screen is covered in Chapter 3.

- ✔ After unlocking the phone, you may hear some alerts or see notifications. These messages inform you of various activities taking place in the phone, such as new e-mail, scheduled appointments, updated apps, and more. See Chapter 3 for information on notifications.

- ✔ Even if the phone has a security pattern, PIN, or password, you can still make emergency calls by touching the Emergency Call button.

- ✔ For information on turning off the phone, see the section "Turning off the phone," at the end of this chapter.

Waking the phone

Most of the time, you don't turn off your phone. Instead, the phone does the electronic equivalent of falling asleep. Either the phone falls asleep on its own (after you ignore it for a while) or you put it to sleep by singing it a lullaby or following the information in the section "Snoozing the phone," later in this chapter.

In Sleep mode, the phone is still on, and it can still receive calls (as well as e-mail and other notifications), but the touchscreen is turned off. See Chapter 5 for specifics on how an incoming call wakes up the phone.

When the phone isn't ringing, you can wake it at any time by pressing the Power Lock button. A simple, short press is all that's needed. The phone awakens, yawns, and turns on the touchscreen display, and you can then unlock the phone as described in the preceding section.

✔ Touching the touchscreen when the screen is off doesn't wake up the phone.

✔ Loud noises don't wake up the phone.

✔ The phone doesn't snore while it's sleeping.

✔ See the later section "Snoozing the phone" for information on manually putting the phone to sleep.

✔ When the Droid 3 is playing music, which it can do while the phone is sleeping, information about the song appears on the lock screen (not shown in Figure 2-1). Touch that information to see controls to play and pause or to skip to the next or previous song. See Chapter 16 for more information on using the Droid 3 as a portable music player.

There's an Android in your phone

You might see or hear the term *Android* used in association with your phone. That's because your phone, like your computer, has an *operating system* — the main program in charge of a computer's hardware. The operating system controls everything. For the Droid 3, the operating system is *Android*.

The Android operating system was developed by Google. Well, actually, it was started by another company that Google gobbled. Anyway: Android is based on the popular Linux operating system, used to power desktop computers and larger, more expensive computers all over the world. Android offers a version of Linux that's customized for mobile devices, such as the Droid 3, but also for other cell phone brands that I can't recall right now.

Because the Droid 3 uses the Android operating system, your phone has access to thousands of software programs. The process of putting those programs on your phone is covered in Chapter 18.

Get Thee a Google Account!

You absolutely need to have a Google account to use with your Droid 3 phone. Perhaps it's the big *with Google*™ hint on the phone's back cover that leads me to write that statement. Or it might be that the phone initially begs you to set things up with a Google account. Whatever. If you don't already have a Google account, set one up right now by following my advice in this section.

Creating your own Google account

If you don't already have a Google account, run — don't walk or mince — to a computer and follow these steps to create your own Google account:

1. **Open the computer's web browser program.**

2. **Visit the main Google page at `www.google.com`.**

   Type **www.google.com** into the web browser's Address box.

3. **Click the Sign In link.**

   Another page opens where you can log in to your Google account, but you don't have a Google account, so:

4. **Click the link to create a new account.**

   The link is typically found beneath the text boxes where you would log in to your Google account. As I write this chapter, the link is titled Create an Account Now.

5. **Continue heeding the directions until you've created your own Google account.**

Eventually, your account is set up and configured. I recommend that you log off and then log back on to Google, just to ensure that you did everything properly. Also create a bookmark for your account's Google page: Pressing Ctrl+D or Command+D does that job in just about any web browser.

Continue reading in the next section for information on synchronizing your new Google account with the Droid 3.

✔ A Google account is free. Google makes zillions of dollars by selling Internet advertising, so it doesn't charge you for your Google account or any of the fine services it offers.

✔ The Google account gives you access to a wide array of free services and online programs. They include Gmail for electronic messaging, Calendar for scheduling and appointments, and an account on YouTube, along with Google Finance, blogs, Google Buzz, and other features that are also instantly shared with your phone.

✔ Information on using the various Google programs on your phone is covered throughout this book — specifically, in Part IV.

Setting up a Google account on your phone

If you haven't yet configured a Google account, follow the steps in the preceding section and then continue with these steps:

1. **Go to the Home screen.**

   The Home screen is the main Droid 3 screen. You can always get there by pressing the Home soft button, found at the bottom of the touchscreen.

2. **Touch the Launcher button.**

   The Launcher button is found to the lower right of the Home screen. Touching this button displays the App menu, which shows icons representing every app (application or program) installed on your phone.

3. **Swipe the list of program icons to locate the My Accounts icon.**

   Swipe the list left and right by using your finger; touch the screen and slide your finger to the right, which displays the next panel of apps.

4. **Touch the Add Account button.**

5. **Choose Google.**

6. **Read the screen and touch the Next button.**

7. **Because you've already read the preceding section and have created your Google account on a computer, touch the Sign In button.**

8. **Touch the Username text box.**

   The onscreen keyboard appears, though you can also pull out the sliding keyboard and use it instead.

9. **Type your Google account username.**

10. **Touch the Password text box.**

11. **Type your Google account password.**

12. **Touch the Sign In button.**

    If you need to, touch the Done button on the onscreen keyboard so that you can find the Sign In button.

    Wait while Google contacts your account and synchronizes any information. It takes longer when you have more information to synchronize.

13. **Ensure that check marks appear by the all the Data & Synchronization options.**

    If they don't, touch the box to place a green check mark by each option. You want the phone to completely synchronize all your Google account information.

14. **Touch the Finish button.**

15. **Touch the Finish Setup button.**

You're done.

You return to the Setup Accounts screen. Press the Home soft button to return to the Home screen.

✔ If you change your Google password and forget to tell the phone about it, you see an alert notification, as shown in the margin. Pull down the notifications and choose Sign In Error for your Google account. Follow the directions on the screen to update your Google password.

✔ See Chapter 3 for more information about the Home screen and the App menu.

✔ Other accounts can be synchronized with your Droid 3, such as Facebook, Twitter, and Skype. Various chapters throughout this book explain how to configure these accounts.

Goodbye, Phone

You can dismiss your Droid 3 from existence in one of three ways. The first way is to put the phone to sleep, to *snooze* it. The second is to turn off the phone. The third involves a flyswatter, a shaved goat, and some crème fraiche, but it's a little too racy for this book.

Snoozing the phone

To snooze the phone, press and release the Power Lock button. No matter what you're doing, the phone's touchscreen display turns off. The phone itself isn't off, but the touchscreen display turns off and ignores your touches. The phone enters a low-power state to save battery life and also to relax.

✔ You can snooze the phone while you're making a call. Simply press and release the Power Lock button. The call stays connected, but the display is turned off.

✔ Snooze mode lets you keep talking on the phone while you put it in your pocket. When the phone is in Snooze mode, your pocket is in no danger of accidentally hanging up or muting it in the middle of a call.

✔ The Droid 3 will probably spend most of its time in Snooze mode.

✔ Snoozing does not turn off the phone; you can still receive calls while the phone is somnolent.

✔ Any timers or alarms you set are still activated when the phone is snoozing, and music continues to play. See Chapter 17 for information on setting timers and alarms; Chapter 16 covers playing music on the Droid 3.

Controlling snooze options

There's no need to manually snooze your Droid 3. That's because it has a built-in time-out: After a period of inactivity, or boredom, the phone snoozes itself automatically using the same techniques honed by high school algebra teachers.

You have control over the snooze timeout value, which can be set anywhere from 15 seconds to 30 minutes. Obey these steps:

1. **At the Home screen, press the Menu soft button.**
2. **Choose Settings.**
3. **Choose Display.**
4. **Choose Screen Timeout.**
5. **Choose a timeout value from the list that's provided.**

   The standard value is 1 minute.

6. **Press the Home soft button to return to the Home screen.**

When you don't touch the screen, or you aren't using the phone, the sleep timer starts ticking. About ten seconds before the timeout value you set (refer to Step 5), the touchscreen dims. Then the Droid 3 goes to sleep. If you touch the screen before then, the sleep timer is reset.

Hibernating the phone

The Droid 3 has another sleep option, a type of Sleep mode that's deeper than regular Sleep mode. I call it *hibernation* because it's similar to the Hibernation mode found on Windows computers. On your Droid 3, however, it's called Sleep, which is utterly confusing, but that's the term they use.

The Hibernation-Sleep mode puts the phone into a very low-power state but doesn't shut it all the way down. The advantage is that the Droid 3 turns itself on faster the next time you press and hold the Power Lock button.

Here's how to put the phone into Hibernation-Sleep mode:

1. **Press and hold the Power Lock button.**

   Eventually, you see the Phone Options menu, shown in Figure 2-4.

2. **Choose the Sleep item.**

   The phone seemingly turns itself off, but it's hibernating.

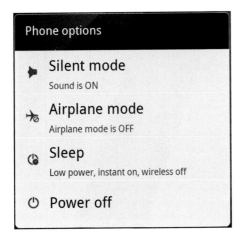

Figure 2-4: The Phone Options menu.

If you change your mind and don't want to hibernate the phone, press the Back soft button to cancel.

The Droid 3 cannot receive phone calls while it's in Hibernation-Sleep mode, but it can be turned on quickly: Press and hold the Power Lock button. The phone snaps back to life a lot faster than had you just turned off the phone. (See the next section.)

Hibernation-Sleep mode is ideal for "turning off the phone" when you're traveling by air. See Chapter 21.

Turning off the phone

To turn off your phone, press and hold the Power Lock button and choose the item Power Off from the Phone Options menu, shown in Figure 2-4. You see some animation as the phone shuts itself off. Eventually, the touchscreen goes dark.

The phone doesn't receive calls when it's turned off. Calls go instead to voice mail. See Chapter 7 for more information on voice mail.

The Droid 3 Tour

In This Chapter

▶ Understanding the soft buttons
▶ Working the touchscreen
▶ Changing the phone's volume
▶ Entering Vibration or Silent mode
▶ Using the phone horizontally
▶ Viewing Home screen panels
▶ Checking notifications
▶ Running applications and working widgets
▶ Accessing recently used apps

*S*imple devices need no fancy introductions. You don't need a diagram describing the items found on a pencil or a full-length chapter describing how a hammer operates, and I don't believe anyone needs a book to tell them which end of the cat eats the food and which end uses the litter box. Such simplicity is absent when it comes to the modern cell phone.

Complex and frightening devices such as the Droid 3 require the proper orientation. Despite the rapid, forgettable orientation you were given at the Phone Store, you'll need more info. To sate this desire, I present this full-size, chapter-long reference that shows you what's what on your phone and how some basic things work.

Basic Droid 3 Operations

The Droid 3 has its own way of doing things, probably different from any other phone you've owned. Further, you'll see some new terms and names over and over. Even if you think you know this basic stuff, consider this your familiarization and orientation section.

Using the soft buttons

Below the touchscreen are four buttons labeled with four icons. They're *soft buttons,* and they perform specific functions no matter what you're doing on the phone. Table 3-1 lists the soft buttons' functions in order, from left to right.

Table 3-1		Droid 3 Soft Buttons		
Button	*Name*	*Press Once*	*Press Twice*	*Press and Hold*
■	Menu	Display menu	Dismiss menu	Nothing
🏠	Home	Go to Home screen	Double Tap Home Launch function	Recent applications
←	Back	Go back, close, dismiss keyboard	Nothing	Nothing
🔍	Search	Open phone-and-web search	Nothing	Voice Actions menu

Not every button always performs the actions listed in Table 3-1. For example, if there's no menu to open, pressing the Menu soft button does nothing.

Pressing the Home soft button always takes you to the primary Home screen panel (the center one) — unless you're already viewing the panel, in which case pressing the Home soft button displays an overview of all five Home screen panels. See the later section "Viewing all Home screen panels" for details.

When you press the Home button twice, you activate the Double Tap Home Launch feature. It's normally configured to do nothing, but you can direct the phone to run one of a handful of popular apps or perform special activities by activating this function. Refer to Chapter 22 for more information.

The soft buttons can still be used when the sliding keyboard is extended. Also, buttons on the sliding keyboard duplicate the functions of the Search and Back soft buttons.

Various sections throughout this book give examples of using the soft buttons. Their icons appear in this book's margins where relevant.

Manipulating the touchscreen

The touchscreen works in combination with one or two of your fingers. You can choose which fingers to use or be adventurous and try using the tip of your nose, but touch the touchscreen you must. Choose among several techniques:

Touch: In this simple operation, you touch the screen. Generally, you're touching an object such as a program icon or a control such as a gizmo you use to slide something around. You might also see the term *press* or *tap*.

Double-tap: Touch the screen in the same location twice. A double-tap can be used to zoom in on an image or a map, but it can also zoom out. Because of the double-tap's dual nature, I recommend using the pinch or spread operation instead.

Long-press: Touch and hold part of the screen. Some operations on the Droid 3, such as moving an icon on the Home screen, begin with the long-press.

Swipe: When you swipe, you start with your finger in one spot and then drag it to another spot. Usually, a swipe is up, down, left, or right, which moves displayed material in the direction you swipe your finger. A swipe can be fast or slow. It's also called a *flick*.

Pinch: A pinch involves two fingers, which start out separated and then are brought together. This effect is used to reduce an image or a map. The pinch is used to zoom out.

Spread: In the opposite of a pinch, you start with your fingers together and then spread them. The spread is used to zoom in.

Rotate: Use two fingers to twist around a central point on the touchscreen, which has the effect of rotating an object on the screen. If you have trouble with this operation, pretend that you're turning the dial on a safe.

You cannot use the touchscreen while wearing gloves, unless they're gloves specially designed for using electronic touchscreens, such as the gloves that Batman wears.

Setting the volume

The phone's volume controls are found on the right side of the phone as it's facing you. Press the Volume Up button to raise the volume. Press the Volume Down button to lower the volume.

A volume control works for whatever noise the phone is making when you use it: When you're on a call, the Volume buttons set the level of the call. When you're listening to music or watching a video, the Volume buttons set the media volume.

The volume can be preset for the phone, media, alarms, and notifications. See Chapter 22 for information.

"Silence your phone!"

You cannot be a citizen of the 21st century and not have heard the admonition "Please silence your cell phones." The quick way to obey this command with your Droid 3 phone is to keep pressing the Volume Down button until the phone vibrates. What you're doing is setting the phone to Silent and Vibration modes.

The Droid 3 can also be silenced by a swipe of your finger. Obey these steps:

1. **Wake up the phone.**

    Obviously, if the phone is turned off, you have no need to turn it on just to make it silent. So assuming that your phone is snoozing, press the Power Lock button to see the unlock screen (refer to Figure 2-1, in Chapter 2).

2. **Slide the Silencer button to the left.**

    You're good.

Finally, you can thrust the Droid 3 into Silent mode by pressing and holding the Power Lock button. From the Phone Options menu, choose Silent mode.

 ✔ When the phone is silenced and in Vibration mode, the Vibration icon appears on the status bar, as shown in the margin.

 ✔ You make the phone noisy again by undoing either step in this section.

 ✔ The phone doesn't vibrate if you turn off that option. See Chapter 22.

 ✔ Also see Chapter 22 for various other methods of silencing the phone.

Going horizontal

The Droid 3 features an *accelerometer* gizmo. It's used by various apps to determine in which direction the phone is pointed or whether you've reoriented the phone from an upright to a horizontal position.

The easiest way to see how the vertical-horizontal orientation feature works is to view a web page on your Droid 3. Obey these steps:

1. Touch the Browser app on the Home screen.

The Droid 3 launches its web browser program, venturing out to the Internet. Eventually, the browser's first page, the *home page,* appears on the touchscreen.

2. Tilt the Droid 3 to the left.

As shown in Figure 3-1, the web page reorients itself to the new, horizontal way of looking at the web. For some applications, it's truly the best way to see things.

Portrait
orientation

Landscape
orientation

Figure 3-1: Vertical and horizontal orientations.

3. Tilt the phone upright again.

The web page redisplays itself in its original, upright mode.

You can also tilt the phone to the right to view the touchscreen in Landscape mode. Either way, the phone displays a web page horizontally, though it's more difficult to use the sliding keyboard when the phone is tilted to the right.

Oh, and don't bother turning the phone upside down and expect the image to flip that way, though some applications may delight you by supporting this feature.

✔ Landscape mode is entered regardless of the phone's orientation when you extend the sliding keyboard. See Chapter 4 for more information on the sliding keyboard.

✔ See Chapter 11 for more information on using your phone to browse the web.

✔ Some applications switch the view from portrait to landscape orientation when you tilt the phone. Most applications, however, are fixed to portrait orientation. Other applications, however, appear only in portrait or landscape orientation, such as games.

 ✔ A useful application for demonstrating the Droid 3 accelerometer is the game *Labyrinth*. It can be purchased at the Android Market, or a free version, *Labyrinth Lite,* can be downloaded. See Chapter 18 for more information on the Android Market.

There's No Screen Like Home

The first thing you see after you unlock your Droid 3 is the *Home screen*. It's the place to go whenever you end a phone call or quit an app, or when you press the Home soft button. Knowing how to work the Home screen is the key to getting the most from your Droid 3.

Looking at the Home screen

The primary Home screen panel is shown in Figure 3-2. The panel has a few things to notice:

status bar: The top of the Home screen is a thin, informative strip that I call the *status bar.* It contains notification icons and status icons, plus the current time.

notifications: These icons come and go, depending on what happens in your digital life. For example, a new notification icon appears whenever you receive a new e-mail message or have a pending appointment. The section "Reviewing notifications," later in this chapter, describes how to deal with notifications.

Phone status: This type of icon represents the phone's current condition, such as the type of network it's connected to, signal strength, and battery status, as well as whether the speaker has been muted or a Wi-Fi network connected, for example.

Status bar

Notifications   Phone status

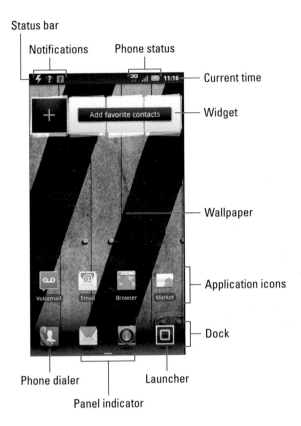

— Current time

— Widget

— Wallpaper

— Application icons

— Dock

Phone dialer   Launcher

Panel indicator

Figure 3-2: The Home screen.

widget: This teensy program can display information, let you control the phone, or access features. Touching a widget can manipulate a phone feature, access a program, or do something purely amusing. You can read more about widgets in Chapter 22.

application icon: The meat of the meal on the Home screen plate is the application icon. Touching this icon runs its program, or *app.*

Dock: The bottom of every Home screen panel contains the same four icons in the *Dock* area. You can change the first three icons; the fourth one is the Launcher, which cannot be changed.

Dialer: It's an application icon, but you use the Dialer, dwelling on the Dock, to make phone calls. It's kind of a big deal.

Launcher: Touching the Launcher button displays the App menu, a paged list of all apps installed on your phone. The section "The App Menu," later in this chapter, describes how it works.

panel indicator: Five panels are on the Home screen, and the panel indicator shows you which one you're viewing. See the next section for more information about Home screen panels.

The terms used in this section describe items on the Home screen and are used throughout this book, as well as in whatever scant Droid 3 documentation exists. Specific directions for using individual Home screen gizmos are found throughout this chapter.

- ✔ The Home screen changes to horizontal, or *landscape,* orientation, but only when you extend the sliding keyboard.

- ✔ The Home screen is entirely customizable. You can add and remove icons from the Home screen, add widgets and shortcuts, and even change the wallpaper images. See Chapter 22 for more information.

- ✔ Touching part of the Home screen that doesn't feature an icon or a control does nothing — unless you're using the *live wallpaper* feature. In that case, touching the screen changes the wallpaper in some way, depending on the wallpaper that's selected. You can read more about live wallpaper in Chapter 22.

Viewing all Home screen panels

And now, the secret: The Home screen is five times wider than the one you see on the front of your Droid 3. The Home screen has left and right wings, as illustrated in Figure 3-3.

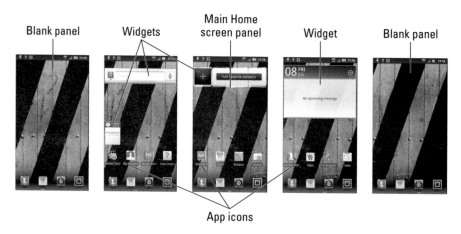

Figure 3-3: All Home screens.

The Home screen panels give you more opportunities to place app icons and widgets on the Home screen. You switch between them by swiping your finger left or right across the touchscreen display. The Home screen slides over one panel in whichever direction you swipe.

For an overview of all five Home screen panels, press the Home soft button twice. The overview is illustrated in Figure 3-4. Touch a Home screen panel thumbnail to visit the panel directly.

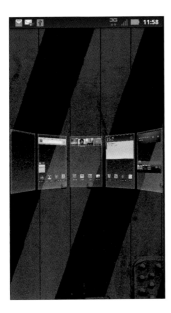

Figure 3-4: Home screen panel overview.

 To return to the Home screen at any time, press the Home soft button.

Using Car Home

The Droid 3 features an alternative Home screen, provided for the scary proposition of using your phone while driving an automobile. The Car Home screen, designed to be easy to see at a glance, offers you access to the phone's more popular features without distracting you too much from the priority of piloting your car.

The Car Home screen appears automatically whenever your Droid 3 is nestled into the car mount phone holder accessory, discussed in Chapter 1. Touch the big buttons to access popular phone features. To return to the standard Droid 3 Home screen, press the Menu soft button and then the Exit command.

See Chapter 13 for information on using the Droid 3 for navigation, a handy feature available directly from the Car Home screen.

I've Been Working on the Home Screen

I recommend getting to know three basic Home screen operations: reviewing notifications, starting programs, and using widgets.

Reviewing notifications

Notifications are represented by icons at the top of the Home screen, as illustrated earlier, in Figure 3-2. To see what the notifications say, peel down the top part of the screen, shown in Figure 3-5.

Notification icons   Touch here.

Drag your finger down
to display notifications.

Figure 3-5: Accessing notifications.

The operation works like this:

1. **Touch the notification icons at the top of the touchscreen.**

2. **Swipe your finger all the way down the front of the touchscreen.**

   This action works like you're controlling a roll-down blind: Grab the top part of the touchscreen and drag it downward all the way. The notifications appear in a list, as shown in Figure 3-6.

   Drag the notification list all the way to the bottom of the touchscreen to prevent it from rolling up again. Use the notification panel control to pull the list all the way down, as shown in Figure 3-6.

3. **Touch a notification to see what's up.**

Touching a notification opens the app that generated the alert. For example, touching the Gmail notification displays a new message in the inbox.

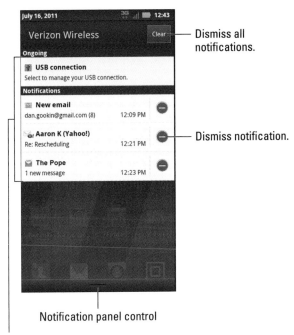

Figure 3-6: The notification list.

If you choose not to touch a notification, you can "roll up" the notification list by sliding the panel control back to the top of the touchscreen or by pressing the Back soft button.

- ✔ A notification icon doesn't disappear after you deal with it — and these icons can stack up!

- ✔ Dismiss individual notifications by touching the red Delete button, as shown in Figure 3-6. You see no confirmation after you touch the Delete button.

- ✔ To dismiss all notification icons, touch the Clear button, shown in Figure 3-6.

- ✔ When more notifications are present than can be shown on the status bar, you see the More Notifications icon displayed, as shown in the margin. The number on the icon indicates how many additional notifications are available.

- ✔ Dismissing notifications doesn't prevent them from appearing again later. For example, notifications to update your programs continue to appear, as do calendar reminders.

- ✔ Some programs, such as Facebook and Twitter, don't display notifications unless you're logged in. See Chapter 12.

- ✔ When new notifications are available, the Droid 3 notification light flashes. Refer to Chapter 1 for information on locating the notification light.

- ✔ Notification icons appear on the screen when the phone is locked. You must unlock the phone before you can drag down the status bar to display notifications.

Starting an application

It's cinchy to run an application on the Home screen: Touch its icon. The application starts.

- ✔ Not all applications appear on the Home screen, but all of them appear when you display the App menu. See the section "The App Menu," later in this chapter.

- ✔ When an application closes or you quit that application, you return to the Home screen.

- ✔ *Application* is abbreviated as *app*.

Using a widget

A *widget* is a teensy program that "floats" over the Home screen, as shown in Figure 3-3. To use a widget, simply touch it. What happens after that depends on the widget.

For example, touching the Google widget displays the onscreen keyboard and lets you type, or dictate, something to search for on the Internet. A weather widget may display information about the current weather, social networking widgets display status updates or tweets, and so on.

Information on these and other widgets appears elsewhere in this book. See Chapter 22 for information on working with widgets.

The App Menu

The place where you find all applications installed on your Droid 3 is the *App menu.* Though you may find shortcuts to applications (apps) on the Home screen, the App menu is where you need to go to find *everything.*

Starting an app from the App menu

To start a program — an *app* — on the Droid 3, heed these steps:

1. **Touch the Launcher button at the bottom of the Home screen.**

   The App menu appears, as shown in Figure 3-7. App icons are listed alphabetically, which still goes from *a* to *z,* as far as I can tell.

2. **If you don't see the all apps displayed, choose All Apps from the Group menu, shown in Figure 3-7.**

3. **Page through the list of app icons by swiping your finger to the left.**

   Each page of the App menu scrolls from right to left, like flipping the pages in a book.

4. **Touch an icon to start its app.**

   The app that opens takes over the screen and does whatever good thing that program is supposed to do.

Applications

Group menu   Android Market

App menu page indicator

Figure 3-7: The App menu shows your phone's apps.

- To help you locate a lost app, or one whose name you might have forgotten, press the Search soft button while viewing the All Apps screen on the App menu. Type all or part of the app's name. As you type, items whose names match the letters you've typed appear in the list. The word *Application* appears beneath the program name of any application in the list.

- Use the Group menu to view different groups of apps, from All Apps, to recently opened apps, to downloaded apps, to groups you create yourself.

- Creating app groups is covered in Chapter 18, along with information on downloading apps from the Android Market.

- The terms *program, application,* and *app* all mean the same thing.

Reviewing your most recently used apps

If you're like me, you probably use the same apps over and over, on both your computer and your phone. You can easily access the list of recent programs on the Droid 3 by pressing and holding the Home soft button. When you do, you see the eight most recently accessed programs, similar to the ones shown in Figure 3-8.

Recently opened applications

Group menu   Android Market

Figure 3-8: Recently used apps.

To exit the list of recently used apps, press the Back soft button.

You can press and hold the Home soft button in any application at any time to see the recently used apps list.

For programs you use all the time, consider creating shortcuts on the Home screen. Chapter 22 describes how to create shortcuts to apps, as well as shortcuts to people and shortcuts to instant messaging and all sorts of fun stuff.

The Keyboard-and-Text Chapter

In This Chapter

▶ Understanding the Droid 3 keyboards

▶ Typing on the Multi-Touch keyboard

▶ Using the sliding keyboard

▶ Getting at special characters

▶ Using word suggestion shortcuts

▶ Editing text on the screen

▶ Selecting, cutting, copying, and pasting text

▶ Dictating text with voice input

*I*t's the year 2134. You wake up in a pleasant though sterile room to the sound of soothing music. A door slides open, and in walks a graceful mechanical being. It introduces itself as your personal Droid Z99, a descendant of what was originally a cell phone more than a century earlier. The Droid Z99 is your slave, dutifully obeying your every whim, supplying whatever you need. It seeks to fulfill any desire you have — as long as you never, ever leave that room.

Though your introduction to the Droid 3 phone may not be as pleasant as a future introduction to a Droid Z99 robot, there's no risk to you that your phone will make you a prisoner. To transmit that message to the phone, you should know how to use the numerous Droid 3 keyboards in addition to voice input. That information is covered in this chapter, which I recommend reading quickly, before your phone gets any wild ideas.

Keyboard Mania

There are plenty of ways to fulfill your typing duties on the Droid 3. You have the option of using an onscreen keyboard or the physical keyboard. The decision to have multiple keyboards was obviously put forward to confuse and intimidate you.

The two keyboards that appear on the touchscreen are the *Multi-Touch* keyboard, which is basically the standard QWERTY keyboard found on a computer, and the *Swype* keyboard. The Swype keyboard looks like the standard QWERTY keyboard but uses a special technique to let you type rapidly. See the following sidebar, "Take a Swype at the old hunt-and-peck," for more information.

The *sliding* keyboard is a physical QWERTY keyboard that slides out from under the touchscreen. The sliding keyboard allows you the luxury of having a physical keyboard on the Droid 3, which many folks find preferable over the onscreen keyboard.

- ✔ *QWERTY* refers to the keyboard layout that's popular in English-speaking countries. The letters in QWERTY are the first six letters in the top row on the keyboard.

- ✔ The Droid 3 also lets you dictate text into your phone. See the section "Voice Input," later in this chapter.

- ✔ The Droid 3 sliding keyboard started out full size. But then the scientists at Motorola zapped it, using that huge shrinking machine the US government built under the Utah desert — you know, the same machine that shrank Stephen Boyd and Raquel Welch in the film *Fantastic Voyage*.

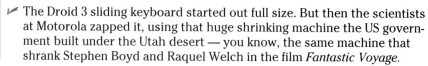

Take a Swype at the old hunt-and-peck

The Swype typing utility is designed to drastically improve your typing speed on a touchscreen phone. The secret to Swype is that you can type without lifting your finger; you literally swipe your finger over the touchscreen to rapidly type words.

Activate Swype by long-pressing any text box or location where you can type on the touchscreen. From the Edit Text menu, choose the Input Method item and then Swype.

To help you best understand Swype, I recommend that you use its onscreen Help: Long-press the Swype key, illustrated nearby, to see the Swype Help menu. You can review the techniques for typing types of words, such as those with capital letters or double letters, and other tips. You can also touch the Tutorial button to see how Swype works and pick up some typing tricks.

Typing on the Multi-Touch keyboard

The Multi-Touch keyboard shows up any time the phone demands text as input, such as when you're composing e-mail, typing a text message, or composing a ransom note in Gmail.

The alphabetic version of the Multi-Touch keyboard is shown in Figure 4-1. The keys a through z (lowercase) are there, plus a Shift/Caps Lock key, Delete key, Space key, and Period key.

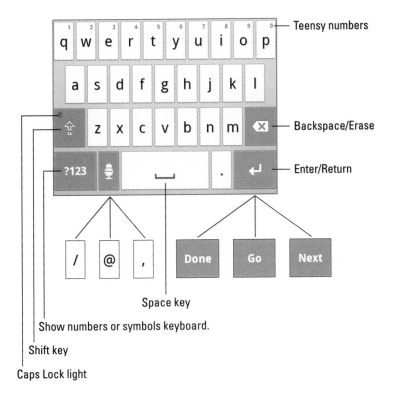

Figure 4-1: The Multi-Touch keyboard.

The key in the lower right corner changes its look depending on what you're typing and where you're typing it. The key has several variations, as shown in the figure. Here's what each one does:

Enter/Return: Similar to pressing the Enter or Return key on a computer keyboard, touching this key ends a paragraph of text. It's used most often when filling in long stretches of text or when multiline input is available.

Done: Use this key to dismiss the onscreen keyboard and view the full-screen app. Normally, this key appears whenever you finish typing text in the final field of a screen with several fields.

Go: This action key directs the app to proceed with a search, accept input, or perform another action.

Next: This key appears when typing information into multiple fields. Touching the key switches from one field to the next, such as when typing a username and password.

The key to the left of the Space key changes as well. It can be a slash, the @ symbol, or a comma, depending on the app. In situations where voice input is accepted, the Microphone icon appears. Touching the Microphone icon key activates voice input, as covered later in this chapter.

?123 Touch the ?123 key to see the number keys as well as the various punctuation symbols shown in Figure 4-2. Pressing the Alt key on the number-and-symbol keyboard displays special symbols, also shown in Figure 4-2. When the Alt key has been pressed, its light turns on, as illustrated in the figure.

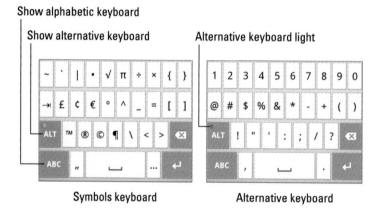

Show alphabetic keyboard

Show alternative keyboard   Alternative keyboard light

Symbols keyboard   Alternative keyboard

Figure 4-2: The numbers-and-symbols keyboard.

To return to the QWERTY keyboard layout (refer to Figure 4-1), touch the ABC key.

✔ Some applications show the keyboard when the phone is in landscape orientation. If so, the keyboard shows the same keys but offers more room for your stumplike fingers to type.

✔ The teensy number keys atop the QWERTY keyboard (refer to Figure 4-1) are accessed by pressing and holding a key. For example, press and hold the q key to type the number 1.

✔ See Chapter 22 for information on how to adjust the onscreen keyboard.

✔ Another type of onscreen keyboard is the Swype keyboard. Using this keyboard requires a bit of training, so it's covered in a later section in this chapter.

Sliding out the sliding keyboard

Like many popular cell phones, the Droid 3 features a real keyboard. The Droid 3 sliding keyboard is ensconced behind the touchscreen. You can slide out this keyboard (to the left as you face the phone) and use it if you prefer a physical keyboard for your cell phone typing chores.

Figure 4-3 illustrates the sliding keyboard, to call out its various parts.

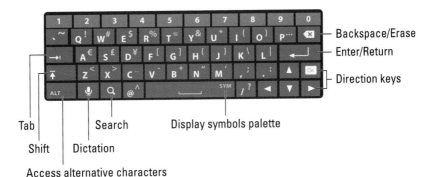

Figure 4-3: Keys on the sliding keyboard.

Two sets of symbols share space on the sliding keyboard: one colored white and the other colored gold. The gold characters are accessed by using the Alt key; see the later section "Typing on your Droid 3" for more information about typing on the sliding keyboard.

The sliding keyboard also features direction keys: up, down, right, and left, plus the OK key. Using these keys is covered later in this chapter, in the section "Text Editing."

When you're done using the sliding keyboard, slide it back into the phone. The touchscreen may reorient itself to Portrait mode when you do so, or the app may stay in its horizontal orientation.

Sliding the keyboard back into the phone doesn't turn off or sleep the Droid 3.

Droid 3 Hunt-and-Peck

Yes, typing on a cell phone is a skill set all its own. Sure, the Droid 3 has a dictation feature. When you're making a call, of course, you use your voice. But for many of the tasks you do, you need to use a keyboard.

Typing on your Droid 3

Using the Droid 3 keyboards works just as you expect: Touch the key you want and its character appears in the program you're using. It's magic!

Typing can be quirky, depending on which keyboard you use, as covered in the sections that follow. For both the Multi-Touch and sliding keyboards, here are some helpful suggestions and thoughts:

 ✔ A blinking cursor on the touchscreen shows where new text appears, which is similar to how typing works on a computer.

 ✔ When you make a mistake, touch the Del key to back up and erase.

 ✔ See the later section "Text Editing" for more details on editing your text.

 ✔ Above all, *type slowly* until you get used to the keyboard.

 ✔ A period is automatically placed at the end of a sentence by pressing the Space key twice. In fact, pressing the Space key twice at any time changes the first space you typed into a period. As a bonus, the next character you type appears automatically in uppercase to start a new sentence.

 ✔ People generally accept that composing text on a phone isn't perfect. Don't sweat it if you make a few mistakes as you type text or e-mail messages, though you should expect some curious replies from unintended typos.

 ✔ One way to get forgiveness for your typos is to include the signature *Sent from my DROID* in your e-mail messages. See Chapter 10.

 ✔ When you type a password, the character you type appears briefly but, for security reasons, is then replaced by a black dot.

 ✔ When you tire of typing, you can always touch the Microphone key on the keyboard and enter Dictation mode. See the section "Voice Input," later in this chapter.

Multi-Touch keyboard typing

As you type on the Multi-Touch keyboard, the button you're touching appears enlarged on the screen, as shown in Figure 4-4. That's how you can confirm that your fingers are typing what you intend to type.

✔ To set the Caps Lock feature, press the Shift key twice. The little light highlighted in Figure 4-1 comes on, indicating that Caps Lock is on.

✔ Press the Shift key again to turn off Caps Lock.

✔ See the later section "Choosing a word as you type" to find out how to deal with automatic spelling corrections.

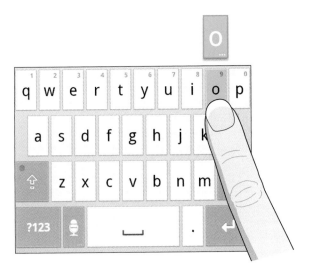

Figure 4-4: Pressing the o key.

Sliding keyboard typing

Despite the capital letters on the sliding keyboard, the text you type appears in lowercase. To create a capital letter, you must press the Shift key (refer to Figure 4-4). Unlike when using a computer keyboard, you don't need to hold down the Shift key; just press and release and then type a letter.

 After the Shift key has been pressed, the cursor changes its appearance, as shown in the margin. It's your clue that the next letter typed will be in uppercase.

 To activate Caps Lock, press the Shift key twice. The cursor changes its appearance, as shown in the margin. Additionally, the tiny light by the Shift key turns on. Press the Shift key again to release Caps Lock.

 Access the gold symbol characters by pressing the Alt key. As with the Shift key, you don't need to press and hold the Alt key; just press and release. The cursor changes, as shown in the margin, to indicate that you're typing symbols and not the letter key.

To lock the symbols, press the Alt key again. The cursor changes again (as shown in the margin), and the Alt Lock light illuminates. When Alt Lock is active, only the gold symbol characters are displayed as you type on the sliding keyboard. Press the Alt Lock key again to return to normal keyboard operation.

The cursor may not change its appearance in every program you use. For example, in the Browser you may see only a vertical line for the cursor.

Accessing special characters

You can type more characters on your phone than are shown on either the Multi-Touch or sliding keyboard. So don't think you're getting gypped when you don't see the key you want.

Multi-Touch keyboard special characters

On the Multi-Touch keyboard, you access a special character by pressing and holding a specific key. When you do, a pop-up palette of options appears, from which you choose a special character.

Not every key on the Multi-Touch keyboard sports extra characters. Those that sport them show three dots on their magnified key cap, as shown earlier, in Figure 4-4. When you press and hold this type of key (the *long-press*), a pop-up palette of options appears, as shown in Figure 4-5. Choose the character you want from the palette.

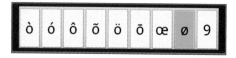

Figure 4-5: Optional characters on the O key.

If you don't want to type an extra character — tough: The highlighted character appears on the screen when you release your finger. Use the Del key on the keyboard to back up and erase.

- Extra characters are available in uppercase as well; press the Shift key before you long-press on the onscreen keyboard.

- Certain symbol keys on the onscreen keyboard also sport extra characters. For example, various currency symbols are available when you long-press the $ key.

Sliding keyboard special characters

Accessing special characters on the sliding keyboard is done by pressing Alt and the Space key, where you find the letters *SYM* shown in gold text. What you see is a pop-up palette of symbols that, yes, you have to choose by touching them on the Droid 3 screen. Figure 4-6 shows the available symbols.

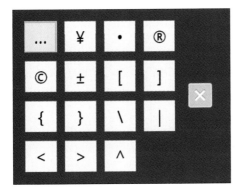

Figure 4-6: The SYM symbols on the sliding keyboard.

Despair not if you don't see the symbol or character you're looking for. Many more characters are available, but you have to know the press-and-hold trick on the sliding keyboard to see them.

To work the press-and-hold trick, press and hold the letter key that most resembles the symbol you want to type. For example, to type the ñ character, press and hold the N key. A palette of accented characters appears onscreen, from which you can choose ñ.

To produce a capital accented character, press the Shift key before you press and hold its letter key.

A palette of accented characters appears for most letter keys on the sliding keyboard; press and hold any key to see its palette onscreen. The vowel keys, specifically, have *many* characters available in their palettes.

Touch the X button to dismiss the pop-up palette when none of the choices pleases you.

Choosing a word as you type

As a "smart" phone, the Droid 3 makes a guess at the words you're typing as you type them. A list of suggestions appears above the Multi-Touch keyboard or at the bottom of the touchscreen when you're using the sliding keyboard. Choose a suggestion by touching it with your finger or by pressing the Space key to choose the highlighted word. The word you choose instantly appears on the screen, saving you time (and potentially fixing your terrible spelling or typing, or both).

You can disable the word suggestions and automatic error corrections. See Chapter 22.

Text Editing

I am but a fool to suggest that you'll edit much text on your cell phone. For most people, the cry is, "Damn the typos — full speed ahead!" If you decide to edit your text, though, this section is worthy of a read.

Moving the cursor

The first part of editing text is to move the *cursor,* that blinking vertical line where text appears, to the correct spot. You can move the cursor in two ways.

The easiest way to move the cursor is simply to touch the part of the text where you want the cursor to blink. This method works, but because your finger is probably fatter than the spot where you want the cursor, it's not usually effective.

To help you deal with fat fingers, you can use the trapezoid icon that appears below the cursor, as shown in the margin. Use your finger to drag the trapezoid around and position the cursor.

A second, and better, way to move the cursor is to use the direction keys, found on the sliding keyboard (refer to Figure 4-3). Pressing a direction key moves the cursor around the text in the direction of the arrow. It works just like pressing the arrow keys on a computer keyboard.

After you move the cursor, you can continue to type, use the Del key to back up and erase, or paste in text copied from elsewhere. See the later section "Cutting, copying, and pasting text" for more information.

Selecting text

You may be familiar with selecting text in a word processor; selecting text on the Droid 3 works the same way. Well, *theoretically,* it works the same way: Selected text appears highlighted on the touchscreen. You can then delete, cut, or copy that block of selected text. It's the method of selecting text on a phone that's screwed up.

Your phone has several methods for selecting text, as covered in the following sections.

After the text is selected, you can do four things with it: Delete it, replace it, copy it, or cut it. Delete the text by touching the Del key on the keyboard. Replace text by typing something new while the text is selected. The later section "Cutting, copying, and pasting text" describes how to cut or copy text.

Text selection with your finger on the touchscreen

To quickly select a word, tap your finger twice on the touchscreen. The word becomes highlighted, as shown in Figure 4-7.

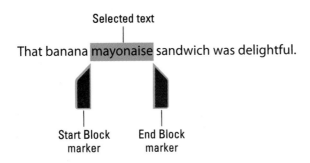

Figure 4-7: Selecting a block of text.

Pay heed to the Start Block and End Block markers on either side of the selected word, as shown in Figure 4-7. Use your finger to drag the start and end markers around the screen, which extends the text selection, as illustrated in the figure.

When dragging the Start Block or End Block marker, keep your finger pressed against the screen: Touch a marker and then drag your finger to move the marker. The text between the two markers is highlighted and selected.

Text selection with the sliding keyboard

You can easily select text by using the sliding keyboard, but it's not the easiest way to select a block. Follow these steps:

1. **Extend the sliding keyboard.**

2. **Move the cursor to the location where you want to start selecting text.**

   You can use your finger, and then make fine adjustments, by using the direction keys on the sliding keyboard.

3. **Press and hold the Shift key.**

4. **Use the direction keys to extend the selection up, down, left, or right.**

   The selected text appears highlighted on the screen.

At this point, you can delete or replace the text, but you can't cut or copy the text. To do that, you long-press the screen and choose the Select Word command from the menu. Choosing this command doesn't deselect the text; instead, the selected block grows little handles, as shown in Figure 4-7. Then you can copy or cut the block, as discussed in the section "Cutting, copying, and pasting text," later in this chapter.

Text selection using the Edit Text menu

Start selecting text by pressing and holding — a *long-press* — any part of the text screen or input box. When you do, the Edit Text menu appears, as shown in Figure 4-8.

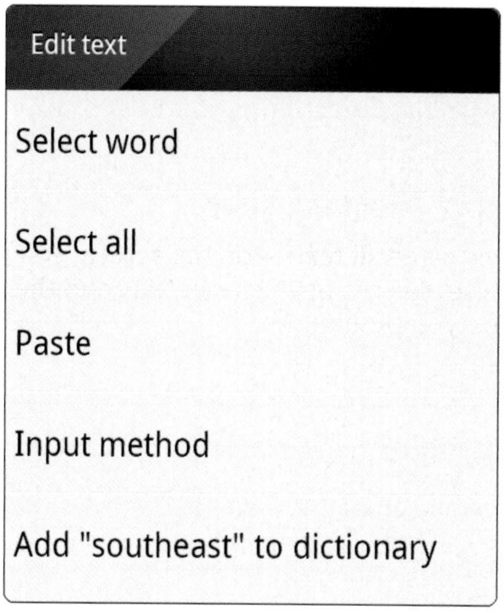

| Edit text |
| Select word |
| Select all |
| Paste |
| Input method |
| Add "southeast" to dictionary |

Figure 4-8: The Edit Text selection menu.

The first two options on the Edit Text menu (refer to Figure 4-8) deal with selecting text:

Select Word: Choose this option to select the word you long-pressed on the screen. You can then extend the selection as illustrated earlier, in Figure 4-7.

Select All: Choose this option to select all text, whether it's in the input box or you've been entering or editing it in the current application.

To back out of the Edit Text menu, press the Back soft button.

You can cancel the selection of text by pressing the Back soft button.

Text selection on a web page

When you're browsing the web on your Droid 3, you select text by summoning a special menu item. Obey these steps:

1. **Press the Menu soft button to summon the web browser's menu.**

2. **Choose the More command, and then choose Select Text.**

3. **Drag your finger over the text on the web page you want to copy.**

   You can extend the selection by dragging the controls at the start or end of the text, similar to the selection shown earlier, in Figure 4-7.

4. **Touch the screen and choose the Copy command.**

   The text is instantly copied.

You can paste the text into any application on your phone that accepts text input. See the next section.

Refer to Chapter 11 for more information on surfing the web with your phone.

Cutting, copying, and pasting text

After selecting a chunk of text — or all text — on the screen, you can cut or copy that text and paste it elsewhere. Copying or cutting and then pasting text works just like it does on your computer.

Follow these steps to cut or copy text on your phone:

1. **Select the text you want to cut or copy.**

   Selecting text is covered earlier in this chapter.

2. **Long-press the selected text.**

   Touch the highlighted text on the touchscreen, and keep your finger pressed down. You see the Edit Text menu with three items: Cut, Copy, and Paste.

3. **Choose Cut or Copy from the menu to cut or copy the text.**

   When you choose Cut, the text is removed; the cut-and-paste operation moves text.

4. **If necessary, start the application you want to paste text into.**

5. **Touch the text box or text area where you want to paste the copied or cut text.**

6. **Move the cursor to the exact spot where the text will be pasted.**

7. **Long-press the text box or area.**

8. **Choose the Paste command from the Edit Text menu.**

   The text you cut or copied appears in the spot where the cursor was blinking.

The text you paste can be pasted again and again. Until you cut or copy additional text, you can use the Paste command to your heart's content.

You can paste text only into locations where text is allowed. Odds are good that if you can type, or whenever you see the onscreen keyboard, you can paste text.

Voice Input

One of the most amazing aspects of the Droid 3 is its uncanny ability to interpret your dictation as text. It pays almost as much attention to what you say as your spouse does, though for legal reasons I can't explain why that's relevant. Suffice it to say that diction is a boon to any cell phone user.

Dictating to your phone

Voice input is available whenever you see the Microphone icon, similar to the one shown in the margin. To begin voice input, touch the icon. The voice input screen appears, as shown in Figure 4-9.

Figure 4-9: The voice input thing.

When you see the text *Speak Now,* speak directly at the phone.

As you speak, the Microphone icon (refer to Figure 4-9) flashes. The flashing doesn't mean that the phone is embarrassed by what you're saying. No, the flashing merely indicates that the phone is listening, detecting the volume of your voice.

After you stop talking, the phone digests what you said. You see your voice input appear as a wavelike pattern on the screen. Eventually, the text you spoke — or a close approximation of it — appears on the screen. It's magical, and sometimes comical.

- ✔ The first time you try to use Voice Input, you might see a description displayed. Touch the OK button to continue.

- ✔ The Microphone key appears on both the onscreen and sliding keyboards, though the onscreen keyboard doesn't *always* sport the Microphone key.

- ✔ The Dictation feature works only when voice input is allowed. Not every application features voice input as an option.

- ✔ The better your diction, the better the results. Try to speak only a sentence or less.

- ✔ You can edit your voice input just as you edit any text. See the section "Text Editing," earlier in this chapter.

- ✔ You have to "speak" punctuation to include it in your text. For example, you say, "I'm sorry comma Belinda period" to have the phone produce the text *I'm sorry, Belinda.*

- ✔ Common punctuation marks that you can dictate include the comma, period, exclamation point, question mark, and colon.

- ✔ Pause your speech before and after speaking punctuation.

- ✔ Voice input may not function when no cellular data or Wi-Fi connection is available.

Controlling the Droid 3 with voice commands

The Voice Commands app, found on the App menu, allows you to bellow verbal orders to your Droid 3. Start the app and wait a second to see a list of command suggestions.

Try out a few of the commands, such as the Call command. The phone may ask you for more detailed information, requiring you to reply "yes" or "no," similar to an annoying voice menu at some Big Impersonal Company.

I admit that this feature is a tad unreliable, especially compared to how well the Dictation feature works overall. Still, it's worth a try if you truly want to play Mr. Spock and dictate your commands to a cold, impersonal piece of electronics.

Uttering f**** words

WARNING!

The Droid 3 features a voice censor. It replaces those naughty words you might utter, placing the word's first letter on the screen, followed by the appropriate number of asterisks.

For example, if *fudge* were a blue word and you utter *fudge* when dictating text, the Droid 3 Dictation feature would place f**** on the screen rather than the word *fudge*.

The phone knows a lot of blue terms, including the infamous "Seven Words You Can Never Say on Television," but apparently the terms *crap* and *damn* are fine. Don't ask me how much time I spent researching this topic.

Part II
Basic Phone

The 5th Wave   By Rich Tennant

Cell Phones

"This model comes with a particularly useful function — a simulated static button for breaking out of long-winded conversations."

In this part . . .

You remember going to the county fair? Remember the pitchmen? Their spiel was all part of the show. "It dices. It slices. It makes julienne fries!" Of course, the item they were huckstering cost twice as much as it did at the local store, and it broke after only a few uses. What's the old phrase? A jack of all trades and a master of none.

Your Droid 3 does a lot of useful things, and it handles them quite well for a jack-of-all-trades: photographs, videos, music, maps, e-mail, and the web. But at its core, your Droid 3 remains a phone. Its primary purpose, its *raison d'être,* is to make phone calls. This basic function is covered in this part of the book.

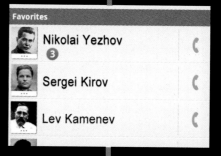

5

Yes, It Can Make Phone Calls

In This Chapter

▶ Calling someone

▶ Connecting with a contact

▶ Calling popular people and favorite friends

▶ Getting a call

▶ Replying to missed calls with a text message

▶ Checking for missed calls

▶ Perusing the Recent Calls list

*I*t would take an entire book to list all the things the Droid 3 is capable of doing. (Hint, hint.) Even so, at its core, the modern smartphone remains a device designed to make phone calls. Just as with the old, heavy telephones of the past century, you can use the Droid 3 to "dial" a phone number and communicate with another human. It isn't sexy smartphone stuff, but it's basic and potentially befuddling on a touchscreen, so I wrote this chapter to clear up any nonsense.

Reach Out and Touch Someone

It's the next best thing to being there, especially when your Uncle Celtus is a fisherman and you detest the smell of bait. Oh, but it's good to hear his voice. Making that connection is simple on the Droid 3, especially after reviewing the information in this section.

Someone asked me to switch, to start wri
old them that I already do.

Placing a phone call

To place a call on your phone, heed these steps:

1. Touch the Dialer app on the Home screen.

The Dialer app is also found on the App menu, but it's traditionally found on the Dock, at the bottom of the Home screen, in the lower left corner.

The Dialer app displays a dialpad, similar to the one shown in Figure 5-1. If you don't see the dialpad, touch the Dialer tab indicated in the figure.

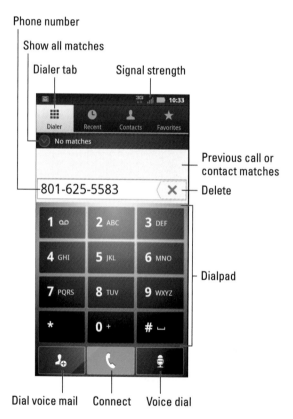

Figure 5-1: Dialing a phone number.

2. Type the number to call.

Use the keys on the dialpad to type the number. If you make a mistake, touch the Delete button, shown in Figure 5-1, to back up and erase.

As you dial, you may hear the traditional touch-tone sound as you input the number. The phone may also vibrate as you touch the numbers. These sound and vibration settings can be changed; see Chapter 22.

Any contacts you have that match the number you dialed appear above the dialpad, as shown in Figure 5-1. Use the Show All Matches button to display the complete list and then touch a contact's name to have that number pasted into the Phone Number field.

3. **Touch the green phone button to make the call.**

   The phone doesn't make the call until you touch the green button.

   As the phone attempts to make the connection, two things happen:

   • First, the Call in Progress notification icon appears on the status bar. The icon is a big clue that the phone is making a call or is actively connected.

   • Second, the screen changes to show the number you dialed, similar to the one shown in Figure 5-2. When the recipient is in your Contacts list, the contact's name and photo (if available) also appear, as shown in the figure. Further, if the contact has social networking information, it may show up as well.

   Even though the touchscreen is pretty, at this point you need to listen to the phone: Put it up to your ear or listen using the earphones or a Bluetooth headset.

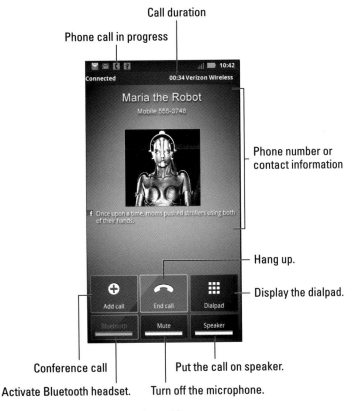

Figure 5-2: Your call has gone through!

4. When the person answers the phone, talk.

What you say is up to you, but I can recommend that you begin with a few pleasantries before asking someone to join your new multilevel marketing campaign.

Use the phone's Volume buttons (on the side of the Droid 3) to adjust the speaker volume during the call.

5. To end the call, touch the red End Call button.

The phone disconnects. You hear a soft *beep,* which is the phone's signal that the call has ended. The Call in Progress notification goes away.

You can do other things while you're making a call on the Droid 3: Just press the Home button to run an application, read old e-mail, check an appointment, or do whatever. Activities such as these don't disconnect you, though your cellular carrier may not allow you to do other things with the phone while you're on a call.

To return to a call after doing something else, swipe down the notifications at the top of the screen and touch the notification for the current call. You return to the Connected screen, similar to the one shown in Figure 5-2. Continue yapping. (See Chapter 3 for information on reviewing notifications.)

✔ You can connect or remove the earphones at any time during a call. The call is neither disconnected nor interrupted when you do so.

✔ If you're using earphones, you can press the phone's Power Lock button during the call to turn off the display and lock the phone. I recommend turning off the display so that you don't accidentally touch the Mute or End button during the call.

✔ You can't accidentally mute or end a call when the phone is placed against your face; a sensor in the phone detects when it's close to something, and the touchscreen is automatically disabled.

✔ Don't worry about the phone being too far away from your mouth; it picks up your voice just fine.

✔ To mute a call, touch the Mute button, shown in Figure 5-2. The Mute icon, shown in the margin, appears as the phone's status (atop the touchscreen).

✔ Touch the Speaker button to be able to hold the phone at a distance to listen and talk, which allows you to let others listen and share in the conversation. The Speaker icon appears as the phone's status when the speaker is active.

✔ Don't hold the phone to your ear when the speaker is active.

✔ If you're wading through one of those nasty voice mail systems, touch the Dialpad button, shown in Figure 5-2, so that you can "Press 1 for English" when necessary.

✔ See Chapter 6 for information on using the Add Call button.

✔ When using a Bluetooth headset, connect the headset *before* you make the call.

✔ If you need to dial an international number, press and hold the 0 (zero) key until the plus-sign (+) character appears. Then input the rest of the international number. Refer to Chapter 21 for more information on making international calls.

✔ The squat U character on the dialpad's pound-sign (#) key is used to produce a space in a telephone number. Aside from aesthetic reasons, I have no idea why you would need a space in a phone number.

✔ To add a pause to a phone number, press the Menu soft key and choose the Add Pause command. The pause shows up as a comma in the phone number. The pause is about 2 seconds long.

✔ You can add a pause prompt to a phone number: Press the Menu soft key and choose the command Add Wait. The wait shows up as a semi-colon character in the phone number. When the Droid 3 dials that character, a prompt appears on the touchscreen; dialing doesn't proceed until you touch the Yes button to continue.

✔ You hear an audio alert whenever the call is dropped or the other party hangs up. The disconnection can be confirmed by looking at the phone, which shows that the call has ended.

✔ You cannot place a phone call when the phone has no service; check the signal strength, as shown earlier, in Figure 5-1. Also see the nearby side-bar, "Signal strength and network information you don't have to read."

✔ You cannot place a phone call when the phone is in Airplane mode. See Chapter 21 for information.

✔ The Call in Progress notification icon (see Figure 5-2) is a useful thing. When you see this notification, it means that the phone is connected to another party. To return to the phone screen, swipe down the status bar and touch the phone call's notification. You can then press the End Call button to disconnect or just put the phone to your face to see who's on the line.

✔ You cannot, using current technology, browse the Internet or receive e-mail (or other data) while you're making a call on the Droid 3. Future changes in the cell network may change this condition.

Signal strength and network information you don't have to read

Two technical-looking status icons appear to the left of the current time atop the Droid 3 screen. These icons represent the network the phone is connected to and its signal strength.

The Signal Strength icon displays the familiar bars, rising from left to right. The more bars, the better the signal. An extremely low signal is shown by zero bars; when there's no signal, you see an X over the bars.

When the phone is out of its service area but still receiving a signal, you see the Roaming icon, where an *R* appears near the bars. See Chapter 21 for more information on roaming.

To the left of the signal bar icon is the Network icon. No icon means that no network is available, which happens when the network is down or you're out of range. The icon might also disappear when you're making a call. Otherwise, you see an icon representing one of the different types of cellular data networks to which the Droid 3 can connect. The 3G icon represents the fastest network to which the Droid 3 can connect.

Also see Chapter 19 for more information on the network connection and how it plays a role in your phone's Internet access.

Dialing a contact

Because your Droid 3 is also your digital Little Black Book, one of the easiest methods for placing a phone call is to simply dial one of the folks on your Contacts list. Follow these steps:

1. **On the Home screen, touch the Dialer app icon.**

2. **Touch the Contacts tab at the top of the screen.**

   See Figure 5-3 for the location of the Contacts tab.

3. **Scroll the list of contacts to find the person you want to call.**

   To rapidly scroll, you can swipe the list with your finger or use the index on the right side of the list, as shown in Figure 5-3.

4. **Touch the contact you want to call.**

5. **Touch the green Phone icon by the phone number of the contact you want to call.**

   The contact is dialed immediately.

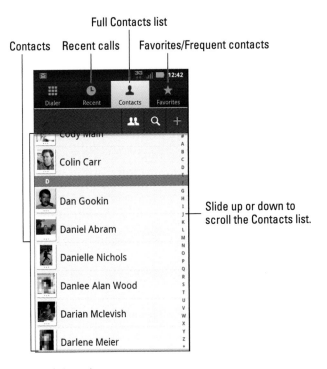

Full Contacts list

Contacts   Recent calls   Favorites/Frequent contacts

Slide up or down to scroll the Contacts list.

Figure 5-3: Perusing contacts.

At this point, dialing proceeds as described earlier in this chapter.

- ✐ You can dial a contact in numerous other ways, including using the Quick Contact list or the contact shortcut icons on the Home screen. These methods are covered throughout this book.

- ✐ See Chapter 8 for more information about the Contacts list.

Phoning someone you call often

Because the Droid 3 is sort of a computer, it keeps track of your phone calls. Also, you can flag as favorites certain people whose numbers you want to keep handy. You can take advantage of these two features to quickly call the people you phone most often or to redial a number.

To use the Recent Calls list to return a call, or to call someone right back, follow these steps:

1. **Touch the Dialer app on the Home screen.**

2. **Touch the Recent tab, found at the top of the window, as shown in Figure 5-3.**

   The Recent tab displays a list of calls you've made and calls received. Though you can choose an item to see more information, to call someone back, it's just quicker to follow Step 3:

3. **Touch the green Phone icon next to the entry.**

   The Droid 3 dials the contact.

People you call frequently, or contacts you've added to the Favorites list, can be accessed by touching the Favorites tab (refer to Figure 5-3). Scroll the list to find a favorite contact and then touch the green Phone icon to dial.

Refer to Chapter 8 for information on how to make one of your contacts a favorite.

Someone's Calling!

I believe that everyone enjoys getting a phone call. It's with a swift, confident motion that you reach for your cell phone, whipping it out to check the screen to see who's calling. Then comes either disgust as the call is banished to voice mail or feigned innocence as you mutter, "Hello," even though Caller ID has already clued you in to who's calling. Oh, I love the drama!

Receiving a call

Several things can happen when you receive a phone call on your Droid 3:

✔ The phone rings or makes a noise signaling you to an incoming call.

✔ The phone vibrates.

✔ The touchscreen reveals information about the call, as shown in Figure 5-4.

✔ The car in front of you explodes, and your crazy passenger starts screaming in an incoherent yet comic manner.

The last item in the list happens only in a Bruce Willis movie. The other three possibilities, or a combination thereof, are your signals that you have an incoming call. A simple look at the touchscreen tells you more information, as illustrated in Figure 5-4.

To answer the incoming call, slide the green Answer button to the right (refer to Figure 5-4). Then place the phone to your ear or, if one's attached, use a headset. Say "Hello" or, if you're in a grouchy mood, say "What?" loudly.

Incoming phone number

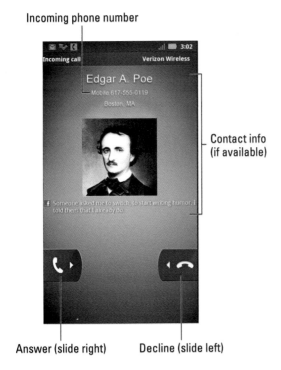

Contact info
(if available)

Answer (slide right)　　　Decline (slide left)

Figure 5-4: You have an incoming call.

To dispense with the incoming call, slide the red Ignore button to the left. The phone stops ringing, and the call is immediately banished into voice mail.

Finally, you can simply silence the phone's ringer by pressing the Volume button up or down.

If you're already using the phone when a call comes in, such as browsing the web or playing Angry Birds, the incoming call screen looks subtly different from the one shown in Figure 5-4. Your choices for what to do with the call, however, are the same: Touch the green Answer button to accept the call or touch the red Ignore button to send the caller to voice mail.

When you're already on the phone and a call comes in, you can touch the green Answer button to accept the call and place the current call on hold. See Chapter 6 for additional information on juggling multiple calls.

✔ The contact's picture, such as Mr. Poe in Figure 5-4, appears only when you've assigned a picture to that contact. Otherwise, the generic Android icon shows up. The contact's social networking information, also shown in Figure 5-4, appears whenever the contact is a social networking buddy.

✔ If you're using a Bluetooth headset, you touch the control on the headset to answer your phone. See Chapter 19 for more information on using Bluetooth gizmos.

✔ The sound you hear when the phone rings is known as the *ringtone*. You can configure the Droid 3 to play a number of ringtones, depending on who is calling, or you can set a universal ringtone. Ringtones are covered in Chapter 6.

✔ Information about which city the call originates from is provided by the City ID app on your Droid 3. You must subscribe to the City ID service to see the city information, though you get a free trial when you first get your phone. Open the City ID app on the App menu for additional details.

Using text message reply

When you dismiss an incoming call, you may see a pop-up menu similar to the one shown in Figure 5-5. That's the Text Message Reply feature in action: Choose an option to send the caller a quick text message, explaining why you didn't answer.

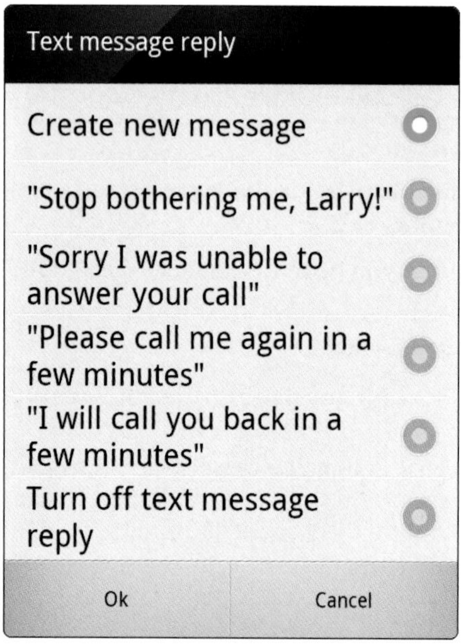

Text message reply	
Create new message	◯
"Stop bothering me, Larry!"	◯
"Sorry I was unable to answer your call"	◯
"Please call me again in a few minutes"	◯
"I will call you back in a few minutes"	◯
Turn off text message reply	◯
Ok	Cancel

Figure 5-5: Choose a text message reply.

If the Text Message Reply feature isn't activated, follow these steps:

1. **At the Home screen, press the Menu soft button.**
2. **Choose Settings.**
3. **Choose Call Settings and then choose Text Message Reply.**
4. **Ensure that a green check mark appears by the option Text Message Reply.**

   You have to scroll down a bit to find the Text Message Reply option.

5. **Choose the Edit Messages option to remove existing text message replies or to create your own.**

   The first message shown in Figure 5-5 is one I created on my own.

After the feature is activated, you see the Text Message Reply menu whenever you dismiss or ignore an incoming call.

Setting the incoming call signal volume

Whether the phone rings, vibrates, or explodes depends on how you've configured the Droid 3 to signal you for an incoming call. Abide by these steps to set the various options (but not explosions) for your phone:

1. **On the Home screen, touch the Launcher button to view all apps on the phone.**
2. **Choose the Settings icon to open the phone's Settings screen.**
3. **Choose Sound.**
4. **Set the phone's ringer volume by touching Volume.**
5. **Manipulate the Ringtone slider left or right to specify how loud the phone rings for an incoming call.**

   After you release the slider, you hear an example of how loudly the phone rings.

6. **Touch OK to set the ringer volume.**

   If you'd rather just mute the phone, touch the Silent Mode option on the main Sound Settings screen.

7. **To activate vibration when the phone rings, touch Vibrate.**
8. **Choose a vibration option from the Vibrate menu.**

   For example, choose Always to always vibrate the phone or Only in Silent Mode so that the phone vibrates only after you mute the volume.

9. **Touch the Home button when you're done.**

When the next call comes in, the phone alerts you using the volume setting or vibration options you've just set.

- See Chapter 3 for information on temporarily silencing the phone.
- Turning on vibration puts an extra drain on the battery. See Chapter 23 for more information on power management for your phone.
- Also refer to Chapter 22 for additional sound options on the Droid 3.

Who's Calling Who When?

Life got easier in my household when I got my Droid 3. Before the Droid 3, my son was the one who answered the old landline phone. He was terrible at remembering who phoned and when they called, let alone what message was left. With the Droid 3, however, I can instantly and boldly confirm who called, and when they called, and then call that person right back. Yes, indeed — another gizmo that the Droid 3 renders unnecessary is the common household teenager.

Dealing with a missed call

The notification icon for a missed call looming at the top of the screen means that someone called and you didn't pick up. Fortunately, the Droid 3 remembers all the details for you.

To deal with a missed call, follow these steps:

1. **Display the notifications.**

   See Chapter 3 for details on how to deal with notifications.

2. **Touch the Missed Call notification.**

   A list of missed calls is displayed. The list shows who called, with more information displayed when the phone number matches someone in your Contacts list. Also shown is how long ago they called.

3. **Touch the green Phone icon by an entry in the Recent Calls list to return the call.**

Also see the next section for more information on the Recent Calls list.

Reviewing recent calls

The Droid 3 keeps a record of all calls you make, incoming calls, and missed calls. Everything is listed on the Recent tab, shown in Figure 5-6. To see the list, open the Dialer app on the Home screen and then touch the Recent tab, as shown in the figure.

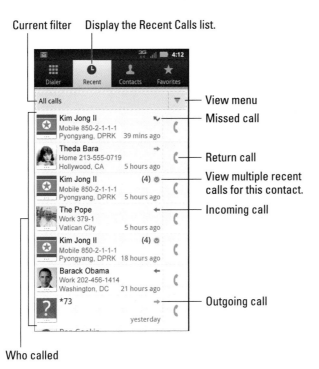

Figure 5-6: The Recent Calls list.

The Recent tab shows a list of people who have phoned you or whom you have called, starting with the most recent call at the top of the list. An icon next to every entry describes whether the call was incoming, outgoing, or missed, as illustrated in the figure.

Touching an item in the Recent Calls list displays contact information for the person who called, if that contact information exists. When contact information doesn't exist, you see a pop-up menu of options for returning the call or sending a text message, for example.

To call someone back, touch the green Phone icon, shown in Figure 5-6.

You can filter the list of recent calls, directing the phone to show only missed calls, only received calls, or only outgoing calls. To do so, touch the View menu triangle (illustrated in Figure 5-6). Choose which type of calls you want to see from the View menu, or choose All Calls to display all recent calls.

Using the Recent Calls list is a quick way to add a recent caller as a contact. Simply touch an item in the list and choose Add to Contacts from the Call Details screen. See Chapter 8 for more information about contacts.

To clear the Recent Calls list, press the Menu soft button. Choose the Clear List command to wipe clean the Recent Calls list.

Advanced Phone Duties

In This Chapter

▶ Calling with speed dial

▶ Handing multiple incoming calls

▶ Setting up a conference call

▶ Configuring call forwarding options

▶ Banishing a contact forever to voice mail

▶ Changing the Droid 3 ringtone

▶ Assigning ringtones to your contacts

▶ Using your favorite song or sound as a ringtone

New phone options began to creep into existence back near the end of Ma Bell's domination of the telephone market in the 1980s. These innovative features seemed exciting at the time, mostly because all a telephone did was make and receive phone calls. Newfangled options such as speed dial, call waiting, and three-way calling were cutting-edge. And don't forget expensive add-ons: I remember caller ID being another $7.95 per month on my old phone bill.

Those days are gone, happily. Today, such fancy features are all part of the Droid 3 right out of the box. They're probably included in your cell phone plan's basic rate as well, so don't avoid 'em — embrace 'em! Oh, and read this chapter so that you can find out what those advanced features are and discover how they work.

arris Glenn Milste

Home 410-555-1019

Towson, MD

Speed Dial

How fast can you dial a phone? Pretty fast — specifically, for eight of your friends or folks you phone most often. The feature is *speed dial.* To set it up on your Droid 3, follow these steps:

1. **At the Home screen, touch the Dialer app icon to start that app.**

2. **Ensure that the Dialer tab is selected and you see the dialpad on the screen.**

3. **Press the Menu soft button.**

4. **Choose Speed Dial Setup.**

   The first speed-dial number is already configured to your carrier's voice mail system. The remaining numbers, 2 through 9, are blank.

5. **Touch a blank item in the list.**

   The blank lines contain the text *Add Speed Dial.* To the left of the blank item is the speed-dial number, 2 through 9.

6. **Choose a contact to speed-dial.**

7. **Repeat Steps 5 and 6 to add more speed-dial contacts.**

When you're done adding numbers, press either the Back or Home button to exit the Speed Dial Setup screen.

Using speed dial is simple: Summon the Dialer (refer to Figure 5-1, in Chapter 5) and then press and hold *(long-press)* a number on the dialpad. When you release your finger, the speed-dial number is dialed.

To remove a speed-dial number, follow Steps 1 through 4 in this section. Touch the red Minus (–) button to the left of the speed-dial number to remove the number. You can then add another speed-dial number in that slot or just leave it empty.

To add a recent caller to the speed-dial list, long-press the recent caller from the Recent Calls list. Choose the option Add to Speed Dial from the menu that appears. This trick works only when you have an available slot for speed-dial numbers. See Chapter 5 for more information on the Recent Calls list.

Speed-dial numbers are referenced on the Favorites list, which you can see by touching the Favorites tab in the Dialer app. The number in the blue circle indicates a speed-dial contact.

Multiple Call Mania

A human being can hold only one conversation at a time. I remember hearing this theory in a lecture, but then the guy next to me started talking and I couldn't focus on what the speaker was saying. So I'll never know for certain. I do, however, know that the Droid 3 is capable of handling more than one call at a time. This section explains how it works.

Receiving a new call when you're on the phone

You're on the phone, chatting it up. Suddenly, someone else calls you. What happens next?

The Droid 3 alerts you to a new call. The phone may vibrate or make a sound. Look at the front of the phone to see what's up with the incoming call, as shown in Figure 6-1.

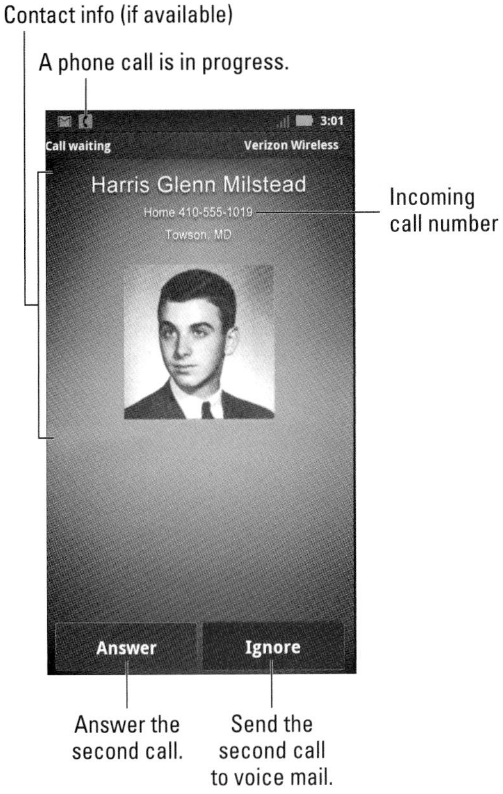

Figure 6-1: Suddenly, there's an incoming call!

You have three options:

Answer the call. Touch the green Answer button to answer the incoming call. The call you're on is placed on hold.

Send the call directly to voice mail. Touch the Ignore button. The incoming call is sent directly to voice mail.

Do nothing. The call eventually goes into voice mail.

When you choose to answer the call and the call you're on is placed on hold, you return to the first call when you end the second call. Or, you can manage the multiple calls as described in the next section.

Juggling two calls

After you answer a second call, as described in the preceding section, your Droid 3 is working with two calls at a time. In this particular situation, you can speak with only one person at a time; juggling two calls is not the same thing as a conference call.

To switch between callers, touch the Switch Calls button that appears on the touchscreen. Every time you touch the Switch Calls button, the conversation moves to the other caller.

To end a call, touch the End Call button, just as you normally do. Both calls might appear to have been disconnected, but that's not the case: In a few moments, the call you didn't disconnect "rings" as though the person is calling you back. No one is calling you back, though: The Droid 3 is simply returning you to that ongoing conversation.

- The number of different calls your phone can handle depends on your carrier. For most of us, it's only two calls at a time. In that case, a third person who calls you either hears a busy signal or is sent directly into voice mail.

- If the person on hold hangs up, you may hear a sound or feel the phone vibrate when the call is dropped.

Making a conference call

Unlike someone interrupting a conversation with an incoming call, a *conference call* is one you set out to make intentionally: You make one call and then *add* a second call. Touch a button on the Droid 3 touchscreen and then everyone is talking. Here's how it works:

1. **Phone the first person.**

   Refer to Chapter 5 if you need to bone up on your Droid 3 phone-calling skills.

2. **After your phone connects and you complete a few pleasantries, touch the Add Call button.**

   The first person is put on hold.

3. **Dial the second person.**

   You can use the dialpad or choose the second person from your Contacts list or Recent Calls list.

   Say your pleasantries, and inform the party that the call is about to be merged.

4. **Touch the Merge button.**

   The two calls are now joined: The touchscreen says *Conference Call,* and the End Last Call button appears. Everyone you've dialed can talk to and hear everyone else.

5. **Touch the End Call button to end the conference call.**

   All calls are disconnected.

When several people are in a room and want to participate in a call, you can always put the phone in Speaker mode: Touch the Speaker button.

Send a Call Elsewhere

Banishing an unwanted call on the Droid 3 is relatively easy. You can dismiss the phone from ringing by touching the Volume buttons. Or, you can send the call scurrying into voice mail by using the red Ignore button, as described in the section in Chapter 5 about receiving a call.

Other options exist for the special handling of incoming calls. They're the forwarding options, described in this section.

Forwarding phone calls

Call forwarding is the process by which you reroute a phone call coming into your Droid 3. For example, you can send to your office all calls you receive while you're on vacation. Then you have the luxury of having your cell phone and still making calls but freely ignoring anyone who calls you.

The options for call forwarding on the Droid 3 are set by the cell phone carrier and not by the phone itself. In the United States, using Verizon as your cellular provider, the call forwarding options work as described in Table 6-1.

Table 6-1	Verizon Call Forwarding Commands	
To Do This	*Input First Number*	*Input Second Number*
Forward unanswered incoming calls	*71	Forwarding number
Forward all incoming calls	*72	Forwarding number
Cancel call forwarding	*73	None

For example, to forward all calls to (714) 555-4565, you input ***727145554565** and touch the green Phone button on the Droid 3. You hear only a brief tone after dialing and then the call ends. After that, any call coming into your phone rings at the other number.

- ✔ You must disable call forwarding on your Droid 3 to return to normal cell phone operations. Dial *73.

- ✔ The Droid 3 doesn't even ring when you forward a call using *72. Only the phone number you've chosen to forward to rings.

- ✔ You don't need to input the area code for the forwarding number when the call is local. In other words, if you need to dial only 555-4565 to call the forwarding number, you need to input only ***725554565** to forward your calls.

- ✔ Call forwarding affects Google Voice voice mail. Unanswered calls that you forward are handled by the forwarding number, not Google Voice. Further, when you cancel call forwarding, you need to reenable Google Voice on your Droid 3 by redialing the Google Voice forwarding number. See Chapter 7 for details.

Sending a contact directly to voice mail

You can configure the Droid 3 to forward any of your cell phone contacts directly to voice mail. This is a great way to deal with a pest! Follow these steps:

1. **Touch the Launcher icon on the Home screen.**

2. **Open the Contacts app.**

3. **Choose a contact.**

   Use your finger to scroll the list of contacts until you find the annoying person you want to eternally banish to voice mail.

4. **Press the Menu soft button.**

5. **Choose Options.**

6. **Touch the square next to the Incoming Calls option.**

   A green check mark appears in the square, indicating that all calls from the contact (no matter which of their phone numbers they use) are sent directly into voice mail.

To unbanish the contact, repeat these steps, but in Step 6 touch the square to remove the green check mark.

   ✔ This feature is one reason you might want to retain contact information for someone with whom you never want to have contact.

   ✔ See Chapter 8 for more information on contacts.

   ✔ Also see Chapter 7, on voice mail.

Fun with Ringtones

I confess: Ringtones can be lots of fun. They uniquely identify your phone's ring, especially when you forget to mute your phone and you're hustling to turn the thing off because everyone in the room is annoyed by your ringtone choice of "Mambo No. 5."

On the Droid 3, you can choose which ringtone you want for your phone. You can create your own ringtones or use snippets from your favorite tunes. You can also assign ringtones for individual contacts. This section explains how it's done.

Choosing the phone's ringtone

To select a new ringtone for your phone, or to simply confirm which ringtone you're using already, follow these steps:

1. **At the Home screen, press the Menu soft button.**

2. **Choose Settings and then choose Sound.**

3. **Choose Phone Ringtone.**

   If you have a ringtone application, you may see a menu that asks you which source to use for the phone's ringtone. Choose Android System.

4. **Choose a ringtone from the list that's displayed.**

   Scroll the list. Tap a ringtone to hear a preview.

5. **Touch OK to accept the new ringtone or touch Cancel to keep the phone's ringtone as is.**

You can also set the ringtone used for notifications: In Step 3, choose Notification Ringtone rather than Phone Ringtone.

Setting a contact's ringtone

Ringtones can be assigned by contact so that when your annoying friend Larry calls, you can have your phone yelp like a whiny puppy. Here's how to set a ringtone for a contact:

1. **Choose the Contacts app from the App Menu screen.**

   Touch the Launcher button on the Home screen to see the App menu.

2. **From the list, choose the contact to which you want to assign a ringtone.**

3. **Touch the Menu soft button and choose Options.**

4. **Choose Ringtone.**

5. **If prompted, choose Android System as the source of the ringtone.**

   Or, if you're using an app such as Zedge, choose it to use that app as the source of the ringtone.

6. **Choose a ringtone from the list.**

   It's the same list that's displayed for the phone's ringtones.

7. **Touch OK to assign the ringtone to the contact.**

Whenever the contact calls, the Droid 3 rings using the ringtone you've specified.

To remove a specific ringtone for a contact, repeat the steps in this section but choose the ringtone named Default Ringtone. (It's found at the top of the list of ringtones.) This choice sets the contact's ringtone to be the same as the phone's ringtone.

Using music as a ringtone

You can use any tune from the Droid 3 music library as the phone's ringtone. The first part of the process is finding a good tune to use. Follow along with these steps:

1. **Touch the Launcher button on the Home screen to display all apps on the phone.**

2. **Touch Music to open the music player.**

3. **Choose a tune to play.**

   See Chapter 16 for specific information on how to use the Music application and use your Droid 3 as a portable music player.

   The song you want must either appear on the screen or be playing for you to select it as a ringtone.

4. **Press the Menu soft button.**

5. **Choose Use As Ringtone.**

   The song — the entire tune — is set as the phone's ringtone. Whenever you receive a call, that song plays.

The song you've chosen is added to the list of ringtones. It plays — from the start of the song — when you have an incoming call and until you answer the phone, send the call to voice mail, or choose to ignore the call and eventually the caller goes away and the music stops.

You can add as many songs as you like by repeating the steps in this section. Follow the steps in the earlier section "Choosing the phone's ringtone" for information on switching among different song ringtones. Refer to the steps in the earlier section "Setting a contact's ringtone" to assign a specific song to a contact.

 A free app at the Android Market, Zedge, has oodles of free ringtones available for preview and download, all shared by Android users around the world. See Chapter 18 for information about the Android Market and how to download and install apps such as Zedge on your phone.

Creating your own ringtones

 You can use any MP3 or WAV audio file as a ringtone for the Droid 3, such as a personalized message, a sound you record on your computer, or an audio file you stole from the Internet. As long as the sound is in the MP3 or WAV format, it can work as a ringtone on your phone.

The secret to creating your own ringtone is to transfer the audio file from your computer to the Droid 3. This topic is covered in Chapter 20, on synchronizing music between your computer and phone. After the audio file is in the phone's music library, you can choose the file as a ringtone in the same way you can assign any music on the Droid 3 as a ringtone, as described in the preceding section.

At the Sound of the Tone . . .

In This Chapter

▶ Configuring basic voice mail
▶ Retrieving messages
▶ Using Visual Voice Mail
▶ Setting up Google Voice for voice mail
▶ Reading a Google Voice voice mail message

*V*oice mail can prove to be handy in so many ways. First, and most obviously, voice mail exists for missed phone calls. When you're unavailable or on the other line, someone can leave you a message. Second, voice mail exists as a sort of digital hell to whence you can banish unwanted calls from annoying pests. Finally, voice mail exists as an excuse: You can dismiss anyone by simply claiming that you've yet to check your voice mail for messages. If only our ancestors had it so good.

email

Alexander Graham Bell
(303) 555-1847
Received: 1:04pm (9 secs)

Boring Ol' Carrier Voice Mail

The most basic, and most stupid, form of voice mail is the free voice mail service provided by your cell phone company. It's a standard feature with few frills and nothing that stands out differently, especially for such a nifty phone as the Droid 3.

Mr. Watson. Come here. I want you.

Carrier voice mail picks up missed calls and calls you thrust into voice mail. The Droid 3 alerts you to a missed call by displaying the Missed Call notification (shown in the margin). You then dial the voice mail system, listen to your calls, and use the phone's dialpad to delete messages or repeat messages or use other features you probably don't know about because no one ever pays attention.

✔ The Missed Call icon does not appear when you've sent a call to voice mail.

✔ You cannot use Visual Voice Mail, covered later in this chapter, until you first set up boring ol' carrier voice mail.

✔ Even when you plan to use something sophisticated, such as Google Voice, as your voice mail service, I still recommend setting up basic carrier voice mail as described in this section.

Setting up carrier voice mail

If you haven't yet done it, you need to set up voice mail on your phone. Even if you believe it to be set up and configured, consider churning through these steps, just to be sure:

1. **From the Home screen, press the Menu soft button.**

2. **Choose Settings.**

   The Settings screen appears.

3. **Choose Call Settings and then Voicemail Service.**

4. **Choose My Carrier, if it isn't chosen already.**

   Or, if it's the only option, you're set.

You can use the Voicemail Settings command to confirm or change the voice mail phone number. For Verizon in the United States, the number is *86.

After performing the steps in this section, call in to the carrier voice mail service to finish the setup: On my carrier (Verizon), I configured my language, set a voice mail password, and then recorded a greeting, following the steps offered by the cheerful Verizon robot.

The Voicemail app on the App menu lists pending messages, though only the quantity of messages and other information. The Call Voice Mail button can be used to have the phone dial into the voice mail system for you, where you can listen to your messages.

Complete your voice mailbox setup by creating a customized greeting. When you don't, you may not receive voice mail messages, or people may believe that they've dialed the wrong number.

Retrieving your messages

When you have voice mail looming, the New Voicemail notification icon appears on the status bar, as shown in the margin. You can either pull down this notification to connect to the voice mail service or simply dial *86 on the phone's dialpad. From the Voicemail app, touch the Call Voicemail button.

Table 7-1 lists the commands for using the Verizon voice mail service (current at the time this book went to press). These commands may change later.

Table 7-1	Verizon Voice-Mail System Commands
Dial This	**To Do This**
*	Go to the Main menu or, from the Main menu, disconnect from voice mail
0	Listen to Help
1	Listen to messages or, if you're listening to a message, rewind the message
2	Send a message to another phone number on the Verizon system
3	Fast-forward (speed up) the message
4	Review or change your personal options, such as the message greeting
5	Restart the session or, if you're listening to a message, get time information
6	Forward the message to someone else
7	Delete the message you just heard
8	After listening to a message, call the sender
9	Save the message you just heard
#	End input

✔ You don't have to venture into carrier voice mail just to see who called you. Instead, check the call log to review recent calls. Refer to Chapter 5 for information on reviewing the Recent Calls list.

✔ Calls you exile into voice mail are not flagged as Missed in the Recent Calls list.

✔ See Chapter 3 for more information on reviewing notifications.

Visual Voice Mail

A better option than carrier voice mail is something Verizon calls Visual Voice Mail. It's an app that lets you organize and listen to your messages in an interactive way, similar to e-mail. The only drawback to using Visual Voice Mail is that it costs extra. You must subscribe to the service, which runs $2.99 per month as this book goes to press.

Setting up Visual Voice Mail

To configure Visual Voice Mail to work on your Droid 3, first set up carrier voice mail, as covered earlier in this chapter. Visual Voice Mail is simply an interface into your existing carrier voice mail.

After you get carrier voice mail up and running, and especially after you set your password or PIN, touch the Launcher button to pop up the list of all apps installed on your phone. You want to start the Voicemail app and then touch the button Subscribe to Visual Voice Mail. Follow the directions on the screen to sign up and subscribe to the service.

You have to input your existing voice mail PIN to proceed, which is why I suggest, earlier in this chapter, that you first set up carrier voice mail.

You may also be required to install a new update to the Voicemail app. Refer to Chapter 18 for information on downloading and updating apps for your Droid 3.

Accessing Visual Voice Mail

Visual Voice Mail serves as your access to all voice mail left on your phone. After Visual Voice Mail is configured (see the preceding section), you never need to dial carrier voice mail again. Simply pull down the Visual Voice Mail notification or start the Voicemail app, and all your messages are instantly available on the screen.

When new voice mail arrives, you see the Visual Voice Mail notification icon, with the number of new messages shown in the icon. To access your messages, pull down the notifications and choose New Voicemail. You see your voice mail inbox, which lists all pending messages. Also shown are any messages you've already listened to but haven't deleted.

Use the controls in the Visual Voice Mail app to listen to messages, call someone back, and otherwise manage your voice mail, similar to the way you manage messages in your e-mail program.

Visual Voice Mail uses the same greeting that was set when you first configured carrier voice mail. To change the greeting, you have to dial carrier voice mail and follow the menus.

The Wonders of Google Voice

Perhaps the best option I've found for working your voice mail is something called Google Voice. It's more than just a voice mail system: You can use Google Voice to make phone calls in the United States, place cheap international calls, and perform other amazing feats. For the purposes of this section, the topic is using Google Voice as the Droid 3 voice mail system.

✔ Even when you choose to use Google Voice, I still recommend setting up and configuring the boring carrier voice mail, as covered earlier in this chapter.

✔ You may need to reset Google Voice after using call forwarding. See Chapter 6 for more information on call forwarding, and see the section "Adding your phone to Google Voice," later in this chapter, for information on reestablishing Google Voice as your phone's voice mail service.

Setting up a Google Voice account

You need to get a Google Voice account on the Internet before you configure the Droid 3 for Google Voice. Start your adventure by visiting the Google Voice home page on the Internet: `http://voice.google.com`.

If necessary, sign in to your Google account. You use the same account name and password you use to access your Gmail.

Your next task is to configure a Google Voice number to be used for your Droid 3, as covered in the next section. Or, if you've just signed up for a Google Voice number, choose the options to use your existing cell phone number and select the "Lite" version of Google Voice. It sets you up with voice mail for your phone, which is the ultimate goal.

✔ If all you want is to use Google Voice as your voice mail service, choose the option that says Just Want Voicemail for Your Cell.

✔ Google Voice offers a host of features: international dialing, call forwarding, and other stuff I am not aware of and, honestly, am quite afraid of.

Adding your phone to Google Voice

After you have a Google Voice account, you add your Droid 3 phone number to the list of phone numbers registered for Google Voice. As in the preceding section, I recommend that you complete these steps on a computer connected to the Internet, but keep your phone handy:

1. **Click the Gear icon in the upper right corner of the Google Voice home page, and choose the Voice Settings command from the menu.**

   The Voice Settings command may change its location in a future update to the Google Voice web page. If so, the purpose of this step is to access the Settings screen, where you register phone numbers for use with Google Voice.

2. **Click the link Add Another Phone.**

3. **Work the steps to verify your phone for use with Google Voice.**

Eventually, Google Voice needs to phone your Droid 3. When it does, use the dialpad on the phone to type the code number you see on your computer's screen. After confirming the code number, you see the Droid 3 listed as a registered phone — but you're not done yet:

4. **Click the Activate Voicemail link.**

You must activate your phone for it to work with Google Voice. This is the most important step!

5. **On your Droid 3, dial the number you see on your computer screen.**

The number starts with *71, which is the command to forward unanswered calls on the Verizon network. Note that the number you're dialing is not the same as your Google Voice phone number.

The number dials and then the Droid 3 hangs up right away. That's normal.

6. **On your computer screen, click the Done button.**

Your Droid 3 is now registered for use with Google Voice.

Retrieving your Google Voice messages

Google Voice transcribes your voice mail messages, turning the audio from the voice mail into a text message you can read. The messages all show up eventually in your Gmail account, just as though someone sent you an e-mail rather than left you voice mail. It's a good way to deal with your messages, but not the best way.

The best way to handle Google Voice is to use the Voice app, available from the Android Market. Use the QR code in the margin, or visit the Android Market to search for and install the Google Voice app. (See Chapter 18 for details on the Android Market; refer to this book's introduction for information on QR codes.)

After the Google Voice app is installed, it provides the best interface for getting your messages. You have to work through some setup, which isn't difficult. Eventually, you see the app's main interface, which looks and works similarly to an e-mail program. You can review your messages or touch a message to read or play it, as illustrated in Figure 7-1.

When new Google Voice messages come in, you see the Google Voice notification icon appear, as shown in the margin. Pull down the notifications, and choose the Voicemail from *Whomever* item to read or listen to the message.

Message text translation

Contact info (if available)

Incoming phone number

Play message.   Turn on speaker.

Figure 7-1: Voice mail with the Google Voice app.

- With Google Voice installed, you see two notices for every voice mail message: one from Google Voice and another for the Gmail message that comes in.

- The Google Voice app works only after you activate Google Voice on your Droid 3, as described in the preceding section.

- You can best listen to the message when using the Google Voice app. In Gmail, you see a transcript of the message, but you must touch the Play Message link to visit a web page and then listen to the message.

- The text translation feature in Google Voice is at times astonishingly accurate and at other times not so good.

- The text *Transcript Not Available* appears whenever Google Voice is unable to create a text message from your voice mail or the Google Voice service is temporarily unavailable.

8

Your Address Book

In This Chapter

▶ Using the Contacts app

▶ Sorting and searching contacts

▶ Creating new contacts

▶ Getting a contact from a map search

▶ Editing contact information

▶ Putting a picture on a contact

▶ Working with favorites

▶ Grouping your contacts

▶ Deleting contacts

*I*t's one of those annoying questions kids ask. Along the lines of "Why do we *dial* a phone" and "How do you *roll up* a window?" they inquire "What's an address book?" You can answer by explaining that, in the olden days, back when Bill Clinton was president of the United States, people would write down names and addresses in a book. And then I'm sure the kids will correct you: "Don't you mean *e-book?*"

One of the handiest apps on your Droid 3 is the Contacts app, which is your phone's digital address book. It just makes sense to keep names, addresses, phone numbers, and e-mail information on your phone rather than tote around a separate book or try to remember all that information in your head. The digital address book is handy, it's part of the digital age, and it's covered in this chapter.

mobile
2-555-1027

Email home
me@theodore-roosevelt.com

View home address
28 East 20th Street
New York, NY 10003

ebook
·h.facebook.com/#/profile.php?

Folks You Know

The name of the program on your Droid 3 that stores information about people you know is Contacts. I would normally write a contact lens joke here, but I just can't be pithy enough, so I'll leave it at that.

Presenting the Contacts app

To peruse your phone's address book, open the Contacts app, found on the App Menu screen. You can also view your contacts by touching the Contacts tab in the Dialer app. Both methods shows you the same list, shown in Figure 8-1.

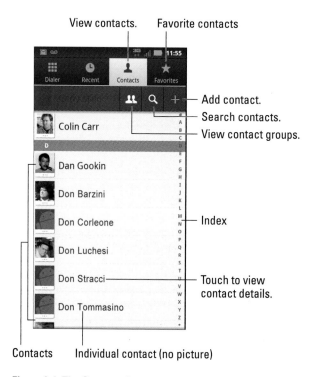

Figure 8-1: The Contacts list.

Scroll the list by swiping your finger. You can use the index on the right side of the screen (refer to Figure 8-1) to quickly navigate up and down through your contacts.

To do anything with a contact, you first have to choose it: Touch a contact name, and you see more information, as shown in Figure 8-2.

Recent calls, texts, and e-mails

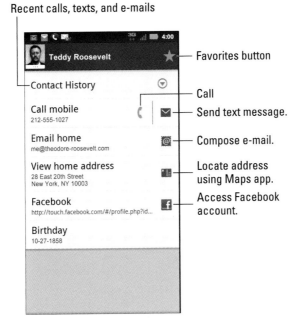

Favorites button

Call

Send text message.

Compose e-mail.

Locate address using Maps app.

Access Facebook account.

Figure 8-2: More detail about a contact.

You can do a multitude of things with the contact after it's displayed, as shown in Figure 8-2:

Make a phone call. To call the contact, touch one of the contact's phone entries, such as Call Home or Call Mobile. See Chapter 5.

Send a text message. Touch the Text Message icon (see Figure 8-2) to open the Text Messaging app and send the contact a message. See Chapter 9 for information about text messaging on your Droid 3.

Compose an e-mail message. Touch the Email link to compose an e-mail message to the contact. When the contact has more than one e-mail address, you can choose to which one you want to send the message. Chapter 10 covers using e-mail on your phone.

View social networking info. Visit the contact's Facebook, Twitter, or other social networking account by touching the appropriate item. See Chapter 12 for additional information on social networking with your Droid 3.

Locate your contact on a map. When the contact has a home or business address, you can touch the little doohickey next to the address, shown in Figure 8-2, to summon the Maps application. Refer to Chapter 13 for all the fun stuff you can do with Maps.

Special and funky contact numbers

Even if you have no friends, or you have friends but don't want them, a smattering of entries are preset in the Contacts list. They represent various phone company services. Here's the list:

#BAL: Receive a free text message indicating your current cell phone charges as well as any previous payments you've made.

#DATA: Receive a free text message indicating your text message or data usage.

#MIN: Receive a free text message indicating the minutes you've used on the Droid 3, including peak, off-hour, weekend, or whatever other categories for cell phone minutes are available.

#PMT: Make a payment using your Droid 3. This operation works only when you've configured your account to make payments via the phone.

#Warranty Center: Contact Verizon for troubleshooting and warranty issues regarding your Droid 3.

Me: That's you! Your own account on your Droid 3 is called *Me.* It has information about you, the person reading this book who owns a Droid 3 phone.

See Chapter 9 for more information about reading text messages on the Droid 3.

Oh, and if you have birthday information there, you can view it as well. Singing "Happy Birthday" is something you have to do on your own.

When you're done viewing the contact, press the Back soft button.

Information about your contacts is pulled from multiple sources: your Google account, the phone's storage, and your social networking sites. When you see duplicated information for a contact, it's probably because the information comes from two or more of those sources. Multiple sources can be viewed when you edit the contact's information, as covered later in this chapter.

Sorting the Contacts list

Your contacts are displayed in the Contacts app in a certain order: alphabetically by first name and first name first. You can change the order, if you like:

1. **Start the Contacts app.**

2. **Press the Menu soft button, and choose Display Options.**

3. **Choose Sort List By.**

4. **Select First Name or Last Name to sort the list accordingly.**

   I prefer sorting by last name, which is how most Rolodex products are organized.

5. **Choose View Contact Names As.**

6. **Choose either First Name First or Last Name First, which specifies how contacts are displayed in the list.**

    The way the name is displayed doesn't affect the sort order. So, if you choose First Name First (as I do), as well as Last Name for the sort order (as I do), you still see the list sorted by last name.

7. **Press the Back soft button when you're done.**

The Contacts list is updated, displayed per your preferences.

Searching contacts

Rather than scroll the Contacts list with angst-riddled desperation, press the Search soft button or the Contact Search button in the Contacts app (refer to Figure 8-1). The Search Contacts text box appears. Type a few letters of the contact's name, and you see the list of contacts narrowed to the few who match the letters you type. Touch a name from the search list to view the contact's information.

There's no correlation between the number of contacts you have and the number of bestest friends you have — none at all.

A New Contact Is Born

You have many ways to get contact information into your phone. You can build them all from scratch, but that's tedious. More likely, you collect contacts as you use your phone. Or, you can borrow contacts from your Gmail contacts. In no time, you'll have a phone full of contact information.

Your social networking friends are automatically merged into your phone's Contacts list whenever you add social networking sites to the Droid 3. See Chapter 12 for details.

Adding a new contact from the Recent Calls list

One of the quickest ways to build up your Contacts list is to add people as they phone you — assuming that you've told them about your new phone number. After someone calls, you can use the Recent Calls list to add the person to your Contacts list. Obey these steps:

1. **Open the Contacts app or the Dialer app.**

2. **Touch the Recent tab at the top of the screen.**

3. **Choose the phone number from the list of recent calls.**

4. **Choose Add to Contacts.**

5. **Choose Create a New Contact.**

6. **Choose your Google account for the location to store the new contact.**

By choosing your Google account, you ensure that the contact's information is duplicated from your phone to your Google account on the Internet. Other options may do the same for you, so if you use Yahoo! Mail more than Google, for example, you can choose that option instead.

You can, optionally, place a green check mark by the setting Remember This Choice so that you're not prompted again.

7. **Touch OK.**

8. **Fill in the contact's information.**

Use either of the Droid 3 keyboards to fill in the blanks, as many as you know about the caller: given name and family name, for example, and other information, if you know it. If you don't know any additional information, that's fine; just filling in the name helps clue you in to who is calling the next time that person calls (using the same number).

Press the Next button on the onscreen keyboard to hop among the various text fields for the contact.

Use the arrow keys on the sliding keyboard to hop among the text fields.

9. **Touch the Save button to create the new contact.**

You can also follow these steps to add a new phone number to an existing contact. In Step 5, choose the contact from your phone's address book. The new phone number is added to the existing contact's information.

Creating a new contact from scratch

Sometimes, it's necessary to create a contact when you meet another human being in the real world. In that case, you have more information to input, and it starts like this:

1. **Open the Contacts app, or touch the Contacts tab in the Dialer app.**

2. **Touch the Add Contact button found near the top of the screen.**

3. **If prompted, choose your main Google account as the place to store the contact and then touch the OK button.**

By saving the contact as a Google contact, you ensure that it's automatically backed up from your phone to the Internet.

4. **Press the Menu soft button and choose Add Contact.**

5. **Fill in the information on the Add Contact screen as the contact begrudgingly gives you information.**

   Fill in the text fields with the information you know: the Given Name and Family Name fields, for example.

   To expand a field, touch the green Plus button on the touchscreen, or highlight that button by using the arrow keys on the sliding keyboard and then press the OK button.

   Touch the gray button to the left of the phone number or the e-mail address to choose the location for that item, such as Home, Work, or Mobile.

   Touch the More button at the bottom of the list to expand that area and add *even more* information!

6. **Touch the Save button to complete editing and add the new contact.**

You can also create new contacts by using your Gmail account on a computer. This option offers you the luxury of using a full-size keyboard and computer screen, though whenever you meet a contact face-to-face, your Droid 3 will have to suffice.

Importing contacts from your computer

Your computer's e-mail program is doubtless a useful repository of contacts you've built up over the years. You can export these contacts from your e-mail program and then import them into the Droid 3. It's not the simplest thing to do, but it's a great way to build up your phone's Contacts list.

The key is to save or export your computer e-mail program's records in the *vCard* (.vcf) file format. These records can then be imported by the Droid 3 into the Contacts app. The method for exporting contacts varies depending on the e-mail program:

- ✔ **In the Windows Live Mail program,** choose Go⇨Contacts and then choose File⇨Export⇨Business Card (.VCF) to export the contacts.

- ✔ **In Windows Mail,** choose File⇨Export⇨Windows Contacts and then choose vCards (Folder of .VCF Files) from the Export Windows Contacts dialog box. Click the Export button.

- ✔ **On the Mac,** open the Address Book program, and choose File⇨Export⇨ Export vCard.

After the vCard files are created, connect the Droid 3 to your computer and transfer the vCard files from your computer to the phone. Directions for making this type of transfer are found in Chapter 20.

After the vCard files have been copied to the Droid 3, follow these steps in the Contacts app to complete the process:

1. **Press the Menu soft button.**

2. **Choose the Manage Contacts option.**

3. **Choose the SD Card option beneath the heading *Import Contacts From.***

   Yeah, it's a dumb design decision to have two SD Card commands on the same menu. Bad, Motorola. Bad!

4. **If prompted, choose your Google account from the list and then touch the OK button.**

5. **If prompted, choose Import All vCard Files.**

6. **Touch the OK button.**

   The contacts are saved on your phone, but also to your Gmail account, which instantly creates a backup copy.

Creating a new contact from a Maps location

When you use the Maps application to locate a restaurant, a livery stable, or a nearby parole office, you can quickly create a contact for that location. Here's how:

1. **After searching for your location, touch the cartoon bubble that appears on the map.**

   For example, in Figure 8-3, a bookstore has been found.

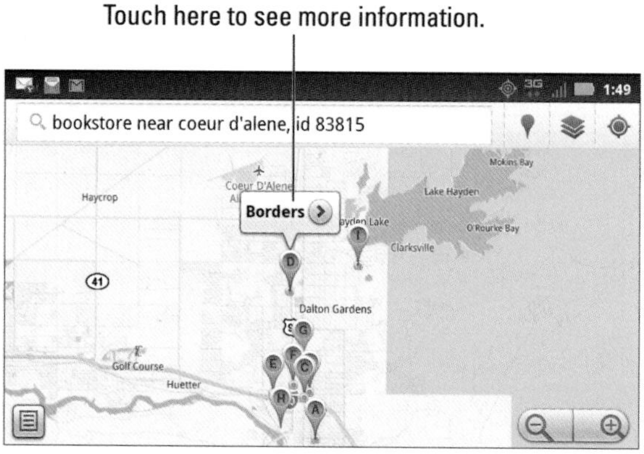

Touch here to see more information.

Figure 8-3: A business has been located.

2. **Press the Menu soft button, and choose the command Add As a Contact.**

3. **If prompted, choose in which account to store the contact.**

   The information from the Maps application is copied into the proper fields for the contact, including the address and phone number, plus other information (if available).

4. **Touch the Save button.**

   The new contact is created.

See Chapter 13 for detailed information on how to search for a location using the Maps application.

Organize and Manage Your Peeps

When things change for a contact, or perhaps your thumbs were a bit too big when you created the contact while you were working a jackhammer, you can edit the contact information. Aside from editing existing information or adding new items, you can do a smattering of other interesting things, as covered in this section.

   ✔ See Chapter 6 for information on configuring contacts so that all their incoming calls go to voice mail.

   ✔ Also refer to Chapter 6 on how to set a contact's ringtone.

Making basic changes

To make minor touch-ups on any contact, start by locating and displaying the contact's information. Press the Menu soft button, and choose Edit Contact.

The contact's information is displayed, organized by source. You may see Google contact information, information stored on the phone, or information culled from web e-mail services or social networking sites.

Change or add information by touching a field and typing on either the onscreen keyboard or the sliding keyboard. You can edit information as well: Touch the field to edit and change whatever you want.

Some information cannot be edited. For example, fields pulled in from social networking sites can be edited only by that account holder on the social networking site.

When you're done editing, touch the Save button.

Adding an image for a contact

Nothing can be more delicious than snapping an inappropriate picture of someone you know and using the picture as their contact picture on your phone. Then, every time they call you, that embarrassing, potentially career-ending photo comes up.

Oh, and I suppose you could use nice pictures as well, but what's the fun in that?

The simplest way to add a picture to one of your Droid 3 contacts is to have the image already stored in the phone. You can snap a picture and save it (covered in Chapter 14), grab a picture from the Internet (covered in Chapter 11), or use any image already stored in the phone's Gallery app (covered in Chapter 15). The image doesn't even have to be a picture of the contact — any image will do.

After the contact's photo, or any other suitable image, is stored on the phone, follow these steps to update the contact's information:

1. **Locate and display the contact's information.**

2. **Press the Menu soft button, and choose the Edit Contact command.**

3. **Touch the Add Picture icon.**

   The icon is found at the top of the screen, where the contact's picture would normally appear.

4. **Choose the option Select Photo from Gallery.**

   If you have other image management apps on your phone, you can instead choose the app's command from the list.

5. **Choose Gallery.**

   The Droid 3 photo gallery is displayed. It lists all photos and videos stored on your phone.

6. **Browse the gallery to look for a suitable image.**

   See Chapter 15 for more information on using the Gallery.

7. **Touch the image you want to use for the contact.**

   The image is now assigned, and it appears whenever the contact is referenced on your Droid 3.

You can add pictures to contacts on your Google account by using any computer. Just visit your Gmail Contacts list to edit a contact. You can then add to that contact any picture stored on your computer. The picture is eventually synced with the same contact on your Droid 3.

- ✔ Pictures can also be added by your Gmail friends and contacts when they add their own images to their accounts.

- ✔ Some images in the Gallery may not work for contact icons. For example, images synchronized with your online photo albums may be unavailable.

- ✔ If you want to crop the image, you can edit it by using the Gallery app. See Chapter 15.

- ✔ To remove or change a contact's picture, follow Steps 1 through 3 in the preceding list. Choose Remove Icon to get rid of the existing image; choose Change Icon to set a new image.

Setting the default phone number and e-mail address

When a contact has multiple phone numbers or e-mail addresses, you can choose which one becomes the *default*. This default number or address is used by various phone features to let you quickly phone or send the contact a message. Here's how to set a contact's default phone number or e-mail address:

1. **Display the contact's information.**

2. **Long-press the phone number you want to use as the main number.**

   Touch and hold the phone number until the Options menu pops up.

3. **Choose Make Default Number.**

   The phone number is appended by a tiny white check mark.

4. **Long-press the e-mail address you want as the contact's primary e-mail contact.**

5. **Choose Make Default Email.**

   As with the phone number, the e-mail address entry grows a tiny white check mark.

Making a favorite

A *favorite* contact is someone you stay in touch with most often. The person doesn't have to be someone you like — just someone you (perhaps unfortunately) phone often, such as your bail bondsman.

The list of favorite contacts is kept on the Dialer app's Favorites tab, as shown in Figure 8-4. The top part of the list shows favorite favorites, or those favorites you've contacted frequently. At the bottom of the list, you see people you contact frequently but who are not (yet) favorites.

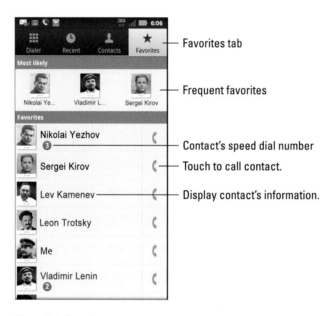

Figure 8-4: Favorite contacts.

To add a contact to the Favorites list, display the contact's information and touch the Star button in the contact's upper right corner, as shown in Figure 8-2. When the star shown in the figure is green, the contact is one of your favorites.

To remove a favorite, touch the contact's star again, and it loses its color. Removing a favorite doesn't delete the contact but instead removes it from the Favorites list.

✔ Occasionally peruse the names in the bottom part of the Favorites list — the frequent contacts. You might consider promoting some of them to your favorites.

✔ Contacts have no idea whether they're favorites, so don't believe that you're hurting people's feelings by not making them favorites.

Creating a contact group

It's possible to corral contacts into groups, which makes it easier to send that group an e-mail or a text message. Heed these steps to create a contact group:

1. **Display the Contacts list.**

2. **Touch the View Contact Groups button at the top of the screen.**

   Refer to Figure 8-1 for the button's location.

   You see any groups already created, such as groups you may have organized in your Google account.

3. **Press the Menu soft button, and choose the New Group command.**

4. **Type a name for the group.**

   For example, type **People I Work with Whom I Don't Despise**.

5. **Touch the OK button.**

   The group is created, but it's empty, and surprisingly, the phone recognizes that the group is empty. The next step is to add members to the group.

6. **Scroll your Contacts list, and place a green check mark by the names of people you want to add to the group.**

7. **Touch the Done button.**

   You see the group listed, along with all its members.

To perform an action with the group, press the Menu soft button and choose Send Message, Send Email, or Create Event. Then follow along with the directions on the screen, as well as elsewhere in this book, for completing your group message or activity.

- ✔ Add members to the group by touching the green Plus button in the upper right part of the screen while you're viewing the group.

- ✔ Remove people from the group by pressing the Menu soft button and choosing the Edit Group command. Touch the red Minus button by a member's name to remove him. Touch the Save button when you're done.

- ✔ Delete a group by pressing the Menu soft button and choosing the Delete Group command. Touch the Yes button to confirm.

Sharing a contact

You know Susie? I know Susie, too! But you don't have her contact information? Allow me to share it with you. Here's what I do:

1. **Summon the contact you want to share from your Contacts list.**

2. **Press the Menu soft button, and choose the Share command.**

3. **Choose the items you want to share about the contact.**

   All items have green check marks by them. Touch a green check mark to deselect an item about the contact you don't want to share.

4. **Touch OK.**

5. **Choose how to send the information: Bluetooth, Email, Gmail, Text Messaging, or whatever else might be displayed.**

   After you choose a method, the appropriate app appears for sharing the contact's name card.

Information about sharing with Email, Gmail, Text Messaging, and other options is explained elsewhere in this book. (I don't cover Bluetooth file sharing because it's a pain to set up.)

What you're sending is a vCard, a common type of file used by databases and personal information software to exchange contact information. You can use the vCard, for example, to import information into your computer's e-mail program.

Removing a contact

Every so often, consider reviewing your phone's contacts. Purge those folks whom you no longer recognize or you've forgotten. It's simple:

1. **Locate the contact in your Contacts list, and display the contact's information.**

2. **Press the Menu soft button, and choose Delete Contact.**

   A warning may appear, depending on whether the contact has information linked from your social networking sites. If so, dismiss the warning by touching the OK button.

3. **Touch OK to remove the contact from your phone.**

Because the Contacts list is synchronized with your Gmail contacts for your Google account, the contact is also removed there.

For some linked accounts, such as Facebook, deleting the account from your phone doesn't remove the human from your Facebook account. The warning that appears (before Step 3 in the preceding list) explains as much.

Part III

Nonverbal Communications

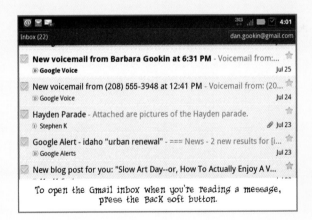

To open the Gmail inbox when you're reading a message, press the Back soft button.

In this part . . .

To say that the Droid 3 is merely a phone is to insult the device. Not that the gizmo has any feelings, but seriously: There's more to staying in touch than the typical, boring phone call. In fact, if you're under 20, you'd probably be surprised to find out that the phone even makes calls. That's because most kids use their cell phones to *text* each other. Verbal communications? Why bother!

The nonverbal communications part of the Droid 3 involves using the phone's keyboards to stay in touch. You can employ text messaging, e-mail, the Internet, and social networking sites to maintain connections to your friends flung far and wide. That's the topic of this part of the book.

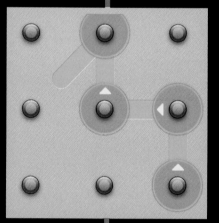

Jim Naiseum — 5:18 PM
Quick medical question: Lawn dart to the head. Remove or keep in?

Ann Oying — 4:53 PM
Just joined FarmVille and now I'm going to bother you about it forever.

Alphanso Gordo — 4:53 PM
I can see my toes!

9

Don't Say It — Text It

In This Chapter

▶ Creating a text message

▶ Getting a text message

▶ Forwarding a text message

▶ Texting pictures, videos, and media items

▶ Managing your text messages

Texting is the cell phone feature that turns your 21st century smartphone into a 19th century telegraph, but without the meddlesome bother of having to learn Morse code. Even though, with the popularity of texting among the teens and tweens, I bet they'd learn Morse code if it were the only way they could still text. Oh, those kids!

Happily, you don't have to learn Morse code to compose and send a text message on your Droid 3. Heck, you don't even have to learn how to type. Just connect with another cell phone user and punch in quick, instant messages until your thumbs grow welts. This chapter explains how it's done, and check out *Repetitive Stress Injury For Dummies* for how to deal with the thumb welts.

Conrad Spirecy
408-555-2013

Yep, them teenagers aren't really human. Th people from Venus. Heard that on the Art Be 'tother night.

at's not what I thought

ohts | thoughtful | thoughtf

Message for You!

The common term for using a cell phone to send a text message to another cell phone is *texting*. I prefer to say it as "sending a text message." The program that handles this job on your Droid 3 is Text Messaging.

✔ Your cellular service plan may charge you per message for every text message you send. Some plans feature a given number of free messages per month. Other plans, favored by teenagers (and their parents), feature unlimited texting.

✔ Though using the Skype Mobile app isn't exactly the same as sending a text message, it does let you send instant messages to folks. The person you're chatting with should have Skype installed, on either a PC or a mobile phone. Unlike text messages, Skype messages are free.

✔ The nerdy term for text messaging is *SMS,* which stands for *Short Message Service.*

Composing a new text message to a contact

Because most cell phones sport a text messaging feature, you can send a text message to just about any mobile number. It works like this:

1. **Open the Contacts icon on the Home screen.**

2. **Choose a contact — someone to whom you want to send a text message.**

   You can also send a message to a contact group by using the group's Contact Quick Action menu. See Chapter 24 for details on Contact Quick Actions.

3. **Touch the Message icon next to the contact's mobile number.**

   The Message icon looks like an envelope, as shown in the margin.

   The message composition window appears, which also tracks your text conversation, similar to the one shown in Figure 9-1.

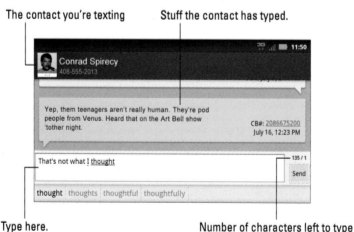

Figure 9-1: Typing a text message.

4. **Type the message text.**

   Be brief. A text message has a 160-character limit. You can check the screen to see whether you're nearing the limit (refer to Figure 9-1). To help you stay under the limit, see the later sidebar "Common text-message abbreviations" for some useful text-message shortcuts and acronyms.

5. **Touch the Send button.**

   The message is sent instantly. Whether the contact replies instantly depends. When the person replies, you see the message displayed (refer to Figure 9-1).

6. **Read the reply.**

7. **Repeat Steps 4 through 6 as needed — or eternally, whichever comes first.**

There's no need to continually look at your phone while waiting for a text message. Whenever your contact chooses to reply, you see the message recorded as part of an ongoing conversation. See the later section "Receiving a text message."

- ✔ You can send text messages only to cell phones. Grandma cannot receive text messages on her landline that she's had since the 1960s.

- ✔ Add a subject to your message by touching the Menu soft button and choosing Add Subject.

- ✔ You can dictate text messages by using the keyboard's Microphone button. See Chapter 4 for more information on voice input.

- ✔ You can send a single text message to multiple recipients: Just type additional phone numbers or contact names in the To field when you're composing a new message.

- ✔ Phone numbers and e-mail addresses sent in text messages become links. You can touch a link to call that number or visit the web page.

- ✔ Continue a conversation at any time: Open the Text Messaging app, peruse the list of existing conversations, and touch one to review what has been said or to pick up the conversation.

- ✔ Do not text and drive. Do not text and drive. Do not text and drive.

Common text-message abbreviations

Texting isn't about proper English. Indeed, many of the abbreviations and shortcuts used in texting are slowly becoming part of the English language, such as LOL and BRB.

The weird news is that these acronyms weren't invented by teenagers. Sure, the kids use them, but the acronyms find their roots in the Internet chat rooms of yesteryear. Regardless of a shortcut's source, you might find it handy for typing messages quickly. Or, maybe you can use this reference for deciphering an acronym's meaning. You can type acronyms in either upper- or lowercase.

2	To, also		NP	No problem
411	Information		OMG	Oh my goodness!
BRB	Be right back		PIR	People in room (watching)
BTW	By the way		POS	Person over shoulder (watching)
CYA	See you		QT	Cutie
FWIW	For what it's worth		ROFL	Rolling on the floor, laughing
FYI	For your information		SOS	Someone over shoulder (watching)
GB	Goodbye		TC	Take care
GJ	Good job		THX	Thanks
GR8	Great		TIA	Thanks in advance
GTG	Got to go		TMI	Too much information
HOAS	Hold on a second		TTFN	Ta-ta for now (goodbye)
IC	I see		TTYL	Talk to you later
IDK	I don't know		TY	Thank you
IMO	In my opinion		U2	You too
JK	Just kidding		UR	Your, you are
K	Okay		VM	Voice mail
L8R	Later		W8	Wait
LMAO	Laughing my [rear] off		XOXO	Hugs and kisses
LMK	Let me know		Y	Why?
LOL	Laugh out loud		YW	You're welcome
NC	No comment		ZZZ	Sleeping

Sending a text message when you know only the phone number

The situation is rare, but it can come up: You have a cell phone number and you need to send a text. Follow these steps:

1. **Open the Text Messaging app.**

   You see a list of current conversations (if any), organized by contact name or phone number. If not, press the Back soft button.

2. **Touch the green Plus button, found at the top of the touchscreen.**

3. **Type a cell phone number in the To field.**

   When the number you type matches one or more existing contacts, you see those contacts displayed. Choose one to send a message to that person; otherwise, continue typing the phone number.

4. **Touch the Compose Message text box.**

5. **Type your text message.**

6. **Touch the Send button to send the message.**

I recommend that the next thing you do after sending the message is to create a new contact for the number: Long-press the phone number you sent a text to (found atop the screen). Choose View Contact and then Create New Contact. Fill in the blanks, using the good information in Chapter 8 to help guide you.

Receiving a text message

Whenever a new text message comes in, you see the message appear briefly at the top of the Droid 3 touchscreen. Then you see the New Text Message notification, shown in the margin.

To view the message, pull down the notifications, as described in Chapter 3. Touch the messaging notification, and that conversation window immediately opens.

Forwarding a text message

It's possible to forward a text message, but it's not the same as forwarding e-mail. In fact, when it comes to forwarding information, e-mail has text messaging beat by well over 160 characters.

Whether to send a text message or an e-mail?

Sending a text message is similar to sending an e-mail message. Both involve the instant electronic delivery of a message to someone else. And both methods of communication have their advantages and disadvantages.

Text messages are short and to the point. They're informal, more like quick chats. Indeed, the speed of reply is often what makes text messaging useful. Like sending e-mail, though, sending a text message doesn't guarantee a reply.

An e-mail message can be longer than a text message. You can receive e-mail on any computer or device that can access the Internet, like your Droid 3. E-mail message attachments (pictures, documents) are handled better, and more consistently, than text message (MMS) media. You can also reply to everyone in an e-mail message by using the Reply All command, whereas you can send only an initial text message to multiple recipients.

Finally, though e-mail isn't considered formal communication, not like a physical letter or a phone call, it's considered more formal than a text message.

The bottom line is that you can forward only the information in a text messaging cartoon bubble, not the entire conversation. Here's how it works:

1. **If necessary, open a conversation in the Messages app.**

2. **Long-press the text entry (the cartoon bubble) you want to forward.**

3. **From the menu that appears, choose Forward Message.**

   From this point on, forwarding the message works like sending a new message from scratch:

4. **Type the recipient's name (if the person is a contact), or type a phone number.**

   The text you're forwarding appears, already written, in the text field.

5. **Touch the Send button to forward the message.**

Multimedia Messages

When a text message contains a bit of audio or video or a picture, it ceases becoming a mere text message and transforms into — *ta-da!* — a multimedia message. This type of message even has its own acronym, MMS, which supposedly stands for Multimedia Messaging Service.

✔ You can send pictures, video, and audio using multimedia messaging.

✔ There's no need to run a separate program or do anything fancy to send media in a text message; the same Text Messaging app is used on the Droid 3 for sending both text and media messages. Just follow the advice in this section.

✔ Not every mobile phone can receive MMS messages. Rather than receive the media item, the recipient may be directed to a web page where the item can be viewed on the Internet.

Composing a multimedia message

The most consistent way to compose a multimedia message is to attach the media to the outgoing message. Obey these steps:

1. **Compose a text message as you normally do.**

2. **Press the Menu soft button, and choose the Insert command.**

   A pop-up menu appears, listing various media items you can attach to a text message. Here's a summary:

   Existing Picture: Choose an image stored in the phone's Gallery.

   New Picture: Take a picture right now and send it in a text message.

   Existing Audio: Attach a song from the music library.

   New Audio: Record an audio clip, such as your voice, and then send it.

   Existing Video: Choose a video you've taken with the phone and stored in the Gallery.

   New Video: Record a video and then send it as media in a text message.

   Slideshow: Create a collection of photos to send together.

   Location: Send a URL of your current, or another, location.

   Name Card: Attach contact information in the form of a vCard.

   More options may appear on the menu, depending on which apps you have installed on your Droid 3.

3. **Choose a media attachment from the pop-up menu.**

   What happens next depends on the attachment you've selected. You're taken to the appropriate app on your phone, where you can choose an existing media item or create a new one.

4. **If you like, compose a message to accompany the media attachment.**

5. **Touch the Send button to send your media text message.**

Opting out of text messaging

You don't have to be a part of the text messaging craze. Indeed, it's entirely possible to opt out of text messaging altogether. Simply contact your cellular provider and tell them that you want to disable text messaging on your phone. They will happily comply, and you'll never be able to send or receive a text message again.

People opt out of text messaging for a number of reasons. A big one is cost: If the kids keep running up the text messaging bill, simply disabling the feature is often easier than continuing to pay all the usage surcharges. Another reason is security: Viruses and spam can be sent via text message. If you opt out, you don't have to worry about receiving these unwanted text messages.

In just a few short cellular moments, the receiving party will enjoy your multimedia text message.

✔ Not every phone is capable of receiving multimedia messages.

✔ Be aware of the size limit on the amount of media you can send; try to keep your video and audio attachments brief.

✔ An easier way to send a multimedia message is to start with the source, such as a picture or video stored on your phone. Use the Share command or button (refer to the icon in the margin), and choose MMS to share that media item. Information about the various Share commands on your phone are covered throughout this book.

✔ Some video attachments can be too large for a multimedia message. The phone warns you when it happens, but more important, review the special options in Chapter 14 for creating multimedia message video attachments.

✔ The Slideshow option presents a second screen, where you collect pictures from the Gallery. Use the icons on top of this screen to add pictures from the Gallery. Use the Preview button to examine the slideshow.

✔ The Name Card option displays the phone's address book. Choose a contact, and that contact's information is then translated into a vCard file and attached to your text message. A *vCard* is a contact-information file format, commonly used by e-mail programs and contact management software. Whether the recipient can do anything with a vCard in a multimedia text message is up to the recipient's phone software.

Receiving a multimedia message

A multimedia attachment comes into your Droid 3 just like any other text message does, but you see a thumbnail preview of whichever media was sent, such as an image, a still from a video, or a Play button to listen to audio. To preview the attachment, touch it. To do more with the multimedia attachment, long-press it. Choose how to deal with the attachment by selecting an option from the menu that's displayed.

For example, to save an image attachment, long-press the image thumbnail and choose the Save Picture command.

Some types of attachments, such as audio, cannot be saved.

Message Management

Even though I'm a stickler for deleting e-mail after I read it, I don't bother deleting my text message threads. That might be because I receive far more e-mail than text messages. Anyway, were I to delete a text message conversation, I would follow these exact steps:

1. **Open the conversation you want to remove.**

   Choose the conversation from the main Text Messaging screen.

2. **Touch the Menu soft button, and choose the Delete command.**

3. **Touch the Delete button to confirm.**

   The conversation is gone.

If I wanted to delete every dang doodle conversation shown on the main Text Messaging screen, I'd follow these steps:

1. **Touch the Menu soft button.**

2. **Choose Select Multiple.**

3. **Touch the box next to each conversation you want to zap.**

   Obviously, if you want to keep a conversation, don't touch its box.

   A green check mark appears by conversations slated for execution.

4. **Touch the Delete button, and then touch Delete again to confirm.**

The selected conversations are gone.

Text messaging alternatives

Life doesn't turn totally dismal when you find yourself unduly bound by text message limitations on your cell phone contract. Just because you're limited to sending (and receiving) only 250 messages a month doesn't mean that you and your friends must stay horribly out of touch or that your thumbs will atrophy from lack of typing. A smattering of free alternatives to text messaging are available, all of which use the Internet and two of which come preinstalled on the Droid 3.

Talk: The Talk app connects you with the Google Talk service on the Internet. It isn't a texting app; it's a chat app. You can summon a list of friends, all configured from your Google account, and chat it up — as long as they're available. My advice is to configure Google Talk on your computer first, and then you can find the same friends available on your Droid 3.

Skype Mobile: The Skype Mobile app can be used to chat as well, if you've set up a slew of friends and they also have Skype Mobile or the full-fledged Skype program on their desktop computers. Chatting on Skype is easy and free.

Of course, these apps use the Internet, so if your phone has a data restriction, you face, theoretically, a surcharge for using more Internet than your cell phone plan allows. Even so, text applications such as Google Talk and Skype Mobile (chat) tend not to eat up much in terms of Internet usage. So type away!

Mail of the Electronic Kind

In This Chapter

▶ Understanding e-mail on the Droid 3

▶ Configuring your e-mail accounts

▶ Receiving a new message

▶ Using the Messaging app

▶ Creating and sending e-mail

▶ Working with e-mail attachments

▶ Making an e-mail signature

▶ Changing the default e-mail account

*I*t has been said that the number-one reason for most people to use the Internet is e-mail. That was probably before Facebook became popular. Even so, e-mail is now the preferred form of written communication, eclipsing the personal handwritten note years ago. Though some nostalgia over the change may linger, I have to confess that I can read none of my relatives' handwriting anyway, so perhaps the whole personal-letter thing was overblown to begin with. Anyway.

As a communications device, your Droid 3 is more than capable of sending and receiving e-mail. In fact, because it's a Google phone, you instantly receive updates of your Gmail on the Droid 3. You can also configure the phone to access your non-Gmail e-mail, making your electronic missives conveniently available wherever you go.

ʌin@gmail.com

ʌ. Xyqz

Teleporter question

Dear Dr. Xyqz,

ˉir, I have received the device I c
ˑ month and I have a small qu
ˑould happen if, just say, t

4 | 5 | 6

Mail Call!

Electronic mail is handled on the Droid 3 by two apps: Gmail and Email.

The Gmail app hooks directly into the Gmail account associated with your Google account. In fact, they're exact echoes of each other: The Gmail you receive on your computer is also received on your phone.

You can also use the Email app on your phone to connect to non-Gmail electronic mail, such as the standard mail service provided by your Internet service provider (ISP) or a web-based e-mail system such as Yahoo! Mail or Microsoft Live mail.

Regardless of the app, electronic mail on your phone works just like it does on your computer: You can receive mail, create new messages, forward e-mail, send messages to a group of contacts, and work with attachments, for example. As long as your phone has a data connection, e-mail works just peachy.

- ✔ You can run the Gmail and Email apps by touching the Launcher on the Home screen and then locating the apps on the App menu.

- ✔ The Email app can be found on the main panel of the Home screen. Adding the Gmail app icon to the Home screen is easy: See Chapter 22.

- ✔ The Email app can be configured to handle multiple e-mail accounts, as discussed later in this section.

- ✔ Although you can use your phone's web browser to visit the Gmail web site, you should use the Gmail app to pick up your Gmail.

- ✔ If you forget your Gmail password, visit this web address:

      www.google.com/accounts/ForgotPasswd

Setting up a web-based e-mail account

You need to configure the Droid 3 to access any non-Gmail e-mail account. The process is easy for web-based e-mail accounts such as Yahoo! Mail; follow through with these steps to get things set up:

1. **Start the My Accounts app.**

   The My Accounts app is found on the App menu, which you access by touching the Launcher button to the lower right of the Home screen.

2. **Touch the Add Account button.**

3. **If your account type is shown in the list, such as Yahoo! Mail, choose it; otherwise, choose the Email icon.**

4. **Type the account's e-mail address.**

5. **Type the password for the account.**

   If you're using the onscreen keyboard, touch the Done button to dismiss the onscreen keyboard.

6. **Ensure that there is a green check mark by the option Automatically Configure Account.**

7. **Touch the Next button.**

   In a few magical moments, the e-mail account is configured and added to the account list.

   If you goofed up the account name or password, you're warned: Try again.

8. **Touch the Done button.**

If your attempt is not met with success, you have to configure the account manually. That's the bad news. The good news is that the phone may help you by providing suggestions. Follow them.

Setting up an ISP e-mail account

For e-mail provided by your Internet service provider (ISP), office, or other large, intimidating organization, you have to work the manual setup. The steps are involved, but as long you have the details from your ISP, things should work smoothly. Heed these steps:

1. **Start the My Accounts app.**

   Look for it on the App menu, along with all other apps on your phone.

2. **Touch the Add Account button.**

3. **Choose the Email icon to add your Internet e-mail account.**

4. **Type the e-mail address you use for the account.**

5. **Type the password for that account.**

   If you're using the onscreen keyboard, touch the Done button to dismiss the onscreen keyboard.

6. **Remove the check mark by the option Automatically Configure Account.**

   You need to supply more information for the Droid 3 to configure a standard Internet e-mail account, such as the one given to you by your ISP.

7. **Touch the Next button.**

8. **Choose General Settings.**

9. **Fill in the information for account name, real name, and e-mail address.**

   In the Account Name field, type a name to recognize the account, such as *Comcast Email* or whatever name helps you recognize the account. For my main e-mail account, I used the name *Main*.

   In the Real Name field, type your name, screen name, or whatever name you want to appear in the From field of your outgoing e-mail messages.

   The Email Address field is the address your recipients use when replying to your messages.

10. **Touch the OK button.**

    Press the Back soft button to dismiss the onscreen keyboard so that you can see the OK button.

11. **Choose Incoming Server.**

12. **Fill in the fields per the information provided by your ISP.**

    For most ISP e-mail, the server type is a POP mail server, shown at the top of the screen.

    The Server field contains the name of the ISP's POP server. The Droid 3 may guess at the name; confirm that it's correct. If not, type in the correct server name.

    The *username* is the name you use to log in to your ISP to retrieve e-mail. The *password* is your ISP e-mail password. Both these fields should be preset for you.

13. **Touch the OK button.**

14. **Choose Outgoing Server.**

15. **Fill in the fields.**

    Fill in the SMTP Server name as provided by your ISP.

    If they aren't already filled in for you, type your username and password.

16. **Touch the OK button.**

17. **Touch OK to create the e-mail account.**

The account is now listed on the My Accounts screen, along with Google and Facebook and whatever other accounts you're accessing from your Droid 3.

You can set up a ton of e-mail accounts on the Droid 3, one for each e-mail account you have.

You've Got Email

The Droid 3 works flawlessly with Gmail. In fact, if Gmail is already set up to be your main e-mail address, you'll enjoy having access to your messages all the time by using your phone.

Regular e-mail, handled by the Email program, must be set up before it can be used, as covered earlier in this chapter. After completing the quick and occasionally painless setup, you can receive e-mail on your phone just as you can on a computer.

Getting a new message

You're alerted to the arrival of a new e-mail message in your phone by a notification icon. The icon differs depending on the e-mail's source.

 For a new Gmail message, you see the New Gmail notification, shown in the margin, appear at the top of the touchscreen.

 For a new e-mail message, you see the New Email notification.

 Yahoo! Mail also features its own New Mail notification icon.

To deal with the new-message notification, drag down the notifications and choose the appropriate one. You're taken directly to your inbox to read the new message.

- ✔ See the later section "Configuring the manual delete option" to set up how the phone gets rid of your e-mail messages.
- ✔ Refer to Chapter 3 for information on notifications.

Checking the Gmail inbox

To peruse your Gmail, start the Gmail app. It can be found on the App menu. The Gmail inbox is shown in Figure 10-1.

Unread missive

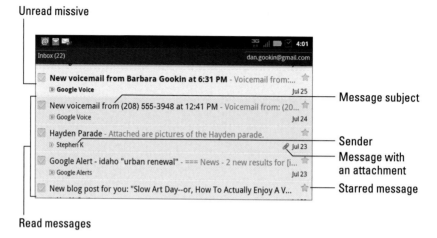

Message subject

Sender

Message with an attachment

Starred message

Read messages

Figure 10-1: The Gmail inbox.

To open the inbox screen when you're reading a message, press the Back soft button.

To check your Email inbox, open the Email app. You're taken to the inbox for your primary e-mail account, though whenever you have multiple e-mail accounts on your Droid 3, you should use the Messaging app, covered in the next section.

✔ Search your Gmail messages by pressing the Search soft key when you're viewing the Gmail inbox.

✔ Gmail is organized using *labels,* not folders. To see your Gmail labels from the inbox, touch the Menu soft button and choose Go to Labels.

Visiting the universal inbox

The Messaging app is your home plate for every account on your Droid 3 that receives messages. It includes all your e-mail accounts as well as social networking sites and even text messaging, as shown in Figure 10-2.

New messages for an account are noted by a number shown in a blue bubble (refer to Figure 10-2).

To view all messages — from e-mail to Facebook updates — touch the Universal Inbox icon.

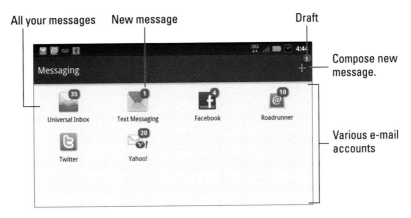

All your messages   New message   Draft

Compose new
message.

Various e-mail
accounts

Figure 10-2: All your messages, in one place.

You compose a new message by touching the green Plus button (refer to Figure 10-2). From the menu that appears, choose an account or a method for creating the new message, or choose a draft to complete. You then see the appropriate program (Email, Facebook, Text Messaging) to craft the new message or finish the draft.

Notice that your Gmail inbox is missing from the Messaging window. Gmail is its own program on the Droid 3; your Gmail messages don't show up in the universal inbox.

The Email app is used to access your primary non-Gmail e-mail account. The Messaging app is used to access all non-Gmail accounts.

Reading an e-mail message

As mail comes in, you can read it by choosing a new e-mail notification, such as the Gmail notification, described earlier in this chapter. You can also choose new e-mail by viewing the universal inbox as covered in the preceding section. Reading and working with the message operate much the same as in any e-mail program you've used.

The way the message looks in the inbox depends on whether you're using the Gmail, Email, or Messaging app. Figure 10-3 shows the Gmail interface; Figure 10-4 shows the Email and Messaging apps' message-reading interface.

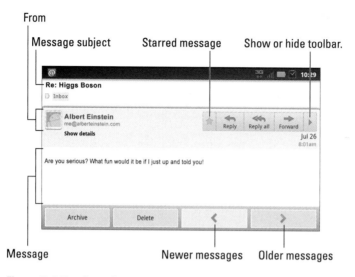

Figure 10-3: Reading a Gmail message on your phone.

Browse messages by touching the arrow buttons at the bottom of the message screen. In Figure 10-3, they point left and right, but in the Email program, shown in Figure 10-4, they point up and down. That difference was created merely to confuse you.

Replying to the message works similarly to composing a new message in the Gmail or Email programs. Refer to the appropriate section later in this chapter.

> ✔ To access additional e-mail commands, touch the Menu soft button. For example, commands in the Email app shuffle messages between folders, flag messages, and print e-mail.

> ✔ See Chapter 19 for information on printing with your Droid 3.

> ✔ Use Reply All only when everyone else *must* get a copy of your reply. Because most people find endless Reply All e-mail threads annoying, use the Reply All option judiciously.

> ✔ To forward a Gmail message, touch the Forward button. In the Email program, the Forward command appears on the same menu as the Reply command, shown in Figure 10-4.

> ✔ When you touch the Star icon in a Gmail message, you're flagging the message. Those starred messages can be viewed or searched separately, making them easier to locate later.

> ✔ If you properly configure the Email program, there's no need to delete messages you read. See the section "Configuring the manual delete option," later in this chapter.

> ✔ I find it easier to delete (and manage) Gmail using a computer.

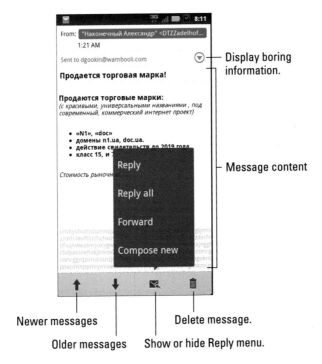

Figure 10-4: Reading an e-mail message.

Make Your Own Mail

Every so often, someone comes up to me and says, "Dan, you're a computer freak. You probably get a lot of e-mail." I generally nod and smile. Then they ask, "How can I get more e-mail?" The answer is simple: To get mail, you have to send mail. Or, you can just be a jerk on a blog and leave your e-mail address there. That method works too, though I don't recommend it.

Composing a new electronic message

Crafting an e-mail epistle on your Droid 3 works exactly like creating one on your computer. Figure 10-5 shows the basic setup.

Here's how to get there:

1. **Start an e-mail program, either Gmail or Email, or use the Messaging app.**

2. **Press the Menu soft button, and choose Compose.**

   You need to be viewing the inbox, not a specific message, for the Compose command to be available.

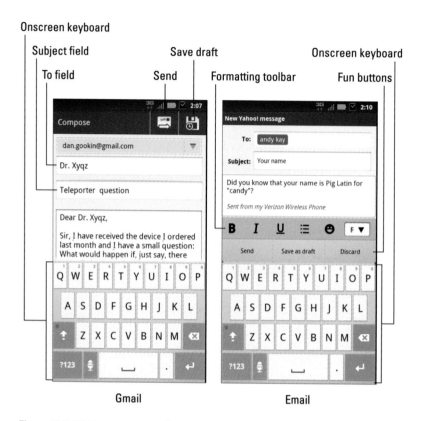

Figure 10-5: Writing a new e-mail message.

3. **If you're using the Messaging app, choose an account from the menu after you touch the green Plus button (refer to Figure 10-2).**

   A new message screen appears, looking similar to Figure 10-5 but with none of the fields filled in. Text-formatting options are available only in the Email program, as shown in the figure.

4. **If necessary, touch the To field to select it.**

5. **Type the first few letters of a contact name, and then choose a matching contact from the list that's displayed.**

   You can also send to any valid e-mail address not found in your Contacts list by typing that address.

6. **Type a subject.**

7. **Type the message.**

8. **Touch the Send button to whisk your missive to the Internet for immediate delivery.**

   In Gmail, you can touch the Save Draft button, and the message is stored in the Drafts folder. You can open this folder to reedit the message. Touch Send to send it.

Copies of the messages you send in the Email program are stored in the Sent mailbox. If you're using Gmail, copies are saved in your Gmail account, which is accessed from your phone or from any computer connected to the Internet.

- To cancel a message, press the Menu soft button and choose the Discard command. Touch either the OK or Discard button to confirm.

- To summon the CC field in Gmail, press the Menu soft button and choose the command Add Cc/Bcc; in the Email program, press the Menu soft button and choose the button Add CC.

- Refer to Chapter 8 for more information on the Contacts list.

- Chapter 4 covers typing, voice input, and text editing.

Starting a new message from a contact

A quick and easy way to compose a new message is to find a contact and then create a message using that contact's information. Heed these steps:

1. **Open the Contacts list.**

2. **Locate the contact to whom you want to send an electronic message.**

   Review Chapter 8 for ways to hunt down contacts in a long list.

3. **Touch the icon next to the contact's e-mail address.**

4. **Choose Email to send an e-mail message using your main e-mail account, or choose Gmail to send the message using Gmail.**

   Other options may appear on the complete Action Using menu. For example, a custom e-mail app you've downloaded may show up there as well.

At this point, creating the message works as described in the preceding sections; refer to them for additional information.

Message Attachments

The Droid 3 lets you view most e-mail attachments, depending on what's attached. You can also send attachments, though it's more of a computer activity, not something that's completely useful on a cell phone. That's because cell phones, unlike computers, aren't designed for creating or manipulating information.

E-mail messages with attachments are flagged in the inbox with the Paperclip icon, which seems to be the standard I-have-an-attachment icon for most e-mail programs. When you open one of these messages, you may see the attachment right away, specifically if it's a picture. Otherwise, you see one of the attachment options illustrated in Figure 10-6.

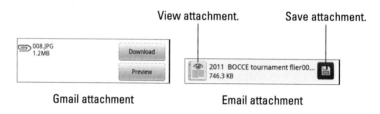

Figure 10-6: E-mail attachment options.

Touch the Preview button to witness the attachment on your phone; touch the Download or Save button to save the attachment to your phone's storage.

What happens after you touch the Preview or View button depends on the type of attachment. Sometimes, you see a list of apps, and you can choose one to open the attachment. Many Microsoft Office documents are opened by the QuickOffice app.

Some attachments cannot be opened. In these cases, use a computer to fetch the message and attempt to open the attachment. Or, you can reply to the message and inform the sender that you cannot open the attachment on your phone.

✓ Sometimes, pictures included in an e-mail message aren't displayed. You find the Show Pictures button in the message, which you can touch to display the pictures.

✓ You cannot save certain e-mail attachments on your phone. Wait until you retrieve these messages on your computer to save their attachments.

✔ The View Attachment button in the Email app (refer to Figure 10-6) shows a thumbnail preview for some image attachments.

✔ You can add an attachment to an e-mail message you create: Touch the Menu soft button and choose either the Attach or Attach Files command. You can then choose what to attach.

✔ See Chapter 15 for more information on the Gallery app and how image and video sharing works on your Droid 3.

E-Mail Configuration

You can have oodles of fun and waste oceans of time confirming and customizing the e-mail experience on your Droid 3. The most interesting things you can do are modify or create an e-mail signature, specify how mail you retrieve on the phone is deleted from the server, and assign a default e-mail account for the Email app.

Creating a signature

I highly recommend that you create a custom e-mail signature for sending messages from your phone. Here's my signature:

```
DAN

This was sent from my Droid 3.
Please forgive the typos.
```

To create a signature for Gmail, obey these directions:

1. **Start Gmail.**

2. **Press the Menu soft button.**

3. **Choose More and then Settings.**

    If you see no settings, choose Back to Inbox and repeat Steps 2 and 3.

4. **Choose Signature.**

5. **Type or dictate your signature.**

6. **Touch OK.**

You can obey these same steps to change your signature; the existing signature shows up after Step 4.

To set a signature for the Email program, heed these steps:

1. **In either the Email or Messaging app, start a new message.**

2. **Press the Menu soft button.**

3. **Choose More and then Email Settings.**

4. **Choose Compose Options.**

5. **If prompted, choose your e-mail account.**

   You create a separate signature for each e-mail account, so when you have multiple accounts, you need to repeat these steps.

6. **Edit the Email Signature area to reflect your new signature.**

   The preset signature is *Sent from my Verizon Wireless Phone.* Feel free to edit it at your whim.

7. **Touch the Done button.**

When you have multiple e-mail accounts, repeat these steps to configure a signature for each one.

Configuring the manual delete option

Non-Gmail e-mail you fetch on your phone is typically left on the e-mail server. That's because, unlike your computer's e-mail program, the Droid 3's Email app doesn't delete messages after it picks them up. The advantage is that you can retrieve the same messages later using your computer. The disadvantage is that you end up retrieving mail you've already read and possibly replied to.

You can control whether the Email app removes messages after they're picked up. Follow these steps:

1. **At the Home screen, press the Menu soft button.**

2. **Choose Settings and then Accounts.**

3. **From the list of accounts, choose the e-mail account you want to configure.**

4. **Choose the command Other Settings.**

5. **Place a green check mark by the option Remove Manually Deleted Emails from the Server.**

6. **Touch the OK button to confirm the new setting.**

7. **Press the Home soft button to return to the Home screen.**

When you delete a message using either the Email or Messaging app, the message is also deleted from the mail server. It isn't picked up again, not by the Droid 3, another mobile device, or any computer that fetches e-mail from that same account.

✔ Mail you retrieve using your computer's mail program is deleted from the mail server after it's picked up. That's normal behavior. Your Droid 3 cannot pick up mail from the server if your computer has already deleted it.

✔ Deleting mail on the server isn't a problem for Gmail. No matter how you access your Gmail, from your phone or from a computer, the inbox has the same messages.

Setting the default e-mail account

When you have more than one e-mail account, the main account — the *default* — is the one used by the Email app. To read or compose mail in another account, you have to access the account via the Messaging app.

Yes, it's confusing.

To change the default mail account, follow these steps:

1. **Start the Messaging app.**
2. **Press the Menu soft button, and choose Messaging Settings.**
3. **Choose Email.**
4. **Choose Default Email Account.**
5. **Choose which e-mail account you want to be the default, or touch Cancel to keep your current choice.**

The account you choose is the one that's displayed when you open the Email app. All your other accounts are still available through the Messaging app.

Fun on the Web

In This Chapter

▶ Looking at a web page on your phone

▶ Browsing around the web

▶ Bookmarking pages

▶ Working with multiple browser windows

▶ Searching the web

▶ Sharing a link

▶ Downloading stuff from the web

▶ Changing the home page

1 don't believe anyone truly sets out to craft web pages for easy viewing on a doinky cell phone screen. Sure, special *mobile* versions of web pages are available; my Wambooli website has such a feature. But web designers secretly desire you to view their work on a lovely, roomy, pixel-rich desktop monitor.

Despite the yearning of web page designers, it's entirely possible to venture out on the web using your Droid 3. Though the screen may not be large enough to show you everything, the browsing experience you enjoy on your computer carries over quite well to your phone. This chapter shows you how everything works and offers some tips to make your mobile web browsing adventures more enjoyable.

✔ If possible, activate the Droid 3 Wi-Fi connection before you venture out on the web. Though you can use the phone's cellular data connection, the Wi-Fi connection can be far faster. See Chapter 19 for more information.

✔ The Droid 3 has apps for Gmail, social networking (Facebook, Twitter, and others), YouTube, and potentially other popular locations or activities on the web. I highly recommend using these applications on the phone over visiting the websites using the phone's browser.

Behold the Web Page

Your World Wide Web cell phone adventure is brought to you by the Browser app. It's found on the App menu, like all apps on your Droid 3. You may also find a copy of the Browser app on the main Home screen panel.

Using the Browser app to explore the web works similarly to using a web browser on a computer, though I've written this section to give you a quick orientation.

Viewing the web

When you first open the Browser app, you're taken to the home page. Figure 11-1 shows the Google website, which is the home screen preconfigured for your Droid 3. You can reset the home page to something else, as described later in this chapter.

Because the Droid 3 screen isn't a full desktop screen, not every web page looks good on it. Here are a few tricks you can use:

✔ Pan the web page by dragging your finger across the touchscreen. You can pan up, down, left, and right.

✔ Double-tap the screen to zoom in or zoom out.

✔ Pinch the screen to zoom out, or spread two fingers to zoom in.

✔ Tilt the phone to its side to read a web page in Landscape mode. Then you can spread or double-tap the touchscreen to make teensy text more readable.

Visiting a web page

To visit a web page, type its address in the Address box (refer to Figure 11-1). You can also type a search word, if you don't know the exact address of a web page. Press the Enter key on the sliding keyboard or touch the Go button by the Address box to search the web or visit a specific web page.

Web page

Address box   Bookmark page   Share

Go   Dictate address   Stop

The button changes depending on your circumstance.

Figure 11-1: The Browser app beholds the Google home page.

If you don't see the Address box, swipe your finger so that you can see the top of the window, where the Address box lurks.

You click links on a page by using your finger on the touchscreen. A better way is to use the arrow keys on the sliding keyboard: Press an arrow key to highlight various links on the page. Press the OK key to select a link.

✔ To reload a web page, press the Menu soft button and choose the Refresh command. Refreshing updates a website that changes often, and the command can also be used to reload a web page that may not have completely loaded the first time.

✔ To stop a web page from loading, touch the Stop button that appears to the right of the Address box. (Refer to Figure 11-1.)

Browsing back and forth

To return to a previous web page, press the Back soft button. It works just like clicking the Back button on a computer's web browser.

The Forward button also exists in the Browser program: Press the Menu soft button and choose the Forward command.

To review the long-term history of your web browsing adventures, follow these steps:

1. **Press the Menu soft button.**
2. **Choose Bookmarks.**
3. **At the top of the Bookmarks page, choose History.**

To view a page you visited weeks or months ago, you can choose a web page from the History list.

To clear the History list, press the Menu soft button while viewing the list and choose the Clear History command.

Using bookmarks

Bookmarks are those electronic breadcrumbs you can drop as you wander the web. Need to revisit a website? Just look up its bookmark. This advice assumes, of course, that you bother to create (I prefer *drop*) a bookmark when you first visit the site. Here's how it works:

1. **Visit the web page you want to bookmark.**
2. **Touch the Bookmark button, found at the top of the Browser window.**

   Refer to Figure 11-1 to see the location of the Bookmark button. After pressing the button, you see the Bookmarks screen, shown in Figure 11-2. The screen lists your bookmarks, showing website thumbnail previews.

3. **Touch the Add button.**

   The Add button appears in the upper left square on the Bookmarks screen (refer to Figure 11-2). The button has the name of the site or page you're bookmarking just below the square.

4. **If necessary, edit the bookmark name.**

   The bookmark is given the web page name, which might be kind of long. I usually edit the name to fit beneath the thumbnail square.

5. **Touch OK.**

Display bookmarks.   Frequently visited web pages

Add bookmark.   Browsing history

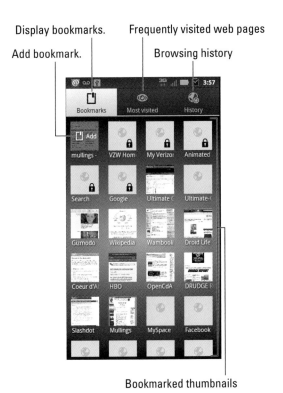

Bookmarked thumbnails

Figure 11-2: Adding a bookmark.

After the bookmark is set, it appears in the list of bookmarks. You can swipe the list downward to see the bookmarks and all their fun thumbnails.

Another way to add a bookmark is to touch the Most Visited tab at the top of the Bookmarks screen (refer to Figure 11-2). This screen lists the web pages you frequent. To add one of these pages, long-press it and choose the command Add Bookmark.

✔ To visit a bookmark, press the Menu soft button and choose the Bookmarks command. Touch a bookmark thumbnail to visit that site.

✔ Remove a bookmark by long-pressing its thumbnail on the Bookmarks screen. Choose the command Delete Bookmark. Touch the OK button to confirm.

✔ Bookmarked websites can also be placed on the Home screen: Long-press the bookmark thumbnail and choose the command Add Shortcut to Home.

- ✔ You can switch between Thumbnail and List views for your bookmarks: When viewing the Bookmarks screen, press the Menu soft button and choose the List View command to switch to List view. To return to Thumbnail view, press the Menu soft button and choose Thumbnail View.

- ✔ When held horizontally, the Droid 3 displays its bookmark thumbnails in a long list that you can swipe left or right.

 ✔ You can obtain the MyBookmarks app at the Android Market. The app can import your Internet Explorer, Firefox, and Chrome bookmarks from your Windows computer into the Droid 3. See Chapter 18 for more information on the Android Market.

- ✔ Refer to Chapter 4 for information on editing text on the Droid 3.

Managing multiple web page windows

Because the Browser app sports more than one window, you can have multiple web pages open at a time on your Droid 3. You can summon another browser window in one of several ways:

- ✔ **To open a link in another window,** press and hold the link by using your finger or holding down the OK key on the sliding keyboard. Choose the command Open in New Window from the menu that appears.

- ✔ **To open a bookmark in a new window,** long-press the bookmark and choose the Open in New Window command.

- ✔ **To open a blank browser window,** press the Menu soft button and choose New Window.

You switch between windows by pressing the Menu soft button and choosing the Windows command. All open Browser windows are displayed on the screen; switch to a window by choosing it from the list. Or, you can close a window by touching the Minus button to the right of the window's name.

New windows open using the home page that's set for the Browser application. See the section "Setting a home page," later in this chapter, for information.

Searching the web

The handiest way to find things on the web is to use the Google Search widget, shown in Figure 11-3. You can often find it floating on the Home screen panel, to the left of the main Home screen panel. Use the Google Search widget to type something to search for, or touch the Microphone button to dictate what you want to find on the Internet.

Figure 11-3: The Google Search widget.

To search for something anytime you're viewing a web page in the Browser app, press the Search soft button. Type the search term into the box. You can choose from a suggestions list or touch the Go button to complete the search using the Google search engine.

To find text on the web page you're looking at, rather than search the entire Internet, follow these steps:

1. **Visit the web page where you want to find a specific tidbit o' text.**

2. **Press the Menu soft button.**

3. **Choose the More command and then choose Find on Page.**

4. **Type the text you're searching for.**

5. **Use the left- or right-arrow button to locate that text on the page — backward or forward, respectively.**

   The found text appears highlighted in a hideous shade of green.

6. **Touch the X button when you're done searching.**

See Chapter 22 for more information on widgets, such as the Google Search widget.

Sharing a page

The Android operating system lets you easily share information you find on your phone. With regard to the web pages you visit, you can easily share a link to the page you're viewing in the Browser app. Follow these steps:

1. **Visit the page you want to share.**

2. **Touch the Share button found at the top of the screen.**

   Refer to Figure 11-1 for the Share button's location, though it sports the traditional Share command icon, as shown in the margin.

3. **Fill in or edit the text field to share the web page link on your social networking sites.**

   Figure 11-4 shows your options. Or, if you'd rather share the link another way, continue with Step 4.

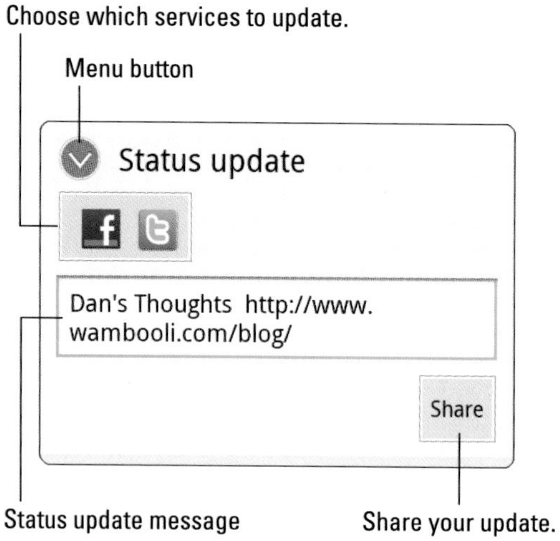

Choose which services to update.

Menu button

Status update

Dan's Thoughts http://www.
wambooli.com/blog/

Share

Status update message   Share your update.

Figure 11-4: Sharing a web page as a status update.

4. **Touch the Menu button to display additional ways to share the web page.**

   A pop-up menu of places to share appears. The variety and number of items on the Share Via menu depends on the applications installed on your phone. For example, you might see a notepad app available for pasting the link, if you have such an app installed.

5. **Choose a method to share the link.**

   For example, choose Email to send the link by mail or Text Messaging to share via a text message.

6. **Do whatever happens next.**

   Whatever happens next depends on how you're sharing the link.

Most likely, whatever happens next opens another application, where you can complete the process. Refer to various parts of this book for details.

The Perils and Joys of Downloading

One of the most abused words in all computerdom is *download*. People don't understand what it means. It's definitely not a synonym for *transfer* or *copy*, though that's how I most often hear it used.

For the sake of the Droid 3, a *download* is a transfer of information from another location to your phone. When you send something from the phone, you *upload* it. There. Now the nerd in me feels much better.

You can download information from a web page into your phone. It doesn't work exactly like downloading does for a computer, which is why I wrote this section.

- There's no need to download program files to your Droid 3. If you want new software, you can obtain it from the Android Market, covered in Chapter 18.

- When the phone is downloading information, you see the Downloading notification. It's an animated icon, though the icon shown in the margin isn't animated in this edition of the book. Completed downloads feature the Download Complete icon, which is not animated.

Grabbing an image from a web page

The simplest thing to download is an image from a web page. It's cinchy: Long-press the image. You see a pop-up menu appear, from which you choose the command Save Image.

- The image is copied and stored on your Droid 3. You can view the image by using the Gallery app; look in the My Library area.

- Refer to Chapter 15 for information on the Gallery.

- You can also use the Downloads app to peruse and review your web page downloads. The Downloads app is found on the App menu.

- Technically, an image is stored on the phone's internal storage in the `download` folder. You can read about storage on the Droid 3 in Chapter 20.

Downloading a file

When a link opens a document on a web page, such as a Microsoft Word document or an Adobe Acrobat (PDF) file, you can download that information to your phone. Simply long-press the download link, and choose the Save Link command from the menu that appears.

You can view the link by referring to the Downloads screen. See the next section.

Reviewing your downloads

You can view downloaded information by perusing the Downloads screen. Summon this screen while using the Browser app by pressing the Menu soft button, choosing the More command, and then choosing Downloads.

The Downloads screen presents a list of downloaded items, organized by date. To view the download, you have to choose an item. The Droid 3 then starts the appropriate app to view the item so that you can see it on your phone.

Well, of course, some of the things you can download you cannot view. When that happens, you see an appropriately rude error message.

You can quickly review any download by choosing the Download notification.

Browser Controls and Settings

More options and settings and controls exist for the Browser app than just about every other app I've used on the Droid 3. It's complex. Rather than bore you with every dang doodle detail, I thought I'd present just a few of the options worthy of your attention.

Setting a home page

The *home page* is the first page you see when you start the Browser app, and it's the first page that's loaded when you fire up a new window. To set your home page, heed these directions:

1. **Browse to the page you want to set as the home page.**

2. **Press the Menu soft button.**

3. **Choose More and then Settings.**

   A massive list of options and settings appears.

4. **Choose Set Home Page.**

5. **Touch the Use Current Page button.**

   Because you obeyed Step 1, you don't need to type the web page's address.

6. **Touch OK.**

   The home page is set.

Unless you've already set a new home page, the Droid 3 comes configured with the Google Mobile search page as your home page.

If you want your home page to be blank (not set to any particular web page), set the name of the home page (in Step 5) to `about:blank`. That's the word *about,* a colon, and then the word *blank,* with no period at the end and no spaces in the middle. I prefer a blank home page because it's the fastest web page to load. It's also the web page with the most accurate information.

Changing the way the web looks

You can do a few things to improve the way the web looks on your phone. First and foremost, don't forget that you can orient the phone horizontally to see the wide view on any web page.

From the Settings screen, you can also adjust the text size used to display a web page. Heed these steps:

1. **Press the Menu soft button.**

2. **Choose More and then Settings.**

3. **Choose Text Size.**

4. **Select a better size from the menu.**

   For example, try Large or Huge.

5. **Press the Back soft button to return to the web.**

I don't make any age-related comments about text size at this time, and especially at this point in my life.

Setting privacy and security options

With regard to security, my advice is always to be smart and think before doing anything questionable or tempting on the web. Use common sense. One of the most effective ways that the Bad Guys win is by using *human engineering* to try to trick you into doing something you normally wouldn't do, such as click a link to see a cute animation or a racy picture of a celebrity or politician. As long as you use your noggin, you should be safe.

As far as the phone's settings go, most of the security options are already enabled for you, including the blocking of pop-up windows (which normally spew ads).

If web page cookies concern you, you can clear them from the Settings window. Follow Steps 1 and 2 in the preceding section, and choose the option Clear All Cookie Data. Touch the OK button to confirm.

You can also choose the command Clear Form Data to remove any memorized information you may have typed on a web page.

Remove the check mark from Remember Form Data. These two settings prevent any characters you've input into a text field from being summoned automatically by someone who may steal your phone.

You might be concerned about various warnings regarding location data. What they mean is that the phone can take advantage of your location on Planet Earth (using the Droid 3 GPS, or *global positioning system*) to help locate businesses and people near you. I see no security problem in leaving this feature on, though you can disable location services from the Browser's Settings screen: Remove the check mark by Enable Location. You can also choose the item Clear Location Access to wipe out any information saved in the phone and used by certain web pages.

See the earlier section "Browsing back and forth" for steps on clearing your web browsing history.

12

Friends and Followers

In This Chapter

▶ Accessing your social networking accounts

▶ Updating your status

▶ Sharing photos on Facebook

▶ Using the Facebook app

▶ Setting up a Twitter client

▶ Accessing other social networking sites

*I*t's the craze of the new century. Social networking is the phenomenon that allows you to be immensely popular without the burden of ever having to leave your house. You can have hundreds, if not thousands, of friends — including people you don't know and have never met — who cling to your every thought, action, and location. That's the miracle of social networking on the Internet.

The Droid 3 is amply equipped to deal with your social networking needs. You can catch up with friends on Facebook, entreat your followers on Twitter, and explore other cyber social opportunities. Using the proper apps on your phone, you can now fete the world with your life broadcast digitally on the Internet in a 24-hour digital oglefest.

News Feed   Profile   Frie

Messages   Places   Gro

Events   Photos   Ch

Droid 3 Social Networking

Your digital social life on the Droid 3 roosts upon the Social Networking app. It lets you access accounts from Facebook, LinkedIn, MySpace, Twitter, and others, all in one spot. It all starts by telling the phone about your social networking accounts.

Adding a social networking account

When you start the Social Networking app for the first time, the only thing you see is the Add a Social Network button. Obviously, the app is trying to tell you something: You need to add some social networking accounts.

I recommend first setting up your social networking accounts on the web, preferably using a computer. That way, you have a full screen and keyboard to help you create the accounts and get things configured.

After setting up an account by using a computer, and getting a login ID and password for that social networking site, it's time to set things up on your phone. Obey these steps:

1. **From the Home screen, press the Menu soft button.**

2. **Choose Settings.**

3. **Choose Accounts.**

4. **Touch the Add Account button, found at the bottom of the screen.**

5. **Choose the social networking site where you already have set up an account.**

   For example, if you have a Facebook account, choose Facebook. If you have a Twitter account, choose Twitter.

6. **Type the account login ID or your e-mail address, whichever is required to access your account on the social networking site.**

   You may need to type only the first part of your e-mail address; if you see a menu with your e-mail address listed, choose it.

7. **Type the account's password.**

   Touch the Done button or press the Back soft button to dismiss the onscreen keyboard when you're done typing the password.

8. **Touch the Next button.**

   The Social Networking app configures and adds your account to its inventory.

9. **Touch the Done button.**

Repeat these steps to add social networking accounts to the Social Networking app's inventory. When you're done, you can press the Home soft button to return to the Home screen.

The Droid 3 is updated immediately with your social networking site information. See the later section "Your Digital Social Life" for information on using the Social Networking app to conduct your digital social life.

Managing your social networking accounts

When you get all huffy and change your online social life, you need to update your account information in the Social Networking app. For example, if you finally make good and quit MySpace, you can remove that account. Or, maybe you clicked a bad link on Facebook and need to update your account password. Those account management chores are handled by following these steps:

1. **Start the Social Networking app.**

   It's found on the Apps screen, along with all other apps on your phone.

2. **Press the Menu soft button.**

3. **Choose Manage Accounts.**

   All the accounts associated with the Droid 3 appear in the My Accounts list. Even your Google account is listed, though it's not officially a social networking app.

You can do three things with the accounts: Change your password, remove the account, or add another account:

Update your password. To change your password, choose an account from the list and type a new password. Touch the OK button when you're done.

Remove an account. To remove an account, choose it from the list and touch the Remove Account button. Touch the Yes button to confirm.

Add an account. Refer to the preceding section for information on adding a new account.

You use the Social Networking app to update your password, not to change it. Change the password using the social networking site on the web, preferably by using a computer. After making the change, you need to update the account information on your phone.

Your Digital Social Life

The whole point of social networking is to be social. The whole benefit to being on the Internet is that you don't have to wear proper social clothing. Of course, when you're out and about with your phone, proper clothing is necessary. Other necessary things for social networking with the Social Networking app are covered in this section.

Finding out what's going on

When you start the Social Networking app, you see a list of status updates, news, and tweets from your social networking pals, similar to the ones shown in Figure 12-1. Tiny icons flag the various social networking sites from which the information is pulled, as illustrated in the figure.

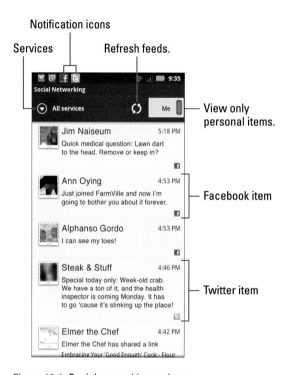

Notification icons

Services   Refresh feeds.

View only personal items.

Facebook item

Twitter item

Figure 12-1: Social networking updates.

To see only information intended for you, touch the Me button at the top of the screen, as shown in Figure 12-1. Or, you can restrict the display to certain sites by touching the Services button (refer to Figure 12-1) and then choosing which social networking site you want to view.

When you want to see all services, touch the Services button again and choose All Services from the Select menu.

Touching an entry displays more details, such as comments, links, or images. For example, if you want to "like" an item in Facebook, touch that item to see the details. Touch the Like button on the details screen to like the post, or touch the Add Comment button to express your opinion.

Updates to your social networking sites are flagged by notification icons, as illustrated in Figure 12-1. Choose the notification icon, as described in Chapter 3, to see what's up.

Setting your status

There's no point in doing the social networking thing if you're not going to be social. When you use the Social Networking app, sharing the most intimate details of your life with the entire online universe is as simple as it can be potentially embarrassing. In the Social Networking app, follow these steps:

1. **Press the Menu soft button, and choose Set Status.**

   The Set Your Status screen appears, as shown in Figure 12-2. You see your current status on all your social networking sites, as shown in the figure. The status you set is posted to the sites you specify.

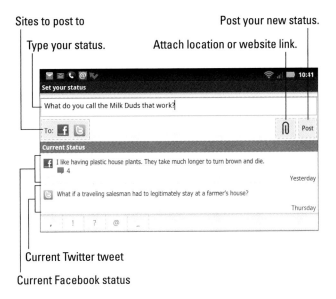

Sites to post to

Type your status.

Post your new status.

Attach location or website link.

Current Twitter tweet

Current Facebook status

Figure 12-2: Sharing your status.

2. **Type in a new status.**

   When you're posting to Twitter, only the first 140 characters of your status appear.

3. **Touch the To field (refer to Figure 12-2) to specify to which social networks you want to post.**

   The icons in the To field show the currently selected services.

4. **Touch the Paperclip icon to attach your current location or a web page link.**

   If you choose Web Page, you see a list of the last several web sites you've been to; there's no need to copy and paste a web page link.

5. **Touch the Post button to send your merry message on its way.**

Your social networking status is updated immediately on whichever sites you selected. The next screen displays your status in the Social Networking app.

✔ When posting to Facebook, your status explains that you posted *via DROID*. This bit of text is a clue to others that you used your phone to set your status.

✔ You can use the Social Networking widget on the Home screen to review your current status or see status updates from your friends. See Chapter 22 for information on installing widgets on the Home screen.

✔ There's no way to unpost a status using the Social Networking app. For that kind of magic, I recommend visiting the social networking site on a computer.

Uploading a picture

There is no direct way to send a picture to your social networking sites using the Social Networking app. Instead, I recommend that you take the picture and then visit the Gallery, as described in Chapter 15. You can then share the picture by following these steps:

1. **View the image you want to share.**

2. **Touch the Share button, found at the bottom of the screen.**

   You may need to touch the screen so that the onscreen menu appears and you can access the Share command.

3. **From the Select an Action menu, choose Photo Share.**

   As this book goes to press, the Photo Share command works only with the Facebook site.

4. **Replace the image's long, cryptic name with a more appropriate description.**

   The name shown is the image's filename as it's stored on the Droid 3. Long-press the name to select it and then type something new.

5. **Touch the Send button to upload the image and its description to Facebook.**

Uploading an image in this manner is more a function of the Gallery app than the Social Networking app. See Chapter 15 for more information on how to use the Gallery app, as well as other ways to share your images.

Also see later sections in this chapter, which cover uploading images using the Facebook and Twitter apps.

Various Social Networking Apps

The Social Networking app is handy, but it's limiting. For example, you can't use it to find new friends or follow new twits. For these activities, you need to obtain and use more specific social networking apps on your phone.

Using the Facebook app

 To get access to more popular Facebook features than the Social Networking app provides for, I recommend that you download the Facebook for Android app. You can scan the QR code shown in the margin or visit the Android Market to search for the Facebook app, as described in Chapter 18.

The main Facebook screen is shown in Figure 12-3. You can use this interface to do most of the Facebook things you can do on the web, including upload a photo or keep your status up to date wherever you go with your Droid 3.

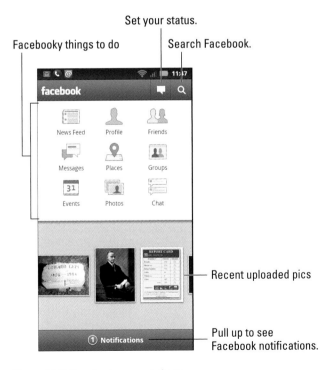

Figure 12-3: Facebook on your phone.

After installing the Facebook for Android app, accept the licensing agreements and sign in. You need to sign in even if you've already configured Facebook for the Social Networking app; they are two separate apps.

Set your Facebook status by touching the Status button, illustrated in Figure 12-3.

To take a picture with the Facebook app, touch the Camera icon, which appears to the left of the text box where you type your status. You get to decide whether to upload a picture you've already taken from the Gallery or choose the Capture a Photo command to take a picture immediately.

After you take the picture, touch the Done button. Add a caption and then touch the Upload button to send the picture to Facebook.

- ✔ Choose the News Feed item to see status updates, newly added photos, and other information from your Facebook friends.

- ✔ Choose Photos to review your Facebook photo albums.

- ✔ Choose Profile to review your personal Facebook page, your status updates, and whatever else you're wasting your time doing on Facebook.

- ✔ To return to the main Facebook screen from another area, press the Back soft button.

- ✔ To sign out of Facebook on your phone, touch the Menu soft button when viewing the main Facebook screen and choose the Logout command. Touch the Yes button to confirm.

Tweeting to other twits

The Twitter social networking site proves the hypothesis that everyone will be famous on the Internet for 140 characters or fewer.

Like Facebook, Twitter is used to share your existence with others or simply to follow what others are up to or thinking. It sates some people's craving for attention and provides the bricks that pave the road to fame — or so I believe. I'm not a big Twitter fan, but your phone is capable of letting you tweet from wherever you are.

The Twitter application provides an excellent interface to many Twitter tasks. You can search for it at the Android Market or use your phone to scan the QR code, shown in the margin. Chapter 18 offers more information on installing new apps for the Droid 3.

After installing the app, sign in. You eventually see the Twitter app's main interface, where you can read tweets from the people you're following.

To tweet, touch the New Tweet icon, shown in the margin. Use the New Tweet screen to send text, upload an image from the Gallery, or take a new picture.

- They say that of all the people who have accounts on Twitter, only a small portion of them actively use the service.
- A message posted on Twitter is a *tweet*.
- You can post messages on Twitter or follow others who post messages.

Exploring other social networking opportunities

The web is brimming with new social networking phenomena. My guess is that each of them is trying to dethrone Facebook as the king of the social networking sites. Good luck with that.

Despite the fact that Facebook and Twitter capture a lot of media attention, other popular social networking sites are out there, such as

- Google Buzz
- LinkedIn
- Meebo
- MySpace

These sites may have special Android apps you can install on your Droid 3, such as the MySpace Mobile app for MySpace.

As with Facebook and Twitter, you should always configure an account by using a computer and then set up options on your phone.

After adding some social networking apps, you may see them appear on various Share menus on the Droid 3. Use the Share menus to help you share media files with your online social networking pals.

Part IV
Magical and Nontraditional Activities

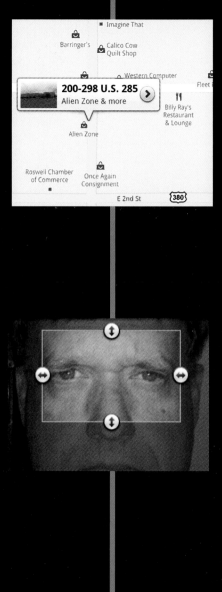

In this part . . .

Imagine the reaction of people from the 1960s to seeing a Droid 3. Sure, they'd be floored that it's so tiny. They'd be astounded that it can make phone calls. But you'd encounter pure apoplexy if you went on to explain all the other nontraditional phone things that the Droid 3 is capable of. Truly, those folks would say it's magic.

Beyond the obvious phone calling and Internet stuff, the Droid 3 can take the place of more than a dozen or so other gizmos you may carry and cling to: GPS, MP3 player, digital camera, video recorder, photo album, movie studio, day planner, calculator, alarm clock, and game playing machine. The Droid 3 handily replaces all these gizmos — and more. The secret to unlocking its potential is held in the chapters in this part of the book.

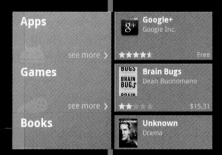

13

There's a Map for That

In This Chapter

▷ Exploring your world with Maps

▷ Adding layers to the map

▷ Finding your location

▷ Sharing your location

▷ Searching for places

▷ Finding a restaurant

▷ Using the Droid 3 as a navigator

▷ Adding a navigation Home screen shortcut

The air smelled great. After six weeks beneath the Earth, inside the cramped Mole Machine, our party was happy to be above-ground, outside, and in the warm sun.

As Dr. Praetorius tended to the Mole Machine, I overheard Benjamin inquire about the location of the nearest Asian fusion restaurant. Before Susan could berate him for his one-track, stomach-fueled mind, I whipped out my Droid 3.

"Why," I exclaimed, "the nearest Asian fusion restaurant is just three blocks from our present location. Indeed, the good people who frequent Google Maps have given it five stars. Let's eat." And the crew beamed with approval.

Basic Map

Your location, as well as the location of things near and far, is found on the Droid 3 by using the Maps app. Good news: You run no risk of improperly folding the Maps app. Better news: The Maps app charts the entire country, including freeways, highways, roads, streets, avenues, drives, bike paths, addresses, businesses, and points of interest.

Using the Maps app

You start the Maps app by choosing Maps from the App menu. If you're starting the app for the first time or it has been recently updated, you can read its What's New screen; touch the OK button to continue.

The Droid 3 communicates with global positioning system (GPS) satellites to hone in on your current location. (See the later sidebar "Activate your locations!") It's shown on the map, similar to Figure 13-1. The position is accurate to within a given range, as shown by a blue circle around your location on the map.

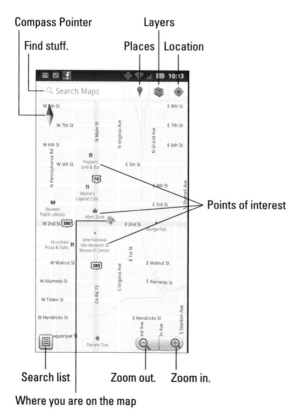

Figure 13-1: An address and your location on a map.

Here are some fun things you can do when viewing the basic street map:

Zoom in: To make the map larger (to move it closer), touch the Zoom In button, double-tap the screen, or spread your fingers on the touchscreen.

Zoom out: To make the map smaller (to see more), touch the Zoom Out button, double-tap the screen, or pinch your fingers on the touchscreen.

Pan and scroll: To see what's to the left or right or at the top or bottom of the map, drag your finger on the touchscreen; the map scrolls in the direction you drag your finger.

Rotate: Using two fingers, rotate the map clockwise or counterclockwise. Touch the Compass Pointer (shown earlier, in Figure 13-1) to reorient the map with north at the top of the screen.

Perspective: Tap the Location button to switch to Perspective view, where the map is shown at an angle. Touch the Location button again (though now it's the Perspective button) to return to flat-map view. Or, if that doesn't work, touch the Compass Pointer.

The closer you zoom in to the map, the more detail you see, such as street names, address block numbers, and businesses and other sites — but no tiny people.

- The blue triangle (refer to Figure 13-1) shows in which general direction the phone is pointing.

- Perspective view can be entered for only your current location.

Adding layers

You add details from the Maps app by applying layers. A *layer* can enhance the map's visual appearance, provide more information, or add other fun features to the basic street map, such as Satellite view, shown in Figure 13-2.

The key to accessing layers is to touch the Layers button, illustrated in Figure 13-2. Choose an option from the Layers menu to add that information to the Map app's display.

You can add another layer by choosing it from the Layers menu, but keep in mind that some layers obscure others. For example, the Terrain layer overlays the Satellite layer so that you see only the Terrain layer.

Touch to exit
perspective view.   Layers button

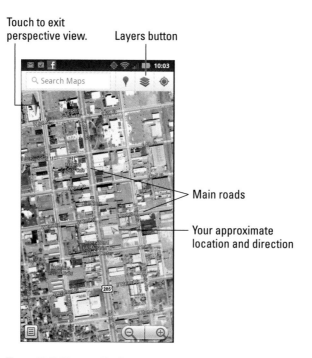

Main roads

Your approximate
location and direction

Figure 13-2: The satellite layer.

To remove a layer, choose it from the Layers menu; any active layer appears with a green check mark to its right. To return to Street view, remove all layers.

✔ The Compass Pointer (refer to Figure 13-1) shows in which direction the phone is pointing. Likewise, the blue triangle also shows the phone's direction (refer to Figure 13-2). These indicators may not always show up.

✔ When all you want is a virtual compass, similar to the one you lost as a kid, you can get the Compass app from the Android Market. See Chapter 18 for more information about the Android Market.

✔ Most of the features found on the Layers menu originated in the Google Labs. To see new features that may be added to the Maps app, visit the Labs by pressing the Menu soft button in the Maps app. Choose More and then Labs to pore over potential new features.

✔ The Droid 3 warns you whenever various applications access the phone's Location feature. The warning is nothing serious — the phone is just letting you know that an app is accessing the phone's physical location. Some folks may view this action as an invasion of privacy; hence, the warnings. I see no issue with letting the phone know where you are, but I understand that not everyone feels that way. If you'd rather not share location information, simply decline access when prompted.

Activate your locations!

The Maps app works best when you activate all the Droid 3 location technology. I recommend that you turn on the following three settings. From the Home screen, press the Menu soft button and choose Settings. Then choose Location & Security. In the Location and Security settings, ensure that green check marks appear by these items:

Google Location Services: Allows software access to your location using Google technology.

Standalone GPS Services: Allows your phone to access the GPS satellites, but it isn't that accurate.

That's why you need to activate more than this service to fully use your phone's location abilities.

VZW Location Services: Allows the phone to use signals from the Verizon cell towers to triangulate your position and refine the data received from GPS Services.

Further, you can activate the phone's Wi-Fi feature for even more exact location information. See Chapter 19 for information on turning on the Droid 3 Wi-Fi setting.

Where You At?

You can look at a physical map all day long and unless you have a sextant or a GPS device, how would you know where you are? Never fear! The Droid 3 knows where you are. Not only does the Droid have GPS but, by using the Maps app, you can also instantly find out where you are and what's nearby and even send your location to someone else.

Finding out where you are

The Maps app shows your location as a blue dot or compass arrow on the screen. But *where* is that? I mean, if you need to phone a tow truck, you can't just say, "I'm the blue triangle on the orange slab by the green thing."

Well, you *can* say that, but it probably won't do any good.

To find your current street address, or any street address, long-press a location on the Maps screen. Up pops a bubble, similar to the one shown in Figure 13-3, that gives your approximate address.

If you touch the address bubble (refer to Figure 13-3), you see a screen full of interesting things you can do, as shown in Figure 13-4.

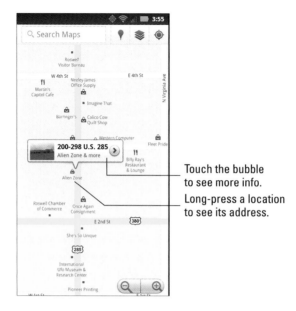

Touch the bubble to see more info.

Long-press a location to see its address.

Figure 13-3: Finding an address.

Return to the map.

Location

Mark the location as a Favorite.

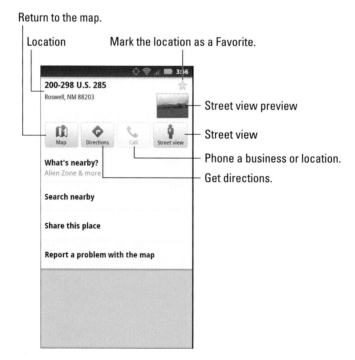

Street view preview

Street view

Phone a business or location.

Get directions.

Figure 13-4: Things to do when you find a location.

When you're searching for a location, the distance and general direction are shown next to the Street view preview (refer to Figure 13-3). Otherwise, if you're just finding out where you are, the distance and direction information isn't necessary.

The What's Nearby command displays a list of nearby businesses or points of interest, some of them shown on the screen (refer to Figure 13-4) and others available by touching the What's Nearby command.

Choose the Search Nearby item to use the Search command to locate businesses, people, or points of interest near the given location.

What's *really* fun to play with is the Street View command. Choosing this option displays the location from a 360-degree perspective. In Street view, you can browse a locale, pan and tilt, or zoom in on details to familiarize yourself with an area, for example — whether you're familiarizing yourself with a location or planning a burglary.

Sending your location to a friend

You can use the Text Messaging app to send your current location to your friends. Your pals who have phones with smarts similar to the Droid 3 can use the coordinates to get directions to your location. Maybe they'll even bring some tacos!

To send your current location in a text message, obey these steps:

1. **Start a new text message to someone desperately wanting to know where you are.**

   Refer to Chapter 9 for information on text messaging with the Droid 3.

2. **Press the Menu soft button, and choose the Insert command.**

3. **Choose Location and then choose Current Location.**

   Your current location appears on the map preview screen, along with your current address (if known).

4. **Touch the Attach Location button.**

   The street address (if available) is inserted into the message, along with a short URL link to your location on a map.

5. **Edit the message to add more details, such as *Bring tacos,* and touch the Send button to send it.**

When recipients receive the text message, they can touch the link to open your location in the Maps app. When the location appears, they can follow my advice in the later section "Getting directions" for getting to your location. And don't loan them this book either; have them buy their own copy. And bring tacos. Thanks.

Find Things

The Maps app can help you find places in the real world, just like the Browser app helps you find places on the Internet. Both operations work basically the same:

Open the Maps app, and press the Search soft button. You can type a variety of terms into the Search box, as explained in this section.

Looking for a specific addresses

To locate an address, type it into the Search box, as in this example:

```
1600 Pennsylvania Ave., Washington, D.C. 20006
```

Touch the Search button on the keyboard, and that location is then shown on the map. The next step is getting directions, which you can read about in the later section "Getting directions."

- ✔ You don't need to type the entire address. Oftentimes, all you need are the street number and street name and then either the city name or zip code.
- ✔ If you omit the city name or zip code, the Droid 3 looks for the closest matching address near your current location.

Finding a business, restaurant, or point of interest

You may not know an address, but you know when you crave sushi or Asian fusion or perhaps Himalayan food. Maybe you need a hotel or a gas station, or you have to find a place that sells suppositories. To find a business entity or a point of interest, type its name in the Search box, as in this example:

```
Movie theater
```

This command flags movie theaters on the current Maps screen or nearby.

Specify your current location, as described earlier in this chapter, to find locations near you. Otherwise, the Maps app looks for places near the area you see on the screen.

Or, you can be specific and look for businesses near a certain location by specifying the city name, district, or zip code, such as

```
Coffee 88201
```

After typing this command and touching the Search button, you see a smattering of coffee huts and restaurants found in Roswell, New Mexico, similar to the ones shown in Figure 13-5.

Search text   Top search result

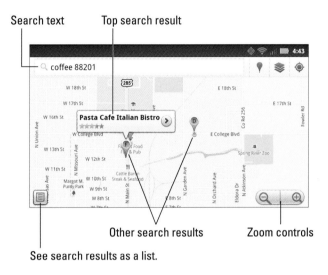

Other search results   Zoom controls

See search results as a list.

Figure 13-5: Search results for sushi in Roswell, New Mexico.

To see more information about a result, touch its cartoon bubble, such as the one for the Pasta Café Italian Bistro in Figure 13-5. The screen that appears offers more information, plus perhaps even a web address and phone number. You can touch the Get Directions button (refer to Figure 13-4) to get directions; see the later section "Getting directions."

🖊 Every letter or dot on the screen represents a search result (refer to Figure 13-5).

🖊 Use the Zoom controls or spread your fingers to zoom in to the map.

TIP

🖊 You can create a contact for the location, keeping it as a part of your Contacts list: After touching the location balloon, touch the More button and choose the command Add As a Contact. The contact is created using data known about the business, including its location and phone number and even a web page address — if that information is available.

Searching for interesting places

Maybe you don't know what you're looking for. Maybe you're like my teenage sons, who stand in front of the open refrigerator, waiting for the sandwich fairy to hand them a snack. The Maps app features a sort of I-don't-know-what-I-want-but-I-want-something fairy. It's the Places command.

Touch the Places button (refer to Figure 13-1) to see the Places screen. It shows categories of places near you: restaurants, coffee shops, bars, hotels, attractions, and more. Touch an item to see matching locations in your vicinity.

You can also use the Places app to directly visit the Places screen. You can find the Places app on the App menu.

Locating a contact

You can hone in on where your contacts are located by using the map. This trick works when you've specified an address for the contact — home or work or another location. If so, the Droid 3 can easily help you find that location or even give you directions.

The secret to finding a contact's location is the little Postcard icon by the contact's address, shown in the margin. Any time you see this icon, you can touch it to view that location by using the Maps app.

The Droid 3 Is Your Copilot

Finding something is only half the job. The other half is getting there. The Droid 3 is ever ready, thanks to the various direction and navigation features nestled in the Maps app.

Getting directions

One command associated with locations on the map is Get Directions. Here's how to use it:

1. **Touch a location's cartoon bubble displayed by an address, a contact, or a business or from the result of a map search.**

2. **Touch the Directions button.**

   You see the Directions screen, shown in Figure 13-6. The information is already filled out, including your current location (shown as My Location in the figure) as the starting point.

3. **Choose a method of transportation.**

   The four methods are car, public transportation, bicycle, and walking, as shown in Figure 13-6.

4. **Touch the Get Directions button.**

   You see a map with a blue line detailing your journey. Use the Zoom controls to make the map larger, if necessary.

5. **Follow the blue line.**

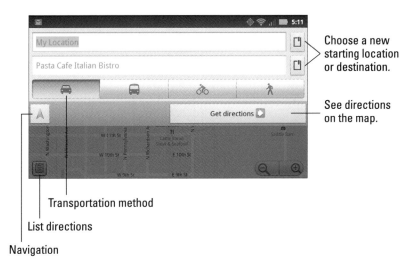

Choose a new
starting location
or destination.

See directions
on the map.

Transportation method

List directions

Navigation

Figure 13-6: Going from here to there.

If you'd rather see a list of directions, touch the List button on the map (refer to Figure 13-6). You can switch back to Map view (with the blue line) by touching the Map button, shown in the margin.

✔ The Maps app alerts you to any toll roads on the specified route. As you travel, you can choose alternative, nontoll routes if available. You're prompted to switch routes during navigation; see the next section.

✔ The Maps app may not give you perfect directions, but for places you've never visited, it's a useful tool.

✔ To receive vocal directions, touch the Navigation button (refer to Figure 13-6) or just read the next section.

Navigating to your destination

Maps and lists of directions are so 20th century. I don't know why anyone would bother, especially when the Droid 3 features a digital copilot, in the form of voice navigation.

To use navigation, choose the Navigation option from any list of directions. Or, touch the Navigation button, as shown earlier, in Figure 13-6. You can also enter the Navigation app directly by choosing it from the Apps screen, though then you must type (or speak) your destination, so it's just easier to start in the Maps app.

In Navigation mode, the Droid 3 displays an interactive map that shows your current location and turn-by-turn directions for reaching your destination. A digital voice tells you how far to go and when to turn, for example, and gives you other nagging advice — just like a backseat driver, albeit an accurate one.

After choosing Navigation, sit back and have the phone dictate your directions. You can simply listen or just glance at the phone for an update of where you're heading.

To stop navigation, press the Menu soft button and choose the Exit Navigation command.

✔ After selecting Navigation, you may be prompted to choose between the Maps app and the VZ Navigation app. VZ Navigation is Verizon's own navigating app, which I've never used.

✔ To remove the navigation route from the screen, exit Navigation mode and return to the Maps app. Press the Menu soft button, and choose the Clear Map command.

✔ When you tire of hearing the navigation voice, press the Menu soft button and choose the Mute command.

✔ I refer to the navigation voice as *Gertrude*.

✔ You can press the Menu soft button while navigating and choose Route Info to see an overview of your journey.

✔ When viewing the Route Info screen, touch the Gears button to see a handy pop-up menu. From this menu, you can choose options to modify the route so that you avoid highways or toll roads, for example.

✔ The neat thing about Navigation is that whenever you screw up, a new course is immediately calculated.

✔ In Navigation mode, the Droid 3 consumes a lot of battery power. I highly recommend that you plug the phone into your car's power adapter (cigarette lighter) for the duration of the trip.

Adding a navigation shortcut to the Home screen

When you visit certain places often — such as the apothecary — you can save yourself the time you would spend repeatedly inputting navigation information by creating a navigation shortcut on the Home screen. Here's how:

1. **Long-press a blank part of the Home screen.**

2. **From the pop-up menu, choose Shortcuts.**

3. **Choose Directions & Navigation.**

4. **Type a contact name, an address, a destination, or a business in the text box.**

   As you type, suggestions appear in a list. You can choose a suggestion to save yourself some typing.

5. **Choose a traveling method.**

   Your options are car, public transportation, bicycle, and on foot.

6. **Scroll down a bit to type a shortcut name.**

7. **Choose an icon for the shortcut.**

8. **Touch the Save button.**

   The navigation shortcut is placed on the Home screen.

To use the shortcut, simply touch it on the Home screen. Instantly, the Maps app starts and enters Navigation mode, steering you from wherever you are to the location referenced by the shortcut.

See Chapter 22 for additional information on creating Home screen shortcuts.

14

Picture This, Video That

In This Chapter

▷ Taking a still picture

▷ Deleting the image you just shot

▷ Turning on the flash

▷ Snapping different types of images

▷ Shooting video with the Droid 3

▷ Recording yourself

▷ Making a video message

As the old adage goes, "A picture is worth a thousand words." That is, unless you're working for a magazine, in which case the rates they pay authors and photographers are not correlated.

Among your phone's many abilities worthy of boasting about is its capacity as both a still camera and video recorder. No longer do you need to fret about not having a camera with you to capture the moment. Armed with your Droid 3, you can snap pictures and record video as life happens around you.

The Droid 3 Has a Camera

When it comes time to snap a picture, someone invariably instructs the photographer's victims to "Say 'Cheese.'" That's because the long ⊠ sound in *cheese* supposedly positions the human mouth into a smile, making it look as though everyone is having the best time. You probably already know that.

What you may not know is how to work your Droid 3's cameras. Yes, it has two of them. This section describes how they work.

Taking a picture

To use your Droid 3 phone as a camera, you have to hold the phone away from your face, which I hear is hell to do when you wear bifocals. Before doing this, start the Camera app, which may be found on the App menu or, more conveniently, on the Dock, right next to the Launcher button.

After starting the Camera app, you see the main Camera screen, as illustrated in Figure 14-1. The controls shown in the figure eventually disappear, leaving the full screen to preview the image.

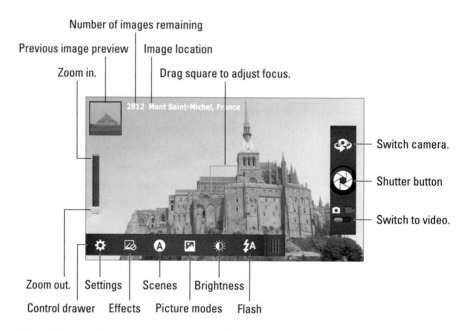

Figure 14-1: Your phone as a camera.

To take a picture, point the camera at the subject and touch the Shutter button, shown in Figure 14-1.

After you touch the Shutter button, the camera will focus, you may hear a mechanical shutter sound play, and the flash may go off. You're ready to take the next picture.

To preview the image you just snapped, touch the little icon that appears in the upper left corner of the screen, as shown in Figure 14-1.

✔ The camera focuses automatically, though you can drag the focus square around the touchscreen to specifically adjust the focus (refer to Figure 14-1).

✔ You can zoom in or out by using the onscreen controls (refer to Figure 14-1) or by pressing the Volume Up or Volume Down button, respectively. Because the zoom is a *digital* zoom, the image is magnified, as opposed to an *optical* zoom, which is done by adjusting the camera's lens.

✔ If the onscreen controls disappear, touch the screen again to bring them back.

✔ Pressing the Menu soft button displays the Control Drawer.

✔ The phone can be used as a camera in either landscape or portrait orientation, though the phone's controls and gizmos are always presented in landscape format (refer to Figure 14-1).

✔ You can take as many pictures with your Droid 3 as you like, as long as you don't run out of storage for them on the phone's internal storage or MicroSD card.

✔ If your pictures appear blurry, ensure that the camera lens on the back of the Droid 3 isn't dirty.

✔ Use the Gallery app to preview and manage your pictures. See Chapter 15 for more information about the Gallery.

✔ The Droid 3 not only takes a picture but also keeps track of where you were located on Planet Earth when you took it. See Chapter 15 for information on reviewing a photograph's location.

✔ The Droid 3 stores pictures in the JPEG image file format. Images are stored in the `DCIM/Camera` folder; they have the `.jpg` file extension. By default, images are stored on the MicroSD card. You can change the storage location by pulling out the Control Drawer and choosing the Gear icon (refer to Figure 14-1). Choose the Storage Location, and select either Internal Phone Storage or SD Card.

Deleting an image immediately after you take it

Sometimes, you just can't wait to delete an image. Either an annoyed person is standing next to you, begging that the photo be deleted, or you're just not happy and you feel the urge to smash into digital shards the picture you just took. Hastily follow these steps:

1. **Touch the image preview that appears in the upper left corner of the screen (refer to Figure 14-1).**

   After touching the preview, you see the full-screen image.

2. **Press the Menu soft button, and choose the Delete command.**

3. **Touch the OK button to confirm.**

   The image has been banished to bit hell.

 To return to the Camera app, touch the Camera button, found in the upper left corner of the preview screen and shown in the margin.

Setting the flash

The camera on the Droid 3 has three flash settings, as shown in Table 14-1.

Table 14-1	Droid 3 Camera Flash Settings	
Setting	**Icon**	**Description**
Auto	⚡A	The flash activates during low-light situations but not when it's bright out.
On	⚡	The flash always activates.
Off	⚡⊘	The flash never activates, even in low-light situations.

To change or check the flash setting, look at the Flash button on the Control Drawer, shown earlier, in Figure 14-1. The button's icon confirms the current flash setting, which is Auto in the figure. Touch the button to change the setting.

 A good time to turn on the flash is when taking pictures of people or objects in front of something bright, such as Aunt Carol holding her prize-winning peach cobbler in front of a forest fire.

Changing the resolution

The Droid 3 nearly does away with the resolution question, where you can set the image resolution (the number of dots in the image) by using the camera. That's because the main camera has only two resolutions: 6MP and 8MP.

To set the resolution in the Camera app, pull out the Control Drawer and touch the Settings button. If a check mark appears by the Widescreen option, the resolution is set to 6MP. Remove the check mark to set the resolution to 8MP.

Press the Back soft button to dismiss the Settings menu, and then press the Menu soft button to close the Control Drawer.

 ✔ The Droid 3's front-facing camera has a fixed resolution of 640 by 480 pixels.

 ✔ A picture's *resolution* describes how many pixels, or dots, are in the image. The more dots, the better the image looks and prints.

 ✔ MP stands for *megapixel* — a measurement of the amount of information stored in an image. One megapixel is approximately 1 million pixels, or individual dots that compose an image.

Doing a self-portrait

Who needs to pay all that money for a mirror when you have the Droid 3? Well, forget the mirror. Instead, think about taking all those self-shots without having to second-guess whether the camera is pointed at your face.

To take your own mug shot, start the Camera app and touch the Switch Camera button, shown earlier, in Figure 14-1. When you see yourself on the screen, you're doing it properly.

Smile. Click. You got it.

Touch the Switch Camera button again to direct the Droid 3 to use the main camera again.

Shooting a panorama

Calm down: A *panorama* is a wide shot, like a landscape, a beautiful vista, or a family photograph where not everyone likes each other. One Droid 3 camera mode allows you to crunch several images into a panoramic shot. Obey these steps:

1. **Start the Camera app.**

2. **Press the Menu soft button to slide out the Control Drawer.**

3. **Choose Panorama from the Picture Modes button's menu.**

   The Picture Modes icon looks like a framed picture of a mountain, as shown earlier, in Figure 14-1.

4. **Hold your arms steady.**

   Pivot on your feet as you scan around you to compose the panoramic image.

5. **Touch the Shutter button.**

   You see a white frame on the screen, which approximates the last shot. Arrows point in the four directions in which you can pan. The Shutter button changes to the Stop button.

6. **Pivot slightly to your right (or left or up or down, but you must continue in the same direction).**

   As you move the camera, the white frame adjusts to your new position. The Droid 3 beeps as the next image in the panorama is snapped automatically. All you need to do is keep moving.

7. **Keep moving as subsequent shots are taken, or touch the Stop button to finish the panorama.**

   After the last image is snapped, wait while the image is assembled.

The Camera app sticks the different shots together, creating a panoramic image.

The Droid 3 camera automatically captures the panoramic shot. You touch the shutter button only when you're done.

Setting the image's location

The Droid 3 not only takes a picture but also keeps track of where you're located on Planet Earth when you take the picture — if you've turned on that option. The feature is called Geo-Tag, and here's how to ensure that it's on:

1. **While using the Camera app, press the Menu soft button.**

2. **Touch the Settings icon on the Control Drawer (refer to Figure 14-1).**

3. **Ensure that a green check mark appears in the Geo-Tag box.**

   If not, touch the gray box to put a check mark there.

4. **Press the Back soft button to close the Settings menu, and then press the Menu soft button to withdraw the Control Drawer.**

Not everyone is comfortable with having the phone record a picture's location, so you can turn the option off. Just repeat these steps, but in Step 3 remove the green check mark by touching the box.

See Chapter 15 for information on reviewing a photograph's location.

Adjusting the camera

Your Droid 3 is more phone than camera — still, it has various camera adjustments you can make. Two such adjustments are found by touching the Control Drawer (refer to Figure 14-1) and choosing either the Effects or Scenes icon.

Effects: Add special visual effects by touching the Effects option and then swiping up or down. The picture preview in the Camera app shows you how the chosen effect changes the way things appear. Choose the Normal option to remove an effect.

Scenes: Choosing this item lets you configure the camera for taking certain types of pictures. After touching the Scenes icon, choose an option that describes the type of images you're capturing, such as Sport for quick action, Night Portrait for low-light situations, or Macro for close-ups. The Auto setting directs the camera to choose the best scene by guessing randomly.

Icons representing the current Effects and Scenes setting appear on the Control Drawer.

Refer to Figure 14-1 for the location of the Effects and Scenes icons.

You Ought to Be on Video

When the action is hot — when you need to capture more than a moment (and maybe the sounds) — you switch the Droid 3 camera into Video mode. Doing so may not turn you into the next Martin Scorsese, because I hear he uses an iPhone to make his films.

Recording video

Video chores on the Droid 3 are handled by the Camcorder app, found on the App menu. It's really just the Camera app, but in Video mode. In fact, you can switch between Camera and Video modes in either app by using the Switch To command, shown in both Figures 14-1 and 14-2.

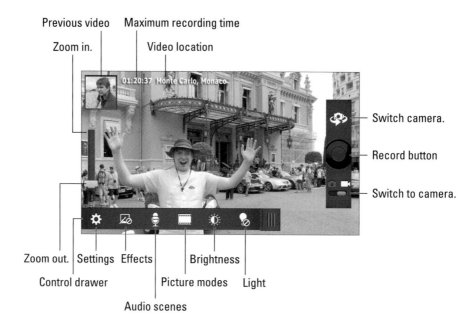

Figure 14-2: Your phone is a video camera.

The Camcorder app is illustrated in Figure 14-2. Start shooting the video by pressing the Record button, as illustrated in the figure.

While the phone is recording, the Shutter button changes to the Stop button. The Mute button appears on the touchscreen. Use it to mute the sound.

To stop recording, touch the Stop button.

✔ Hold the phone steady! The camera still works when you whip around the phone, but wild gyrations render the video unwatchable.

✔ The video's duration depends on its resolution (see the next section) as well as on the storage available on your phone. The maximum recording time is shown on the screen before you shoot (refer to Figure 14-2). While you record, elapsed time appears.

✔ In addition to the zoom controls on the screen, you can use the volume controls to zoom in or out as you record video.

✔ Visual effects (the cheap kind, not the movie SFX kind) can be applied to the video. Touch the Effects button on the Control Drawer to review the available visual effects.

- Chapter 15 covers the Gallery app, used to view and manage videos stored on your phone. Directions are also found in Chapter 15 for uploading your video to YouTube.

- Recorded video is saved in the phone's storage — primarily, the MicroSD card. You can change this location by dragging out the Control Drawer and touching the Settings icon. Choose Storage Location, and then choose either Internal Phone Storage or SD Card.

- The video is stored on the Droid 3 using the MPEG-4 video file format. The video files are located in the `DCIM/Camera` folder and have the `.mp4` file extension.

Setting video quality

Though it may seem that choosing high quality or HD (high definition) all the time for videos is the best option, that's not always the case. For example, video you shoot for YouTube need not be of HD quality. Multimedia text messaging (known as *MMS*) video should be of very low quality or else the video doesn't attach to the message. Also, HD video uses up a heck of a lot more storage space on the Droid 3.

To set the video quality while using the Camcorder app, press the Menu soft button to pull out the Control Drawer and then touch the Settings icon. Choose the Video Resolution command. Here's a rundown of the options and my recommendations for using them:

HD+ (1080p): The highest-quality setting is best suited for video you plan to show on a large-format TV or computer monitor. It's useful for video editing or for showing important events, such as UFO landings.

High Definition (720p): The second-highest-quality setting, which would be a good choice if you need to record longer but still want high quality. This setting is the one that the Camcorder app uses automatically.

DVD (720 x 480): This option has good quality for shooting video when you don't know where the video will end up.

VGA (640 x 480): This setting, good for quality Internet video, doesn't enlarge well.

CIF (352 x 288): This choice is good for medium-quality YouTube and web videos. The files are small and load quickly over an Internet connection. This setting isn't good for viewing videos in a larger format.

QVGA (320 x 240): This setting is designed for use with text messaging video attachments.

Check the video quality *before* you shoot! Especially if you know where the video will end up (on the Internet, on a TV, or in an MMS message), it helps to set the quality first.

Taping a confession

You don't have to record a confession, but when you want to record yourself and you have no friends available — and the dog lacks opposable thumbs — you have to switch to the Droid 3's front-facing camera to do the recording.

The secret is to touch the Switch to Camera button, shown earlier, in Figure 14-2. As soon as you see your face on the touchscreen, you've done things properly.

The front-facing camera uses only VGA resolution (refer to the preceding section), though it's ideal for attaching to an e-mail or text message.

Making a video message

You have two modes to choose between for shooting video on the Droid 3: Normal Video and Video Message. Video Message mode is especially designed for quick uploading to the Internet or for adding an attachment to an MMS (multimedia) text message.

To set Video Message mode, follow these steps in the Camcorder app:

1. **Press the Menu soft button to pull out the Control Drawer.**

2. **Touch the Picture Modes icon, and choose Video Message.**

3. **If you're recording yourself, touch the Switch Camera button to use the front-facing camera.**

4. **Touch the Record button to start.**

   Do something interesting.

5. **Touch the Stop button when you're done.**

The recorded message is ideal for attaching to an e-mail or a text message. That's because in this recording mode, the resolution is set low so that the message's file size is smaller.

✔ To attach video to a text message, press the Menu soft button. Choose the Insert command, and then select Existing Video. Refer to Chapter 9 for more information on text messaging.

✔ To add the video to an e-mail message composed in the Email app, press the Menu soft button and choose Attach Files. Choose Gallery from the Attach Files menu, and choose your video from the Select an Item screen.

✔ Refer to Chapter 9 for more information on text messaging; Chapter 10 covers sending e-mail.

✔ Keep the video message short! Short is good for a video message attachment.

Turning on the light

You don't need a flash when recording video, but occasionally you need a little more light. You can manually turn on the Droid 3's LED flash to help: From the Control Drawer, touch the Light icon. Choose Light On to turn on the LED light on the back of the camera.

Turning on the LED light consumes a hefty portion of the phone's battery power. Use this light sparingly.

Your Digital Photo Album

In This Chapter

▶ Viewing images and videos stored on your phone
▶ Organizing your media into library albums
▶ Tagging images
▶ Finding an image's location
▶ Printing an image at a local developer
▶ Editing images
▶ Sharing images and videos
▶ Publishing a video on YouTube

To understand the need to carry around pictures, it helps to have children. If the need doesn't hit you then (and you're probably too overwhelmed), the onslaught of grandchildren will definitely turn you into one of those humans who constantly carries around pictures in your purse or wallet. Yeah, a load of pictures is something else to carry around — but not when you have the Droid 3. That's because your phone is also your photo album.

The Droid 3 stores copies of the digital pictures you snap, and the videos you record, right there inside the phone. It can also store pictures you've synchronized from your computer or from the Internet. It even has a nifty slideshow program that you can show people, if you first trap them in an elevator and get it stuck between floors. All of that (except for the elevator part) is covered in this chapter.

The Droid 3 Gallery

The app in charge of showing you the phone's pictures and videos is aptly named Gallery. You use the Gallery app to not only look at pictures and view videos, but also organize them, edit them, and eventually share them with the known universe.

To start the Gallery app, choose it from the App menu. The Gallery's main screen is shown in Figure 15-1. The primary part of the screen (at the top) displays image updates from your social networking sites. You can scroll these images by flicking them left or right.

Organized images

Figure 15-1: The Gallery's main screen.

To view the images and videos you've taken with the Droid 3, touch the Camera Roll button. Figure 15-2 illustrates the Camera Roll screen.

Touching a thumbnail in the Camera Roll, or any similar display in the Gallery app, displays the full-screen image or presents the video for playback. Flick the touchscreen left or right to page through full-screen images. Press the Back soft button to return to the thumbnail overview.

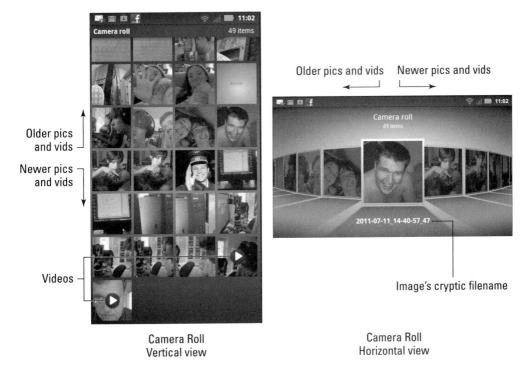

Figure 15-2: Viewing the Camera Roll.

Image Organization

Eventually, you have dozens, if not millions, of images in your phone. They're all stored in one long spaghetti string in the Gallery app, visible by endlessly scrolling through the Camera Roll. If you want to exert a little energy and organize your pictures and videos, you need to create an album.

Viewing albums in the library

The Gallery app automatically creates two albums for you — one for still images and a second for videos. You can view these albums, as well as any others you've created, by touching the My Library button on the main Gallery screen (refer to Figure 15-1).

The Library screen is shown in Figure 15-3. In the figure, Album view is shown, along with Locations view. You can touch the Menu button (refer to the figure) to display your phone's images by their locations or tags, or chronologically.

Menu button

Library organized
by album

Library organized
by image location

Figure 15-3: Albums in the Gallery app.

To view an album, touch its thumbnail. The album opens and displays its contents, similar to the way the Camera Roll appears in Figure 15-2.

Press the Back soft button to back out of an album and return to the Library screen.

Creating a new album

Putting pictures in their own album is a great way to not only keep your photos and videos organized but also keep your friends from going insane as you wildly scan the Camera Roll for the exact pictures you want. Rather than risk ruining a friendship, create a new album during your spare time by following these steps:

1. **Open the Gallery app, and touch the Camera Roll button.**

   The Camera Roll is the source for images you place into a new album; don't bother visiting the Library first.

2. **Long-press the thumbnail image you want to place into an album in the library.**

3. **Choose the command Add to Album.**

   The Add to Album screen appears. It lists not only albums you've created on the phone but also social networking albums, albums from online photo-sharing websites, and potentially others.

4. **Touch the New Album button.**

   The button is found in the upper left corner of the screen.

5. **Fill in the text fields on the Create Album screen.**

   The most important field is Title, which is the name you see beneath the album's thumbnail on the My Library screen.

6. **Touch the Save button to create the new album.**

   The image you long-pressed (in Step 2) is added to the album.

To add more images to the new album, or to any album, repeat Steps 2 and 3, but in Step 4 choose the album from the list on the Add to Album screen.

 By choosing an online album in Step 4, you can quickly upload an image to one of your online photo-sharing websites. See the section "Share Your Pics and Vids with the World," later in this chapter, for information on adding your online photo-sharing website account to the Droid 3.

About Those Thousand Words . . .

Pictures stored in the Droid 3 Gallery aren't merely a collection of colored pixels on the touchscreen. The images have a little depth to them — and not in a cheesy, Hollywood 3D way, either. Additional information about each picture is stored in the picture itself, or you can add it as described in this section.

Tagging an image

Because images contain visual information, searching and organizing images tend to be haphazard tasks. One method to help you keep your pictures and videos organized is to tag them.

A *tag* is simply a tidbit of text, short and punchy — for example, *vacation, beach, 2011, Oregon,* or *kidney stone.* By itself, a tag may seem useless, but the key to properly tagging an image is to apply more than one tag. An image tagged with all its descriptions — *vacation, beach, 2011, Oregon, kidney stone* — is quite descriptive.

To apply a tag to an image in the Gallery, follow these steps:

1. **Touch an image to view it by itself on the Droid 3 touchscreen.**

2. **Press the Menu soft button, and choose the Edit command.**

3. **Choose Tags.**

   Dismiss the Face Tags notice, if one pops up.

4. **Type text to describe the image, and then touch the green Plus button to add the tag.**

   Short, descriptive text works best. Use single words, if possible. Try to think about the words you'd use to search for the image and then create tags using those words.

5. **Touch the Done button when you're finished adding tags.**

   The tags are applied to the image.

To see the tags, view the full-screen image. The tags show up at the bottom of the screen, similar to the ones shown in Figure 15-4. Touch the screen again if the tags (and other information) hides from view.

Figure 15-4: Image tags.

- A tag you can quickly add to any image is the face tag: Long-press on someone's head when you're viewing an image. You see a list of face tag options at the bottom of the screen. Choose *Me* to tag yourself. Choose *Contact* to tag a contact in the photo. You can also choose *Keyword* to add a text tag to the image.

- Tags can be used to organize your images when using Library view, as described in the section "Viewing albums in the library," earlier in this chapter.

- Tagging works only when you remember to do it!

Finding an image location on a map

In addition to snapping a picture, the Droid 3 saves the location where you took the picture. This information is obtained from the phone's GPS, the same tool used to find your location on a map. In fact, you can use the information saved with a picture to see exactly where the picture was taken.

For example, Figure 15-5 shows the location where I took the image shown in Figure 14-1 (from Chapter 14). That location was saved by the phone's GPS technology and is available as part of the picture's data.

Figure 15-5: A picture's location.

To see where you've taken a picture, follow these steps for the Droid 3 gallery:

1. **View the image in the Gallery.**

2. **Press the Menu soft button.**

3. **Choose More and then Map.**

Not every image has location information. In some cases, the Droid 3 cannot read the GPS to store the information. When this happens, location information is unavailable.

Printing a picture

Add another item to the list of amazing things the Droid 3 can do: Print a picture. As long as you've set up and configured a printer for your Droid 3, you can print any image stored in the Gallery. Obey these steps:

1. **View the image you want to print.**

2. **Press the Menu soft button, and choose More and then Print.**

3. **Choose the printing method, such as Print with MOTOPRINT.**

4. **Select your printer.**

5. **Touch the Print button to print the image.**

More specific directions, including information on getting your Droid 3 and a Wi-Fi printer on speaking terms, are provided in Chapter 19.

Picture Editing

The best tool for image editing is a computer amply equipped with photo-editing software, such as Adobe Photoshop or one of its less expensive alternatives. Even so, it's possible to use the Gallery app to perform some minor photo surgery. This section highlights a few of the more useful things you can do.

Cropping an image

To make an image smaller or to cut out someone you don't want in the picture, you use the *crop* tool. Heed these steps:

1. **Display in the Gallery app the image you want to crop.**

2. **Press the Menu soft button, and choose Edit.**

3. **Choose the Crop command from the Edit menu.**

4. **Use the onscreen controls to crop the image.**

   Refer to Figure 15-6 for help with using the onscreen controls.

5. **Touch the Save button to crop the image.**

   The image's size and content are changed immediately.

Rotating your pics

Images that flop when they should flip might be oriented properly in the phone, but definitely not on the touchscreen. To rotate an image to the left or right, follow these steps:

Resize cropping box.

Drag to select area to keep.

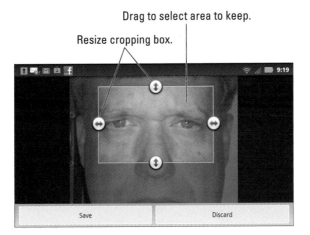

Figure 15-6: Cropping an image.

1. **Display the image in the Gallery app.**

2. **Press the Menu soft button, and then choose Edit and then Rotate.**

3. **Use the circle gizmo on the screen to rotate the image.**

   Though it seems as though you can rotate the image to any angle, the circle gizmo snaps to 90-degree increments.

4. **Touch the Apply button when you're done.**

   The image takes on its new orientation.

Setting an image for a contact or as wallpaper

Images need not be anchored to the Gallery app. You can set them free, to set a friend's pretty face as the contact icon or to convert that sunset you just snapped into your Home screen background or wallpaper. Both operations work similarly and use the same Set As command.

To assign an image to a contact, follow these steps:

1. **Summon the image in the Gallery app.**

2. **Press the Menu soft button, and choose Set As.**

3. **Choose Contact Icon.**

4. **Choose the contact from the list of contacts in your phone.**

5. **Optionally, crop the image.**

   Refer to the earlier section "Cropping an image" for cropping directions.

6. **Touch the Save button to apply the image to the contact.**

Repeat these steps to set an image as the phone's wallpaper, though in Step 4 you choose Wallpaper. Optionally, crop the image and then touch the Save button to set your phone's Home screen background.

See Chapter 8 for more information on editing contact information. Chapter 22 offers details on setting the Home screen wallpaper.

Deleting an image

To prune an image you no longer want in the Gallery, summon it by itself. Press the Menu soft button, and choose the Delete command. You're prompted before the image is removed; touch the OK button to delete the image. It's gone.

There's no way to undelete an image you've removed from the Gallery.

Some images cannot be edited, such as images brought in from social networking sites or from online photo-sharing albums.

Share Your Pics and Vids with the World

There's no need to keep your pictures and videos locked up inside the phone. Thanks to the Share command, you can send your images far and wide, using other apps on the phone, social networking sites, online photo-sharing sites, and other locations.

Using the Share button

The Share button lurks at the bottom of the screen whenever you view an image or a video, similar to the one shown earlier, in Figure 15-4. If you don't see the button, touch the screen and it shows up.

Touching the Share button displays a menu chock-full of methods or apps you can use to share the image or video. The variety of items depends on the apps installed on your phone as well as on which accounts you've added. Here's a run-through of the more popular sharing options:

Photo/Video Share: These items work in conjunction with social networking sites as well as with any photo-sharing or hosting sites. You must set up your account on the Droid 3 for these options to work: Refer to Chapter 12 to add social networking. After this option is configured, you choose either the Photo Share or Video Share command, choose a site to send the image, add a comment if you want, and then send the image to that site.

Email and Gmail: Choosing Email or Gmail for sharing sends the media file from your Droid 3 as a message attachment. Fill in the To, Subject, and Message text boxes as necessary. Touch the Send button to send the media.

Picasa: The Picasa photo-sharing site is one of those free services you get with your Google account. Choose this option to upload a photo to your Picasa account: Type a caption, choose an online album, and then touch the Upload button.

Print to Retail: Here's a crazy idea: Connect your phone to a local photo developer, such as Costco, and have it send your images electronically so that they can be printed. After choosing the Print to Retail option, you can do exactly that: The Droid 3 uses its GPS powers to locate a printer near you. You can then fill in the various forms to have your pictures sent and printed. (Also see Chapter 19 for more information on printing with your Droid 3.)

Text Messaging: Media can be attached to a text message, which then becomes the famous MMS, or multimedia message, that I write about in Chapter 9. After choosing the Messaging sharing option, input the contact name or phone number to which you want to send the media. Optionally, type a brief message. Touch the Send button to send the media and the message.

YouTube: The YouTube sharing option appears whenever you choose to share a video from the Gallery. See the later section "Uploading a video to YouTube."

Additional options may appear on the menu in the Downloaded Apps section. For example, if you have the Facebook app or a Twitter client, these items appear on the menu for sharing.

- Some images and videos may be too large to send as multimedia text messages. The Droid 3 may offer to automatically resize the images in some cases, but not all.

- To configure your Picasa account for use on your Droid 3, open the My Accounts app on the Apps menu. Touch the Add Account button, choose Picasa (Gallery), and then fill in your Google account information.

- Because Picasa may automatically sync images with your Droid 3, you can end up with two copies of the image on the phone. If so, you can delete the non-Picasa version of the image from its original gallery.

- Picasa is for sharing images only, not video.

- You can visit picasaweb.google.com on the Internet to access your Picasa albums from any computer.

- Not every cell phone has the ability to receive multimedia text messages.

Uploading a video to YouTube

The best way to share a video is to upload it to YouTube. As a Google account holder, you also have a YouTube account. You can use the YouTube app on the Droid 3 along with your account to upload your phone's videos to the Internet, where everyone can see them and make rude comments upon them. Here's how:

1. **Activate the Wi-Fi connection for your Droid 3.**

   The best — the only — way to upload a video is to turn on the Wi-Fi connection, which is oodles faster than using the cell phone digital network. See Chapter 19 for information on how to turn on the Wi-Fi connection.

2. **From the App menu screen, choose the Gallery app.**

3. **View the video you want to upload.**

   Or, simply have the video displayed on the screen.

4. **Touch the Share button, and choose YouTube from the menu.**

5. **Type the video's title.**

6. **Touch the More Details button.**

7. **Optionally, type a description, specify whether to make the video public or private, add tags, or change other settings.**

8. **Touch the Upload button.**

   You return to the Gallery as the video is being uploaded. It continues to upload, even if the phone gets bored and falls asleep.

To view your video, open the YouTube app on the App menu, press the Menu soft button, and choose the My Channel command. If necessary, choose your Google account from the pop-up list. Your video should appear in the Uploads list.

You can share your video by sending its YouTube web page link to your pals. I confess that using a computer for this operation is easier than using your phone: Log in to YouTube on a computer to view your video. Use the Share button that appears near the video to share it via e-mail or Facebook or other methods.

See Chapter 17 for more information on using YouTube on your Droid 3.

Music, Music, Music

In This Chapter

▷ Checking into music on your Droid 3

▷ Listening to a song

▷ Copying music from your computer

▷ Purchasing music for the Droid 3

▷ Organizing your tunes into playlists

▷ Making a new playlist

▷ Using your phone as a radio

*I*f you long to listen to your phone even when you're not making a phone call, you can employ the Droid 3 as your portable music player. Enjoying music is another way you can while away your time with your phone, especially when you tire of watching videos on YouTube, playing games you download from the Android Market, texting, taking pictures or videos, or doing any of the other boring little things your phone does.

.ecently added

1980s- the good stuff

Beatles

Driving (mellow)

˙riving (traffic)

The Hits Keep On Coming

Your Droid 3 is ready to entertain you with music whenever you want to hear it. Simply plug in the headphones, summon the Music app, and choose tunes to match your mood. It's truly blissful — well, until someone calls you and the Droid 3 ceases being a musical instrument and returns to being the ball-and-chain of the modern digital era.

Browsing your music library

Music Headquarters on your phone is the app named, oddly enough, Music. You can start this app by touching its icon, found on the App menu. Soon, you discover the main Music browsing screen, similar to the one shown in Figure 16-1.

Music categories   Show current song.

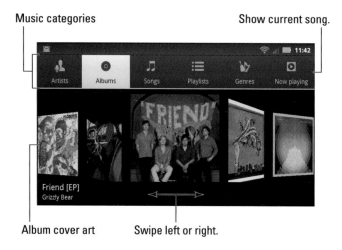

Album cover art   Swipe left or right.

Figure 16-1: The Music library.

All music stored on your phone can be viewed by category, as shown in Figure 16-1:

Artists: Songs are listed by recording artist or group. Choose Artist to see the list of artists. Then choose an artist to see their albums. Choosing an album displays the songs for that album. Some artists may have only one song, not in a particular album.

Albums: Songs are organized by album. Choose an album to list its songs.

Songs: All songs are listed alphabetically.

Playlists: Only songs you've organized into playlists are listed by their playlist names. Choose a playlist name to view songs organized in that playlist. The section "Organize Your Music," later in this chapter, discusses playlists.

Genres: Tunes are organized by their themes, such as classical, rock, or irritating.

Now Playing: This item isn't a category, but a quick link to the currently playing (or paused) song. When the phone is held in a vertical orientation, this item appears at the bottom of the screen.

These categories are merely ways that the music is organized, ways to make tunes easier to find when you may know an artist's name but not an album title or you may want to hear a song but not know who recorded it.

- Music is stored on the Droid 3's internal storage as well as on the MicroSD card.

- The size of the phone's storage limits the total amount of music you can keep on your phone. Also, consider that pictures and videos stored on your phone horn in on some of the space that can be used for music.

- See the later section "More Music for Your Phone" for information on getting music into your phone.

- Album artwork generally appears on imported music as well as on music you purchase online. If an album doesn't have artwork, it cannot be manually added or updated.

- When the Droid 3 is unable to recognize an artist, it uses the title *Unknown Artist.* This happens with music you copy manually to the Droid 3. Music that you purchase, or import or synchronize with a computer, generally retains the artist and album information. (Well, the information is retained as long as it was supplied on the original source.)

Playing a tune

To listen to music on the Droid 3, you first find a song in the library, as described in the preceding section, and then you touch the song title. The song plays in another window, shown in Figure 16-2.

While the song is playing, you're free to do anything else with the phone. In fact, the song continues to play even if the phone goes to sleep.

After the song is done playing, the next song in the list plays. Touch the Song List button (refer to Figure 16-2) to review the songs in the list.

The next song doesn't play if you have the Shuffle button activated (refer to Figure 16-2). In that case, the phone randomizes the songs in the list, so who knows which one is next?

The next song also might not play if you have the Repeat option on. The three repeat settings are illustrated in Table 16-1, along with the shuffle settings. To change settings, simply touch either the Shuffle or Repeat button.

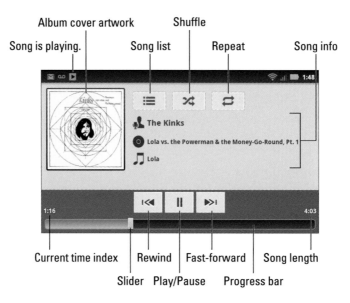

Figure 16-2: A song is playing.

Table 16-1	Shuffle and Repeat Button Icons	
Icon	*Setting*	*What Happens When You Touch the Icon*
⤭	Shuffle Is Off	Songs play one after the other.
⤭	Shuffle Is On	Songs are played in random order.
⇄	Repeat Is Off	Songs don't repeat.
⇄	Repeat All Songs	All songs in the list play over and over.
⇄	Repeat Current Song	The same song plays over and over.

To stop the song from playing, touch the Pause button (refer to Figure 16-2).

 When music plays on the phone, a notification icon appears, as shown in the margin. Use this notification to quickly summon the Music app to see which song is playing or to pause the song.

Information about the current song playing also appears on the phone's lock screen. In fact, you can use the music controls on the phone's lock screen without unlocking the phone.

- ✔ Volume is set by using the Volume switches on the side of the phone: Up is louder, down is quieter.

- ✔ When you're browsing your music library, you may see the green Play icon, similar to the one shown in the margin. This icon flags any song that's playing or paused.

- ✔ Determining which song plays next depends on how you chose the song that's playing. If you choose a song by artist, all songs from that artist play, one after the other. When you choose a song by album, that album plays. Choosing a song from the entire song list causes all songs in the phone to play.

- ✔ To choose which songs play after each other, create a playlist. See the section "Organize Your Music," later in this chapter.

- ✔ After the last song in the list plays, the phone stops playing songs — unless you have the Repeat option on, in which case the song or list plays again.

More Music for Your Phone

Odds are good that your Droid 3 came with no music preinstalled. It might have: Some resellers may have preinstalled a smattering of tunes, which merely lets you know how out of touch they are musically. Regardless, you can add music to your phone in a number of ways, as covered in this section.

Stealing music from your computer

Your computer is the equivalent of the 20th century stereo system — a combination tuner, amplifier, and turntable, plus all your records and CDs. If you've already copied your music collection to your computer, or if you use your computer as your main music storage system, you can share that music with the Droid 3.

In Windows, you can use a music jukebox program, such as Windows Media Player, to synchronize music between your phone and the PC. Here's how it works:

1. **Connect the Droid 3 to the PC.**

2. **Pull down the USB Connection notification.**

3. **Choose the item Windows Media Sync, and touch the OK button.**

4. **On your PC, start Windows Media Player.**

   You can use most any media program, or "jukebox." These steps are specific to Version 12 of Windows Media Player, though they're similar to the steps you take in any media-playing program.

5. **If necessary, click the Sync tab in Windows Media Player.**

   The Droid 3 appears in the Sync list on the right side of Windows Media Player, as shown in Figure 16-3.

Click to sync.   Sync tab   Droid 3

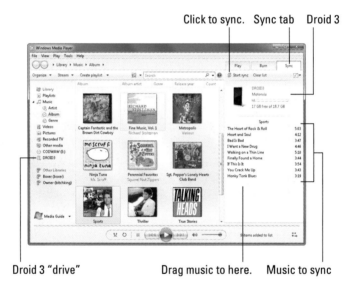

Droid 3 "drive"   Drag music to here.   Music to sync

Figure 16-3: Windows Media Player meets Droid 3.

6. **Drag to the Sync area the music you want to transfer to the Droid 3 (refer to Figure 16-3).**

7. **Click the Start Sync button to transfer the music to the Droid 3.**

8. **Close the Windows Media Player when you're done transferring music.**

   Or, you can keep it open — whatever.

9. **Unmount the Droid 3 from the PC's storage system.**

   Refer to Chapter 20 for specific unmounting instructions, also known as turning off USB storage.

When you have a Macintosh, or if you detest Windows Media Player, you can use the doubleTwist program to synchronize music between your Droid 3 and your computer. Refer to the section about synchronizing with doubleTwist in Chapter 20 for information.

✔ The Droid 3 can store only so much music! Don't be overzealous when copying over your tunes. In Windows Media Player (refer to Figure 16-3), a capacity-thermometer thing shows you how much storage space is used and how much is available on your phone. Pay heed to the indicator!

✔ You cannot use iTunes to synchronize music with the Droid 3.

✔ Okay, I lied in the preceding point: You *can* synchronize music using iTunes, but only when you install the iTunes Agent program on your PC. You then need to configure the iTunes Agent program to use your Droid 3 with iTunes. After you do that, iTunes recognizes the Droid 3 and lets you synchronize your music. Yes, it's technical — hence the icon in the margin.

✔ The Droid 3 cannot access its storage (music, photos, contacts) while it's mounted to a computer for music syncing. You can access this information after you unmount the phone from the computer.

Buying music at the Amazon MP3 store

When you don't have any music, and you're not creative enough to write your own, you need to buy it. The Android Market may at some point sell music, but for now you need to turn to another source for your music shopping needs. The place I recommend is the app called Amazon MP3 Store.

Use the QR Code in the margin or visit the Android Market to download a copy of the Amazon MP3 app to your Droid 3.

To get the most from the Amazon MP3 app, you need an Amazon account. If you don't have one set up, use your computer to visit www.amazon.com and create one. You also need to keep a credit card on file for the account, which makes purchasing music with the Droid 3 work O so well.

Follow these steps to buy music for your phone:

1. **Ensure that you're using a Wi-Fi or high-speed digital network connection.**

   Activating the phone's Wi-Fi is described in Chapter 19.

2. **From the App menu, choose the Amazon MP3 app.**

The Amazon MP3 app connects you with the online Amazon music store, where you can search or browse for tunes to preview and purchase for your Droid 3.

The Amazon MP3 store presents you with two options for purchasing music: Store and Player. The Store option is where you buy music to download to your phone. The Player option, which I don't cover here, lets you save your music on the Internet, where you can play it from any device connected to the Internet.

3. **Touch the Store button.**

4. **Touch the Search button to begin your music quest.**

   Or, you can browse by top-selling songs and albums or new releases, or browse by category.

5. **Type some search words, such as an album name, a song title, or an artist name.**

6. **Touch a result.**

   If the result is an album, you see the contents of the album. Otherwise, an audio preview plays.

   When the result is an album, choose a song in the album to hear the preview.

   Touch the song again to stop the preview.

7. **To purchase the song, touch the big button with the amount in it.**

   Some buttons say *FREE,* for free songs.

   Touching the button changes the price into the word *BUY.*

8. **Touch the word *BUY.***

9. **If necessary, you may need to accept the license agreement.**

   This step happens the first time you buy something from the Amazon MP3 store.

10. **Sign in to your Amazon.com account: Type your account name or e-mail address and password.**

    Your purchase is registered, account authorized, and download started. If they aren't, touch the Retry button to try again.

11. **Wait while the music downloads.**

    Well, actually, you don't have to wait: The music continues to download while you do other things on the phone.

No notification icon appears when the song or album has finished downloading. Notice, however, that the MP3 Store Downloading icon vanishes from the notification part of the screen. It's your clue that the new music is in the phone and ready for your ears.

✔ Amazon e-mails you a bill for your purchase. That's your purchase record, so I advise you to be a good accountant and print it and then input it into your bookkeeping program or personal finance program at once!

✔ You can review your Amazon MP3 store purchases by pressing the Menu soft button in the MP3 Store app and choosing the Downloads command.

Organize Your Music

A *playlist* is a collection of tunes you create. You build the list by combining songs from an album or artist or from whatever music you have on your phone. You can then listen to the playlist and hear the music you want to hear in the order you want to hear it. That's how to organize music on your Droid 3.

Reviewing your playlists

Any playlists you've already created, or that have been preset on the Droid 3, appear under the Playlists heading on the Music app's main screen. Touching the Playlists heading displays playlists, similar to the ones shown in Figure 16-4.

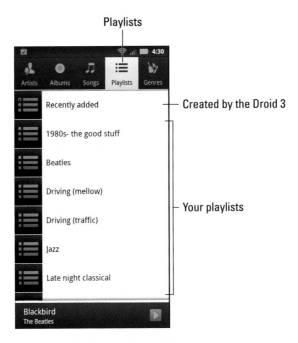

Figure 16-4: Playlists on the Droid 3.

To listen to a playlist, long-press the playlist name and choose the Play command from the menu that appears.

You can also touch a playlist name to open the playlist and review the songs listed. You can touch any song from the list to start listening to that song.

A playlist is a helpful way to organize music when a song's information may not have been completely imported into the Droid 3. For example, if you're like me, you probably have a lot of songs by Unknown Artist. The quick way to remedy this situation is to name a playlist after the artist and then add those unknown songs to the playlist. The next section describes how it's done.

Creating a playlist

The Droid 3 ships with one playlist already set up for you — the Recently Added playlist, shown in Figure 16-4. This playlist contains all the songs you've purchased for, or imported to, your phone. Obviously, having more playlists would be a good idea.

Playlists aren't created from scratch on the Droid 3. Instead, you must choose a song and then add it to a new playlist. Follow these steps:

1. **Long-press the song you want to use to start a new playlist.**

   Use the Music app to locate the song. You don't have to play the song — just locate its name on the screen.

2. **Choose Add to Playlist.**

3. **Choose New from the Add to Playlist menu.**

4. **Type the playlist name.**

   Erase whatever silly text already appears in the input field. Type or dictate a new, better playlist name.

5. **Touch the Save button.**

   The new playlist is created, and the song you long-pressed (refer to Step 1) is added to the playlist.

A new playlist has only one song. That's not much of a playlist, unless, of course, the song is by the Grateful Dead. To add more songs to a playlist, follow these steps:

1. **Long-press the song you want to add to the playlist.**

2. **Choose Add to Playlist.**

3. **Choose an existing playlist.**

   You may have to scroll down the list to see all your playlists.

You can continue adding songs to as many playlists as you like. Adding songs to a playlist doesn't noticeably affect the phone's storage capacity.

✔ Songs in a playlist can be rearranged: Use the tab on the far left end of the song's title in the list to drag the song up or down.

✔ To remove a song from a playlist, long-press the song in the playlist and choose the command Remove from Playlist. Removing a song from a playlist doesn't delete the song from your phone. (See the next section for information on deleting songs from the Music library.)

✔ To delete a playlist, long-press its name in the list of playlists. Choose the Delete command. Touch the OK button to confirm. Though the playlist is removed, none of the songs in the playlist has been deleted.

Deleting music

To purge unwanted music from your Droid 3, follow these brief, painless steps:

1. **Long-press the music that offends you.**

   It can be an album, a song, or even an artist.

2. **Choose Delete.**

   A warning message appears.

3. **Touch the OK button.**

   The music is gone.

As the warning says (before Step 3), the music is deleted permanently from the phone's storage. By deleting music, you free up storage space, and you cannot recover any music you delete. If you want the song back, you have to reinstall or sync it or buy it again, as described elsewhere in this chapter.

Your Phone Is a Radio

Though they're not broadcast radio stations, some sources on the Internet — *Internet radio* — play music. You can listen to this Internet music if you put one of these two apps on your Droid 3:

✔ Pandora Radio

✔ StreamFurious

 Pandora Radio lets you select music based on your mood and customizes what you listen to according to your feedback. The app works like the Internet site www.pandora.com, in case you're familiar with it.

StreamFurious streams music from various radio stations on the Internet. Though not as customizable as Pandora, it uses less bandwidth.

Both apps are available at the Android Market. They're free, though a paid, *Pro,* version of StreamFurious exists.

✔ Various apps are also available at the Android Market that can turn your cell phone into an FM radio. I have nothing specific to recommend, mostly because the good apps aren't free. But keep your eyes peeled for FM radio apps for your Droid 3.

✔ See Chapter 18 for more information about the Android Market.

Even More Apps

In This Chapter

▷ Using the Calendar
▷ Checking your schedule
▷ Adding an event
▷ Using the Droid 3 as a calculator
▷ Setting alarms
▷ Reading e-books
▷ Watching and renting videos
▷ Playing games

*Y*our phone is limited in its abilities only by the software — the *apps* — it has, and the Droid 3 comes with a lot of apps. Too many to write about all in one book, in fact. Too many to try all at once. Yet just enough to keep the task of scrolling the App menu just a notch above tedious.

Though other chapters cover some of the major apps tied into the secondary (nonphone) duties of the Droid 3, a few apps are still worthy of a look. Some are useful, some are for diversion, and some can be dangerously fun. They're covered in this chapter.

August 2011				
Mon	Tue	Wed	Thu	F
1	2	3	4	5
7	8	9	10	11	1
	15	16	17	18	1

An Appointment to Remember

Some people have date books. Others might write down appointments on business cards or on their palms. These methods might be effective, but they pale in comparison to the power of using your Droid 3 as your calendar and date keeper. Your phone can easily serve as a reminder of obligations due or delights to come. It all happens thanks to Google Calendar and the Calendar app on your phone.

If all you need is a To Do list, check out the Tasks app, found on the Apps menu. It offers a simple interface for creating tasks, honey-do lists, and reminders.

Understanding the Calendar

The Droid 3 takes advantage of Google Calendar on the Internet. If you have a Google account (and I'm certain that you do), you already have Google Calendar. You can visit Google Calendar by using your computer to go to this web page:

```
http://calendar.google.com
```

If necessary, log in using your Google account. You can use Google Calendar to keep track of dates or meetings or whatever else occupies your time. You can also use your phone to do the same thing, thanks to the Calendar app.

✓ I recommend that you use the Calendar app on your phone to access Google Calendar. It's a better way to access your schedule on the Droid 3 than using the Browser app to get to Google Calendar on the web.

✓ The Droid 3 comes with a Calendar widget, which is preinstalled on the first Home screen panel to the right of the main Home screen. The Calendar widget is useful for reminding you of upcoming appointments. See Chapter 22 for details on adding widgets to the Home screen.

Browsing dates

To see your schedule or upcoming important events, or just to know which day of the month it is, summon the Calendar app. Touch the Launcher button at the bottom of the Home screen to display a list of all apps on the phone; choose the one named Calendar.

The first screen you see is most likely the monthly calendar view, shown in Figure 17-1. The calendar looks like a typical monthly calendar, with the month and year at the top. Scheduled appointments appear as colored highlights on various days.

Use the View button (refer to Figure 17-1) to view your appointments by week or day. You can choose the Agenda item from the Change View menu to see your appointments in a list format.

Figure 17-2 shows both Week and Day views in the Calendar. In these views, you can see the color coding used to identify different calendar categories.

View today, month, week, day, agenda

Event reminder   Today   New event

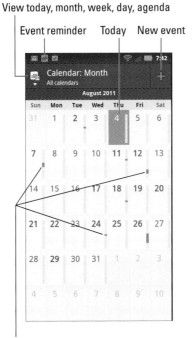

Events

Figure 17-1: The Calendar's Month view.

All-day events

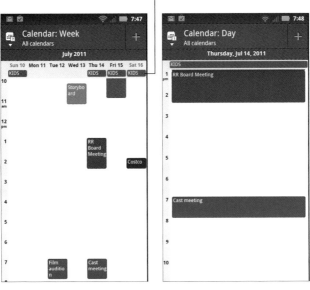

Week view   Day view

Figure 17-2: The Calendar's Week and Day views.

You can return to the Month view at any time by touching the View button and choosing Month. Or hop quickly to today's date by choosing the command Show Today from the View button.

- ✔ See the later section "Making a new event" for information on reviewing and creating events.

- ✔ Use Month view to see an overview of what's going on, but use Week or Day view to see your appointments.

- ✔ I check Week view at the start of the week to remind me of what's coming up.

- ✔ Events on the Calendar are color-coded, which helps you not only organize events but also show and hide different types of events. To control the colors and event categories in the Calendar app, press the Menu soft button and choose Settings and then Manage Calendars.

- ✔ Also see the later section "Making a new event" for information on color-coded calendars.

- ✔ Use your finger to flick the Week and Day views up or down to see your entire schedule, from midnight to midnight.

- ✔ Navigate the days, weeks, or months by flicking the screen with your finger. Months scroll up and down; weeks and days scroll from left to right.

- ✔ To go to a specific date, press the Menu soft button and choose the Go to Date command. Use the onscreen gizmo to enter a date and touch the Go button.

Reviewing your schedule

To see all upcoming events, choose Agenda from the View button's menu (refer to Figure 17-1). Rather than list a traditional calendar, the Agenda screen lists only those dates with events and the events themselves.

To see more detail about an event, touch it. Details about the event appear similarly to the ones shown in Figure 17-3.

Not every event has the level of detail shown in Figure 17-3. The minimum amount of information necessary for an event is a name and the date and time.

- ✔ Use the sliding keyboard's arrow keys to move around the selected date or time. The selected date or time comes in handy when creating events.

- ✔ Touching a location, as shown in Figure 17-3, conjures up the Maps app, where you see the event's location on the map. From there it's easy to get directions, as described in Chapter 13.

- ✔ See the next section for information on event reminders.

Repeating-event schedule   Forward event via Gmail.

Calendar category   Edit event.

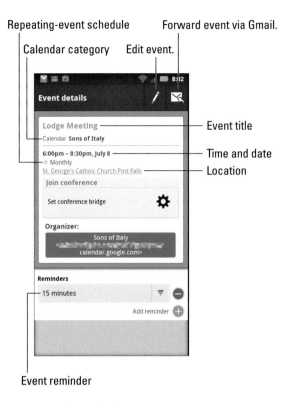

Event title

Time and date

Location

Event reminder

Figure 17-3: Event details.

Making a new event

The key to making your calendar work is to add events: appointments, things to do, meetings, or full-day events such as birthdays and earthquakes. To create a new event, follow these steps in the Calendar app:

1. **Select the day for the event.**

    Use Month or Week view, and touch the day of the new event.

    To save time, use Day view, and touch the hour at which the event starts.

2. **Touch the New Event button (refer to Figure 17-1).**

    The Create Event screen appears, where you add details about the event.

3. **Choose the event Calendar.**

   Calendars are best set up on the Internet using a computer. Basically, they let you organize your events by category and color. Also, you can show or hide individual calendar categories when you have a particularly busy schedule.

4. **Type the event name.**

   For example, type **Vasectomy**.

5. **Use the buttons by Start to set the starting date and time.**

6. **Use the buttons by End to set the ending date and time.**

   When an event lasts all day, such as visiting your mother-in-law for an hour, simply touch the All Day button to put a check mark there. All-day events appear at the top of the day when the Calendar is shown in Week view (refer to Figure 17-2).

   At this point, you've entered the minimum amount of information for creating an event. Any details you add are okay but not necessary.

7. **Touch the Where field to enter a location.**

   The location can be used by the Maps app to help you get to your appointment. My theory is that you should specify a location as if you're typing something to search for on the map. See Chapter 13 for more information on the Maps app.

8. **Optionally set or dismiss a reminder.**

   Reminders are nice, but if you forget about them they can be annoying. For example, if you forget to remove the reminder for an all-day event, the phone will make a noise at 15 minutes to midnight. Don't ask how long it took me to figure that out.

9. **Touch the Save button.**

   The Calendar app creates the event.

You can change an event at any time: Simply touch the Edit Event button when viewing the event (refer to Figure 17-3).

To remove an event, long-press it in Week or Day view. Choose the Delete Event command. Touch the OK button to confirm.

  ✓ Use the Repetition button to create repeating events, such as weekly or monthly meetings, anniversaries, and birthdays.

  ✓ Reminders can be set so that the phone alerts you before an event takes place. The alert can show up as a notification icon (shown in the margin), or it can be an audio alert or a vibrating alert.

✔ To deal with an event notification, pull down the notifications and choose the event. You can touch the Dismiss button to remove event alerts.

✔ Alerts for events are set by pressing the Menu soft button in the Calendar app and choosing the Settings command. Use the Select Ringtone option to choose an audio alert. Use the Vibrate option to control whether the phone vibrates to alert you of an impending event.

Your Phone, the Calculator

The Calculator is perhaps the oldest of all traditional cell phone apps. It's probably also the least confusing and frustrating app to use.

Start the Calculator app by choosing its icon from the App menu. The Calculator appears, as shown in Figure 17-4.

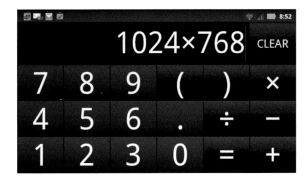

Figure 17-4: The Calculator.

✔ You can swipe the screen (refer to Figure 17-4) to the left to see a panel of strange, advanced mathematical operations you'll probably never use.

✔ Use the sliding keyboard's up- and down-arrow keys to scroll back through the previous calculations you've made.

✔ Long-press the calculator's text (or results) to cut or copy the results.

✔ I use the Calculator most often to determine my tip at a restaurant. It takes me almost as long to use the Calculator as it does for smarty-pants Barbara to do the 15 percent calculation in her head. That's when I tip 18 percent.

No Need to Alarm You

The Droid 3 keeps constant and accurate track of the time, which is displayed at the top of the Home screen and also when you first wake up the phone. When you'd rather have the phone wake you up, you can take advantage of the Alarm & Timer app.

Start the Alarm & Timer app by choosing its icon from the App menu. The Alarm Clock is shown in Figure 17-5.

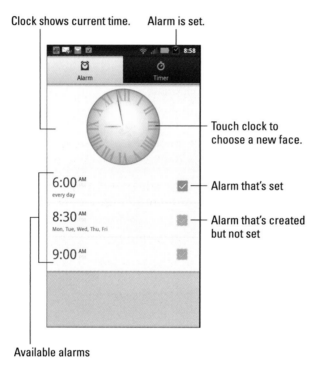

Clock shows current time.   Alarm is set.

Touch clock to choose a new face.

Alarm that's set

Alarm that's created but not set

Available alarms

Figure 17-5: The Alarm & Timer app.

If you see an alarm you want to set, touch the gray square (refer to Figure 17-5) to set that alarm. A green check mark in a square indicates that an alarm is set.

To create your own alarm, follow these steps while using the Alarm Clock app:

1. Press the Menu soft button, and choose Add Alarm.

2. **Choose Alarm Name to type in a name for the alarm.**

   Be descriptive. A good alarm name would be *Get up and go to work!*

3. **Choose Time to set the alarm time.**

   Use the gizmo to set the hour and minute and specify AM or PM. Touch the Set button when you're done setting the time.

4. **Touch the Sound button to choose a ringtone for the alarm — something suitably annoying.**

5. **Specify whether the phone vibrates by placing a check mark next to the Vibrate option.**

6. **Choose whether the alarm repeats.**

   Choose which days of the week you want the alarm to sound.

7. **Touch the Done button to create the alarm.**

   The alarm appears in a list on the main Alarm Clock screen, along with any other available alarms.

Alarms must be set or else they will not trigger. To set an alarm, touch it in the alarm list. Place a check mark in the gray box (refer to Figure 17-5).

✓ For a larger time display, you can add a Clock widget to the Home screen. Refer to Chapter 22 for more information about widgets on the Home screen.

✓ Turning off an alarm doesn't delete the alarm.

✓ To delete an alarm, long-press it in the list and choose the Delete Alarm command. Touch the OK button to confirm.

✓ The alarm doesn't work when you turn off the phone. The alarm does, however, go off when the phone is sleeping.

✓ A notification icon appears whenever an alarm is set, as shown in Figure 17-5. Another notification appears whenever an alarm has gone off but has been ignored.

✓ So tell me: Do alarms go *off,* or do they go *on?*

Something to Read

An *e-book* is an electronic version of a book. The words, formatting, figures, pictures — all that stuff is simply stored digitally so that you can read it on something called an e-book reader. Or, because Droid 3 comes with two e-book reader apps preinstalled, you can read e-books on your phone as well.

- Your Droid 3's preinstalled e-book reader apps are Google Books and the Amazon Kindle app.

- The advantage of an e-book reader is that you can carry an entire library of books with you without developing back problems.

- Rather than buy a new book at the airport, consider getting an e-book instead, though you can still read a real book during take-off and landing.

- Lots of e-books are free, such as quite a few of the classics, including some that aren't that boring. Current and popular titles cost money, though the cost is often cheaper than the book's real-world equivalent.

- Magazine and newspaper subscriptions are also available for e-book readers.

- You aren't limited to using the Google Books and Amazon Kindle apps as your e-book readers. Other apps are available, including Aldiko, FBReader, Kobo, Laputa, and more. You can locate these e-book readers by perusing the Android Market, as described in Chapter 18.

- Not every title is available as an e-book.

Reading with Google Books

The Books app allows you to read e-books purchased at the Android Market. It organizes the books into a library and displays the books for reading on your Droid 3. The reading experience happens like this:

1. **Open the Books app, found on the App menu.**

   If you're prompted to turn on Synchronization, touch the Turn On Sync button.

   You see your e-book library, which lists any titles you've obtained for your Google Books account, or, when you're returning to the Books app after a break, you see the current page of the e-book you were last reading.

2. **Touch a book to open it.**

3. **Start reading.**

   Use Figure 17-6 as your guide for reading a Google Books e-book. Basically, you just swipe the pages left to right.

Also see Chapter 18 for information on purchasing books for your Droid 3 at the Android Market.

Synchronization allows you to keep copies of your Google Books on all your Android devices, as well as the `http://books.google.com` website.

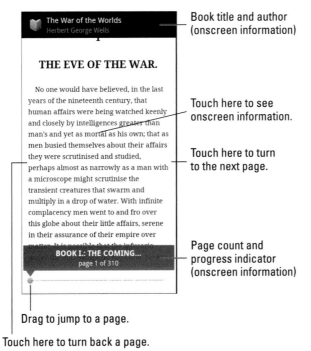

Book title and author (onscreen information)

Touch here to see onscreen information.

Touch here to turn to the next page.

Page count and progress indicator (onscreen information)

Drag to jump to a page.

Touch here to turn back a page.

Figure 17-6: Reading an e-book in the Books app.

Using the Amazon Kindle app

The good folks at Amazon recognize that you probably don't want to buy a Kindle e-book reader gizmo because you already have a nifty portable do-everything device, the Droid 3. Therefore, the Kindle app serves as your e-book reader software and also provides access to the vast library of existing Kindle titles at Amazon.com.

Start the Amazon Kindle app by touching its icon, found on the App menu. Upon starting the Amazon Kindle app, you see the Registration screen. Log in using your e-mail address and Amazon password.

If you already have an Amazon Kindle account, after you touch the Register button, your Droid 3 synchronizes with your existing Kindle library.

Choose a book from the Kindle bookshelf, and start reading. The e-book-reading operation works on the Kindle similar to the Google Books app (refer to Figure 17-6), though on the Kindle you can highlight text, bookmark pages, look up word in a dictionary, and do other keen stuff that Google will no doubt add to a future update of the Books app.

✒ Books for the Kindle app are purchased at the Kindle store using your existing Amazon account. In the Kindle app, press the Menu soft button and choose Kindle Store.

✒ Yes, you need an Amazon.com account to purchase e-books (or even download freebies), so I highly recommend that you visit `www.amazon.com` to set up an account if you don't already have one.

✒ To ensure that you get your entire Kindle library on the Droid 3, turn on the Wi-Fi connection, press the Menu soft button, and choose the Archived Items command.

Movies in the Palm of Your Hand

The first commercially available television sets were about 12 inches across. Today, the screens can be 72 inches across or more. In a dramatic reversal of that trend, your Droid 3 has the ability to let you view movies, TV shows, and Internet video on its relatively diminutive 4-inch screen.

Viewing vids on YouTube

The cheapest — and by that I mean free — way to view video on your phone is to access YouTube. It's the Internet phenomenon that proves Andy Warhol right: In the future, everyone will be famous for 15 minutes. Or, in the case of YouTube, they'll be famous on the Internet for the duration of a 10-minute video. That's because YouTube is *the* place on the Internet for anyone and everyone to share video creations.

To view the mayhem on YouTube or to contribute something yourself, start the YouTube app. Like all apps on the Droid 3, it can be found on the App menu. The main YouTube screen is depicted in Figure 17-7.

To search for a video, press the Search soft button while using the YouTube app. Type or dictate what you want to search for, and then peruse the results.

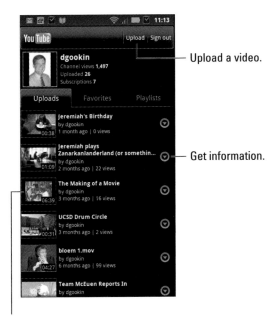

Upload a video.

Get information.

Touch a video to watch.

Figure 17-7: YouTube.

To view a video, touch its name or icon in the list.

Turn the phone to Landscape mode to view a video full-screen. You can touch the screen to see the onscreen video controls.

✔ Use the YouTube app to view YouTube videos rather than use the Browser app to visit the YouTube website.

✔ Because you have a Google account, you also have a YouTube account. I recommend that you log in to your YouTube account when using YouTube on the Droid 3: Press the Menu soft button, and choose the command My Channel. Log in, if necessary. Otherwise, you see your account information, your videos, and any video subscriptions.

✔ Not all YouTube videos can be viewed on mobile devices.

✔ You can touch the Upload button (refer to Figure 17-7) to shoot and then immediately send a video to YouTube. Refer to Chapter 14 for information on recording video with your Droid 3.

Renting movies

Movies that you rent at the Android Market can be viewed on the Droid 3 for up to a 24-hour period after you first start the film. The process involves renting the film at the Market and then using the Video app to watch it. Follow these steps:

1. **Visit the Android Market; open the Market app on your phone.**

2. **Choose the Movies category.**

   All movies are rentals.

3. **Browse or search for a movie.**

4. **Touch the movie's Rent button, which also lists the rental price.**

   You aren't charged for touching the Rent button. Instead, you see more details, such as the rental terms. Typically, you have 30 days to watch the film, and you can pause and resume and watch it over and over during a single 24-hour period.

5. **Choose a payment method.**

   If you don't yet have an account set up at Google Checkout, you can configure one by touching the Add Payment Method button. Otherwise, choose your Google Checkout credit card, shown on the screen.

6. **Touch the Accept & Buy button to rent the movie.**

7. **Touch the Play button to view the movie.**

If you don't already have the Videos app, you're prompted to download it. Follow the directions on the screen.

The move is *streamed* to your phone, which means it's sent to the Droid 3 as you watch it. Therefore, I highly recommend two things when you're ready to watch. First, plug the Droid 3 into a power source. Second, turn on the Wi-Fi network so that you don't incur any data overages.

You don't have to view the movie right away. You can wait as long as 30 days. When you're ready, start the Videos app, and choose your rental from the My Rentals list.

You can also start the Videos app from the App menu to review and view your rentals, as well as any personal videos you've installed on the Droid 3.

The rental is available for 30 days, but once you start watching it, you have only 24 hours to finish.

✔ The Droid 3 also comes with the Blockbuster app, which can be used to rent or purchase mainstream movies that you can view right on your phone. The key is to have an account at Blockbuster. When you do, you can follow the directions on the screen after starting the Blockbuster app and get everything signed up and configured.

✔ Connect the Droid 3 to a large-screen HDMI monitor or TV to view the rental. See Chapter 20 on instructions on making the HDMI connection.

✔ See Chapter 18 for additional information on the Android Market, though most of that chapter is dedicated to purchasing and organizing apps.

The Droid 3 Does Games

For all its seriousness and technology, one of the best uses of a smartphone is to play games. I'm not talking about the silly arcade games (though I admit that they're fun). No, I'm talking about some serious portable gaming.

To whet your appetite, the Droid 3 comes with a small taste of what the device can do in regard to gaming, such as the Nova game app, shown in Figure 17-8.

Figure 17-8: A game on the Droid 3.

Game apps use phone features such as the touchscreen or the accelerometer to control the action. It takes some getting used to, especially if you regularly play using a game console or PC, but it can be really fun.

Also, the preinstalled games are generally previews only; if you want to continue using the games you have to buy the full version. The app lets you know how much it costs as soon as you complete the first few levels or laps or kill off a given number of aliens.

Of course, Droid 3 gaming isn't limited to the few games that come with the phone. Many games — arcade, action, and puzzle — can be found in the Android Market. See Chapter 18.

Behold the Android Market

In This Chapter

▷ Using the Market app

▷ Searching for apps, books, and movies

▷ Downloading a free app

▷ Getting a paid app

▷ Reviewing apps you've downloaded

▷ Sharing an app

▷ Updating an app

▷ Managing apps

Your phone isn't limited to merely the smattering of interesting and diverse apps that come preinstalled. There is a whole galaxy of apps available out there. Not only that, there are books to read and movies to rent. It's all found in a handy place called the Android Market. Not only that, most of the apps and lots of the books are free. Oh, you can really go nuts at the Market.

Shop at the Android Market

Obtaining new apps, books, and movie rentals for your Droid 3 can be done anywhere that you and your phone just happen to be. You don't even need to know what you want; like many a mindless ambling shopper, you can browse until the touchscreen is smudged and blurry with your fingerprints.

✔ You obtain items from the Market by *downloading* them into your phone. This type of file transfer works best at top speeds. Therefore:

✔ I highly recommend that you connect to a Wi-Fi network if you plan to obtain apps, books, or movies at the Android Market. See Chapter 19 for details on connecting the Droid 3 to a Wi-Fi network.

✔ The Market app is frequently updated, so its look may change from what you see in this chapter. It may also add a Music category in the near future. Updated information on the Market can be found on my website:

    www.wambooli.com/help/phone

Visiting the Market

New apps, books, and movies await delivery into your phone, like animated vegetables shouting, "Pick me! Pick me!" To get to them, open the Market icon, which can be found on the center Home screen panel or accessed from the App menu.

After opening the Market app, you see the main screen, similar to the one shown in Figure 18-1. You can browse for apps, games, books, and movie rentals. The categories are listed on the top left part of the screen, with the other parts of the screen highlighting popular or recommended items. Those recommendations are color-coded to let you know what they are: green for apps, blue for books, and red for video rentals.

Find items by choosing a category from the main menu (refer to Figure 18-1). The next screen lists popular and featured items, plus categories you can browse by swiping the screen right to left. The category titles appear toward the top of the screen.

When you have an idea of what you want, such as an app's name or even what it does, searching works fastest: Touch the Search button at the top of the Market screen (refer to Figure 18-1). Type all or part of the app's name, book or movie title, or perhaps a description. Touch the keyboard's Search or Go button to begin your search.

To see more information about an item, touch it. Touching something doesn't buy it, but displays a more detailed description, screen shots, a video preview, comments, plus links to similar items.

✔ The first time you enter the Android Market, you have to accept the terms of service; touch the Accept button.

✔ Books you get from the Market are read by the Books app. See Chapter 17 for information.

✔ Chapter 17 covers renting movies from the Market.

Search

Featured and
recommended

More recommendations

Featured items

Figure 18-1: Android Market.

Finding apps at the Market

The most common and traditional things to hunt down at the Android Market
are more apps for your phone. Presently, more than 200,000 apps are available at the Market. That's good news. Better news: Most of the apps are free.
Even the paid apps have "lite" versions you can try without having to pay.

> ✔ Apps you download are added to the App menu, made available like any
> other apps on your phone.

> ✔ You can be assured that all apps that appear in the Market on your
> phone can be used with the Droid 3. There's no way that you can
> download or buy something that's incompatible with your phone.

> ✔ Pay attention to an app's ratings. Ratings are added by people who use
> the apps, like you and me. Having more stars is better. You can see
> additional information, including individual user reviews, by choosing
> the app.

> ✔ In addition to getting apps, you can download widgets for the Home
> screen as well as wallpapers for the Droid 3. Just search the Market for
> *widget* or *live wallpaper.*

> ✔ See Chapter 22 for more information on widgets and live wallpapers.

Getting a free app

After you locate an app you want, the next step is to download it. Follow these steps:

1. **If possible, activate the phone's Wi-Fi connection.**

   Downloads complete much faster over the Wi-Fi connection than over the digital cellular connection. See Chapter 19 for information on connecting your Droid 3 phone to a Wi-Fi network.

2. **Open the Market app.**

3. **Locate the app you want, and open its description.**

   You can browse for apps or use the Search button to find an app by name or what it does.

4. **Touch the Download button.**

   The Download button is found at the bottom of the app's list o' details. Free apps feature an Download button. Paid apps have a button with the app's price on it. (See the next section for information on buying an app.)

   After touching the Download button, you're alerted to any services that the app uses. The alert isn't a warning, and it doesn't mean anything bad. It's just that the Droid 3 is telling you which of your phone's features the app uses.

5. **Touch the Accept & Download button to begin the download.**

   As the app is downloaded you see a progress bar dance across the screen. When it's done the app has been installed.

6. **Touch the Open button to run the app.**

   Or, if you were doing something else while the app was downloading and installing, choose the Installed App notification, as shown in the margin. The notification features the app's name, with the text `Successfully Installed` beneath it.

At this point, what happens next depends on the app you've downloaded. For example, you may have to agree to a license agreement. If so, touch the I Agree button. Additional setup may involve signing in to an account or creating a profile, for example.

After the initial setup is complete, or if no setup is necessary, you can start using the app.

- The new app's icon is placed on the App menu, along with all the other apps on the Droid 3.

- Peruse the list of services an app uses (in Step 4) to look for anything unusual or out of line with the app's purpose. For example, an alarm clock app that uses your contact list and the text messaging service would be a red flag, especially if it's your understanding that the app doesn't need to text message any of your contacts.

- You can also place a shortcut icon for the app on the Home screen. See Chapter 22.

- Chapter 26 lists some Android apps that I recommend, all of which are free.

- Don't forget to turn off Wi-Fi after downloading your app; Wi-Fi is a drain on the phone's battery.

Buying an app

Some great free apps are available, but many of the apps you dearly want probably cost money. It's not a lot of money, especially compared to the price of computer software. In fact, it seems odd to sit and stew over whether paying 99 cents for a game is "worth it."

I recommend that you download a free app first, to familiarize yourself with the process.

When you're ready to pay for an app, follow these steps:

1. **Activate the phone's Wi-Fi connection.**

2. **Open the Market app.**

3. **Browse or search for the app you want, and choose the app to display its description.**

   Review the app's price.

4. **Touch the price button.**

   For example, if the app is $0.99, the button reads $0.99.

5. **Choose your credit card.**

   The card must be on file with Google Checkout. If you don't yet have a card on file, choose the option Add Payment Method. Choose Add Card and then fill in the fields on the Credit Card screen to add your payment method to Google Checkout.

6. **Touch the Accept & Buy button.**

   Your payment method is authorized, and the app is downloaded and installed.

The app can be accessed from the App menu, just like all other apps available on your Droid 3. Or, if you're still at the app's screen in the Market, touch the Open button.

Eventually, you receive an e-mail message from Google Checkout, confirming your purchase. The message explains how you can get a refund from your purchase. Generally speaking, you can open the app's info screen (see the section "Controlling your apps," later in this chapter) and touch the Refund button to get your money back.

Be quick on that refund: Some apps allow you only 15 minutes to get your money back. Otherwise, the standard refund period is 24 hours. You know when the time is up because the Refund button changes its name to Uninstall.

Also see the section "Removing downloaded apps," later in this chapter.

Manage Your Apps

The Market is not only where you buy apps — it's also the place you return to for performing app management. That task includes reviewing apps you've downloaded, updating apps, organizing apps, and removing apps you no longer want or that you severely hate.

Reviewing your downloaded apps

If you're like me, and if I'm like anyone (and my editor says that I'm not), you probably sport a whole host of apps on your Droid 3. It's kind of fun to download new software and give your phone new abilities. To review the apps you've acquired, follow these steps:

1. **Start the Market app.**

2. **Press the Menu soft button, and choose My Apps.**

3. **Scroll your downloaded apps.**

The list of downloaded apps should look similar to the one shown in Figure 18-2.

Besides reviewing the list, you can do other things with an installed app, as covered in the sections that follow.

The list of downloaded apps is accurate in that it represents apps you've downloaded. Some apps in the list, however, might not be installed on your Droid 3: They were downloaded, installed, and then removed. To review all apps installed on the phone, see the section "Controlling your apps," later in this chapter.

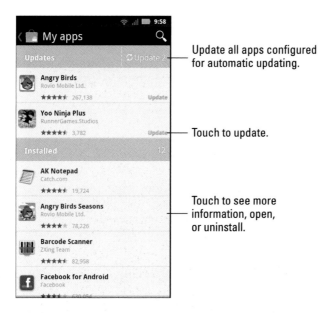

Update all apps configured for automatic updating.

Touch to update.

Touch to see more information, open, or uninstall.

Figure 18-2: Apps downloaded on the Droid 3.

Sharing an app

When you love an app so much that you just can't contain your glee, feel free to share that app with your friends. You can easily share a link to the app in the Market by obeying these steps:

1. **Visit the app on your download list.**

   Refer to the preceding section. Or the app doesn't have to be on your list of downloaded apps; it can be any app in the Market. You just need to be viewing the app's description screen.

2. **Touch the Share button.**

   A menu appears, listing various apps and methods for sharing the app's Market link with your pals.

3. **Choose a sharing method.**

   For example, choose Text Messaging to send a link to the app in a text message.

4. **Use the chosen app to send the link.**

   What happens next depends on which sharing method you've chosen.

The result of following these steps is that your friend receives a link. They can touch that link on their phone, or another mobile Android device, and be whisked instantly to the Market, to view the app and easily install it on their gizmo.

Methods for using the various items on the Share menu are found throughout this book.

Updating an app

One nice thing about using the Android Market to get new software is that the Market also notifies you of new versions of the programs you download. Whenever a new version of any app is available, you see it flagged for updating, as shown in Figure 18-2. Updating the app to get the latest version is cinchy.

From the downloads list (refer to Figure 18-2), touch the Update button to update all the apps for which automatic updating is allowed.

Some apps must be updated individually. To do so, touch the Update item in the downloads list (refer to Figure 18-2) to see the app's information screen. Touch the Update button on the app's information screen and then choose Accept & Download.

To make updating easier, open an app's information screen and place a green check mark by the item Allow Automatic Updating.

> ✔ The updating process often involves downloading and installing a new version of the app. That's perfectly fine; your settings and options are not changed by the update process.

> ✔ Update to apps might also be indicated by the Updates Available notification icon, shown in the margin. Choose the Updates Available notification to be instantly whisked to the My Apps screen, where you can update your apps as described in this section.

Removing downloaded apps

You're free to remove any app you've added to the Droid 3, specifically those apps you've downloaded from the Market. To do so, heed these steps:

1. **Start the Market app.**

2. **Press the Menu soft button, and choose My Apps.**

3. **Touch the app that offends you.**

4. **Touch the Uninstall button.**

5. **Touch the OK button to confirm.**

   The app is removed.

The app continues to appear on the Downloads list even after it's been removed. After all, you downloaded it once. That doesn't mean that the app is installed.

✔ In most cases, if you uninstall a paid app right away, your credit card or account is fully refunded. The definition of "right away" depends on the app and is stated so on the app's description screen. It could be anywhere from 15 minutes to 24 hours.

✔ You can always reinstall paid apps that you've uninstalled. You aren't charged twice for doing so.

✔ Preinstalled software cannot be removed from your Droid 3. Only if you hack into your phone through a process called *rooting* can you remove that software. I don't recommend it.

Controlling your apps

The Droid 3 has a technical place where you can review and manage all apps you've installed on your phone. To visit that place, follow these steps:

1. **At the Home screen, press the Menu soft button.**

2. **Choose Settings and then choose Applications.**

3. **Choose Manage Applications.**

   A complete list of all applications installed on your phone is displayed. Unlike the list of downloaded apps in the Market app, only installed applications appear.

4. **Touch an application name.**

   An application info screen appears, showing lots of trivia about the app.

Among the trivia on the application's info screen, you'll find some useful buttons. Among them, these are my favorites:

Force Stop: Touch this button to halt a program run amok. For example, I had to stop an older Android app that continually made noise and offered no option to exit.

Uninstall: Touch the Uninstall button to remove the app, which is another way to accomplish the same steps described in the preceding section.

Move to Media Area: Touch this button to transfer the app from the phone's internal storage to the MicroSD card. Doing so can help reduce storage overload on the phone.

Move to Phone: Touch this button to transfer an app from the MicroSD card to the phone's internal storage. (This button replaces the Move to Media Area button when an app is already dwelling on the MicroSD card.)

Share: Touch the Share button to send a text or e-mail message to a friend. In the message is a link the recipient can use to install the app on her phone.

There's brewing controversy in the Android community about whether to store apps on the phone's internal storage or the MicroSD card. I prefer the internal storage because the app stays with the phone and is always available.

Creating app groups

There are three ways to organize your apps on the Droid 3.

The first way is not to organize your apps at all. That duty is handled by the App menu screen, which lists all the apps in your phone.

The second way is to place frequently used apps on the Home screen. That technique is covered in Chapter 22, but it has its limitations.

The third way is to create App menu groups. Heed these steps:

1. **Touch the Launcher to display the App menu.**

2. **Touch the Groups button, and choose New Group.**

   The Groups button is in the upper left corner of the screen.

3. **Name the group.**

   For example, Games.

4. **Choose an appropriate icon from the icons menu (found to the left of the group name text field).**

5. **Touch the Save button.**

   The group is created, but it's empty. The next step is to add apps to the group.

6. **Touch the green Plus button.**

   The Select Apps menu appears. It lists all the apps installed on your phone.

7. **Scroll through the list of apps, placing a green check mark by the apps you want to add to your group.**

   The apps are not moved; only a copy of the app (a shortcut or alias) is placed into your new group.

8. **Touch the OK button when you're done adding apps.**

   The group is created and filled with apps.

You can redisplay all the phone's apps by choosing the All Apps command from the Group menu. Or you can choose any other group from the Groups menu, or create even more groups to further organize your apps.

You can edit or remove the group by long-pressing it on the Groups menu. You can even add the group to the Home screen as a shortcut, which is yet another way to organize your apps.

Part V
Nuts and Bolts

The 5th Wave   By Rich Tennant

PCS PHONES

"So, what kind of roaming capabilities does this thing have?"

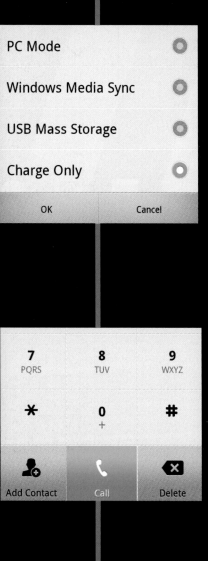

*B*eyond using your Droid 3 to make phone calls, and enjoying all the other wonderful things the phone does, there comes the "whatever's left" part of the book, which I call Nuts and Bolts. In this part of the book, you'll find information that doesn't really have to do with what the phone does but, rather, with what you can do with the phone. The chapters here contain tidbits on connecting your phone, customizing its appearance and functionality, taking the phone abroad, and maintaining the device, along with some helpful troubleshooting info.

No Wires Ever!

In This Chapter

▶ Understanding wireless networking

▶ Using Wi-Fi on the Droid 3

▶ Connecting to a Wi-Fi network

▶ Setting up a 3G mobile hotspot

▶ Sharing the Internet connection

▶ Configuring a Bluetooth

▶ Using a Bluetooth headset

▶ Printing wirelessly

Technology was once easy to spot: Simply look for the wires. The more wires something had, the more technically advanced it was. When I was growing up, the inside of my family's TV had hundreds of miles of wires inside. It was truly high-tech. Here in the 21st century, however, it's the lack of wires that demonstrates a gizmo's sophistication.

The Droid 3 can live a nearly wireless existence. After charging the device, you're free to wander the earth, all while communicating with other gizmos without the horrid fashion faux pas of an ugly wire. The phone can use the digital cellular network, Wi-Fi, or Bluetooth to make its wireless connections. This chapter shows you the ropes, er, well, the lack of ropes.

nnected to Imperial Wambooli

etwork notification

Open network
Notify me when an open network is availa

Secure network
lotify me when a secure network is availa

etworks

Wambooli

Wireless Network Access

Though you can't see it, wireless communications is going on all around. No need to duck — the wireless signals are intercepted only by items such as cell phones and laptop computers. The Droid 3 uses these signals to let you talk on the phone and communicate over the Internet and other networks.

Understanding the digital network

You pay your cellular provider a handsome fee every month. The fee comes in two chunks. One chunk (the less expensive of the two) is the telephone service. The second chunk is the data service, which is how the Droid 3 gets on the Internet. This system is the *cellular data network.*

There are several types of cellular data networks with which the Droid 3 can communicate. Regardless, you see only two status icons, representing the various networks:

3G: The *third generation* of wide-area data networks is several times faster than the previous generation of data networks. A 3G network also provides for talking and sending data at the same time, though such a feature may not be enabled by the cellular carrier.

1X: The slower data connection comes in several technical flavors, but only one icon appears on the phone's status bar. The 1X network is actually the second generation of cellular data technology. It's a lot slower than 3G, but it's better than nothing.

Your phone always uses the best network available. So if the 3G network is within reach, it's the network the Droid 3 uses for Internet communications. Otherwise, a 1X network is chosen.

✔ Accessing the digital cellular network isn't free. Your Droid 3 most likely has some form of subscription plan for a certain quantity of data. When you exceed this quantity, the costs can become prohibitive.

✔ See Chapter 21 for information on how to avoid cellular data overcharges when taking your Droid 3 out and about.

Understanding Wi-Fi

Wi-Fi is the same wireless networking standard used by computers for communicating with each other and the Internet. To make Wi-Fi work on your Droid 3 requires two steps. First, you must activate Wi-Fi, by turning on the phone's wireless radio. The second step is connecting to a specific wireless network.

Activating Wi-Fi

Follow these steps to activate Wi-Fi on your Droid 3:

1. **At the Home screen, press the Menu soft button.**
2. **Choose Settings and then choose Wireless & Networks.**
3. **Choose Wi-Fi to place a green check mark by that option.**

   A green check mark indicates that the phone's Wi-Fi radio is now activated.

The next step is to connect the Droid 3 to a Wi-Fi network, which is covered in the next section.

A quicker way to activate the Droid 3's Wi-Fi radio is to use the Power Control widget, shown in Figure 19-1. The widget isn't preinstalled on the phone; you need to add it to one of the Home screen panels. I highly recommend that you do so; see Chapter 22 for directions on adding widgets to the Home screen.

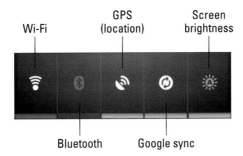

Figure 19-1: The Power Control widget.

Touch the Power Control widget's Wi-Fi button, and the Droid 3 turns on its Wi-Fi abilities.

To turn off Wi-Fi, repeat the steps in this section. Doing so turns off the phone's Wi-Fi access, disconnecting you from any networks.

✔ Using Wi-Fi to connect to the Internet doesn't incur data usage charges.

✔ The Wi-Fi radio places an extra drain on the battery, but it's truly negligible. If you want to save a modicum of juice, especially if you're out and about and don't plan to be near a Wi-Fi access point for any length of time, turn off the Wi-Fi radio.

Accessing a Wi-Fi network

After activating the Droid 3's Wi-Fi radio, you can connect to an available wireless network. Heed these steps:

1. **Press the Menu soft button while viewing the Home screen.**

2. **Choose Settings and then Wireless & Networks.**

3. **Choose Wi-Fi Settings.**

   You see a list of Wi-Fi networks displayed, as shown in Figure 19-2. If no wireless network is displayed, you're sort of out of luck regarding wireless access from your current location.

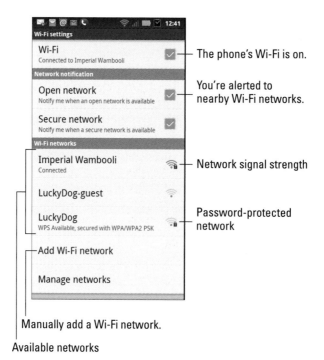

Manually add a Wi-Fi network.
Available networks

Figure 19-2: Hunting down a wireless network.

4. **Choose a wireless network from the list.**

   In Figure 19-2, I chose the Imperial Wambooli network, which is my office network.

5. **If prompted, type the network password.**

   Putting a green check mark in the box by Show Password makes it easier to type a long, complex network password.

6. **Touch the Connect button.**

You should be immediately connected to the network. If not, try the password again.

When the Droid 3 is connected, you see the Wi-Fi status icon appear atop the touchscreen. This icon means that the phone's Wi-Fi is on, connected, and communicating with a Wi-Fi network.

Some wireless networks don't broadcast their names, which adds security but also makes accessing them more difficult. In these cases, choose the Add Wi-Fi Network command (refer to Figure 19-2) to manually add the network. You need to input the network name, or *SSID,* and the type of security. You also need the password, if one is used. You can obtain this information from the little girl with the pink hair and pierced lip who sold you coffee or from whoever is in charge of the wireless network at your location.

✔ Not every wireless network has a password.

✔ Some public networks are open to anyone, but you have to use the Browser app to get on the web and find a login page that lets you access the network: Simply browse to any page on the Internet, and the login page shows up.

✔ The phone automatically remembers any Wi-Fi network it's connected to as well as its network password.

✔ To disconnect from a Wi-Fi network, simply turn off Wi-Fi on the phone. See the preceding section.

✔ A Wi-Fi network is faster than the 3G cellular data network, so it makes sense to connect with Wi-Fi whenever you can.

✔ Unlike a cellular data network, a Wi-Fi network's broadcast signal goes only so far. My advice is to use Wi-Fi when you plan to remain in one location for a while. If you wander too far away, your phone loses the signal and is disconnected.

Share the Connection

You and your Droid 3 can get on the Internet anywhere you receive a digital cellular signal. But pity the poor laptop that sits there, unconnected, seething with jealousy.

Well, laptop, be jealous no more! You can easily share your Droid 3's digital cellular signal in one of two ways. The first is to create a mobile hotspot, which allows any Wi-Fi–enabled gizmo to access the Internet through your phone. The second is a direct connection between your phone and another device, which is a concept called *tethering.*

Creating a mobile hotspot

You can direct the Droid 3 to share its cellular data network connection with as many as eight other devices. These devices connect wirelessly with your phone, accessing a shared 3G network. The process is referred to as *creating a mobile wireless hotspot,* though no fire is involved.

To set up a 3G mobile hotspot with your Droid 3, heed these steps:

1. **Turn off the Wi-Fi radio.**

   There's no point in creating a Wi-Fi hotspot is one is already available.

2. **From the App menu, open the Mobile Hotspot icon.**

   You may see text describing the process. If so, dismiss the text.

3. **Touch the box to place a green check mark by Mobile Wi-Fi Hotspot.**

   A warning message appears, recommending that you plug your Droid 3 into a power source because the mobile hotspot feature sucks down a lot of battery juice.

4. **Touch the OK button to dismiss the warning.**

   If you've not yet set up a mobile hotspot, you need to supply some information, such as the name of your hotspot and the password. You can change the name and password provided or just keep them as is.

   Make a note of the password. You need it to log in to the mobile hotspot.

5. **Touch the OK button or the Save button to save your settings and start the hotspot.**

   You're done.

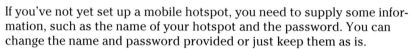

When the 3G hotspot is active, you see either the Tethering or Hotspot Active notification icon appear, as shown in the margin. You can then access the hotspot by using any computer or mobile device that has Wi-Fi capabilities.

To turn off the 3G hotspot, open the Mobile Hotspot app and remove the green check mark.

   ✔ The range for the mobile hotspot is about 30 feet, and it gets shorter when items such as walls and elephants are standing in the way.

   ✔ Data usage fees apply when you use the mobile hotspot. Those charges can add up quickly.

   ✔ Don't forget to turn off the mobile hotspot when you're done using it.

Tethering the Internet connection

A more intimate way to share the Droid 3's digital cellular connection is to connect the phone directly to a computer and activate the tethering feature.

Yes, I am fully aware that tethering goes against the wireless theme of this chapter. Still, it remains a solid way to provide Internet access to another gizmo, such as a laptop or desktop computer. Follow these steps to set up Internet tethering on your Droid 3:

1. **Connect the phone to another device by using the USB cable.**
2. **On the Droid 3, at the Home screen, press the Menu soft button.**
3. **Choose Settings and then choose Wireless & Networks.**
4. **Choose Tethering & Mobile Hotspot.**
5. **Place a green check mark by the item USB Tethering.**

    Internet tethering is activated.

The other device should instantly recognize the Droid 3's network access. Further configuration may be required, which depends on the device using the tethered connection. For example, you may be prompted on the PC to locate and install software for the Droid 3. Do so: Accept the installation of new software when prompted by Windows.

 When tethering is active on the Droid 3, the Tethering notification icon appears. The icon looks nearly the same as the standard USB Connection icon, but it's green.

- ✔ There's no need to disable the Wi-Fi radio to activate USB tethering on the Droid 3.

- ✔ Sharing the digital network connection incurs data usage charges against your cellular data plan. Be careful with your data usage when you're sharing a connection.

Bluetooth Gizmos

One type of computer network you can confuse yourself with is Bluetooth. It has nothing to do with the color blue or any dental problems. *Bluetooth* is simply a wireless protocol for communication between two or more Bluetooth-equipped devices.

For your Droid 3, the primary Bluetooth peripheral you'll consider using is one of those ear-clingy earphones. There's far more to Bluetooth, however, than walking around looking like you have a stapler stuck to your ear.

Activating Bluetooth

You must turn on the phone's Bluetooth networking before you can use one of those Borg-earpiece implants and join the ranks of walking nerds. Here's how to turn on Bluetooth for the Droid 3:

1. **At the Home screen, press the Menu soft button.**

2. **Choose Settings and then choose Wireless & Networks.**

3. **Choose Bluetooth.**

   Or, if a little green check mark already appears by the Bluetooth option, Bluetooth is already on.

You can also turn on Bluetooth by using the Power Control widget (refer to Figure 19-1). Just touch the Bluetooth button to turn it on.

To turn off Bluetooth, repeat the steps in this section.

✔ When Bluetooth is on, the Bluetooth status icon appears, as shown in the margin.

✔ Activating Bluetooth on the Droid 3 can quickly drain its battery. Be mindful to use Bluetooth only when necessary, and remember to turn it off when you're done.

Using a Bluetooth headset

To make the Bluetooth connection between the Droid 3 and a set of those I'm-so-cool earphones, you *pair* the devices. That way, the Droid 3 picks up only your earphone and not anyone else's.

To pair the phone with a headset, follow these steps:

1. **Ensure that Bluetooth is on.**

2. **Turn on the Bluetooth headset.**

3. **At the Home screen, press the Menu soft button and choose Settings.**

4. **Choose Wireless & Networks and then Bluetooth Settings.**

   The Bluetooth Settings screen appears.

5. **Choose Scan for Devices.**

6. **If necessary, press the main button on the Bluetooth gizmo.**

   The main button is the one you use to answer the phone. You may have to press and hold the button.

   Eventually, the device should appear on the screen, or you see its code number.

   Bluetooth headsets feature the Headset icon by their name, as shown in the margin.

7. **Choose the device.**

8. **If necessary, input the device's passcode.**

   It's usually a four-digit number, and quite often it's simply 1234.

When the device is connected, you can stick it in your ear and press its main Answer button when the phone rings.

After you've answered the call (by pressing the main Answer button on the earphone), you can chat away.

If you tire of using the Bluetooth headset, you can touch the Bluetooth button on the touchscreen to use the Droid 3 speaker and microphone. (Refer to Figure 5-2, in Chapter 5, for the location of the Bluetooth button.)

✓ You can turn the Bluetooth earphone on or off after it's been paired. As long as Bluetooth is on, the Droid 3 instantly recognizes the earphone when you turn it on.

✓ The Bluetooth status icon changes when a device is paired. The new icon is shown in the margin.

✓ You can unpair a device, after you locate it on the Bluetooth Settings screen. Long-press the device, and choose either the Disconnect or the Disconnect & Unpair command.

✓ Don't forget to turn off the earpiece when you're done with it. The earpiece has a battery, and it continues to drain when you forget to turn the thing off.

Fun with Wireless Printing

The concept of printing from a cell phone is rather new and certainly unique. No longer are documents and pictures permanently entombed in your Droid 3. Follow the advice in this section, and you'll be printing wirelessly in no time.

Printing to a Bluetooth printer

Perhaps the most insane way to print is to connect the Droid 3 to a Bluetooth printer. I refer to this method as insane because it takes quite a few steps — plus, Bluetooth printers are kind of rare. Still, if you have a Bluetooth printer and are willing to gamble with your sanity and follow these steps, you'll be successful.

Before you can print, ensure that your Droid 3 is paired with the Bluetooth printer. Refer to the section "Using a Bluetooth headset," earlier in this chapter. Pairing a printer works the same as pairing a headset: You need to make the printer discoverable and possibly input the printer's passcode on your phone to complete the connection.

You may also need to make the Droid 3 discoverable to get it connected to the printer. On the Bluetooth Settings screen, choose the item Discoverable. Then direct the printer to search for Bluetooth devices. Choose the Droid 3 on the printer's control panel to pair it with the phone.

When the printer and the Bluetooth printer are properly paired, you see the printer listed under Bluetooth Devices on the Bluetooth Settings screen. Even if it says "Paired but not connected," you're ready to go.

Assuming that the Bluetooth printer is on and ready to print, obey these steps to print something on your Droid 3 phone by using the Share command:

1. **View the document, web page, or image you want to print.**

2. **Choose the Share command.**

   If a Share button isn't visible in the app, press the Menu soft button to look for the Share command.

3. **Choose Bluetooth from either the Share or Share Via menu.**

4. **Choose your Bluetooth printer from the list of items on the Bluetooth Device Picker screen.**

5. **If prompted on the printer, confirm that the phone is printing a document.**

   The document prints.

Not everything on your phone can be printed on a Bluetooth printer. When you can't find the Share command or the Bluetooth item isn't available on the Share menu, you cannot print using Bluetooth.

You might be able to print using MOTOPRINT or the Print to Retail option, as covered later in this chapter.

Bluetooth printers sport the Bluetooth logo somewhere.

Using MOTOPRINT

The Droid 3 comes with the wireless network printing app MOTOPRINT. You can use this app to print from your phone to any wireless printer on a computer Wi-Fi network. Follow these steps:

1. **Ensure that your Droid 3 is connected to a wireless (Wi-Fi) network.**

   The network should have a network printer available for sharing.

2. **Start the MOTOPRINT app.**

3. **Choose something to print from the MOTOPRINT menu.**

   For example, to print a saved Gmail message, choose the Saved Emails option.

4. **Browse for the item to print.**

   When no items to print are available, you're rudely informed. Try another category or use another printing method.

5. **If prompted by the Complete Action Using menu, choose the command Print with MOTOPRINT.**

6. **Choose your printer from the Favorites list, or touch the Search Printers button to locate a wireless printer.**

   When you use the Search Printers command, choose the printer to use from the Available Printers screen.

7. **Choose optional printer settings on the Print screen.**

   You can set the number of copies and choose the paper size and orientation, for example.

8. **Touch the Print button.**

   The item is queued up and printed.

The MOTOPRINT command is available from other apps, such as Gmail and the Gallery. If the command doesn't appear on the screen, press the Menu soft button and look for the Print or MOTOPRINT command.

 Printing options are also available on the various Share menus on the Droid 3, though the option may not exist for all document types or in all apps.

To make a Wi-Fi printer a favorite, long-press it from the Available Printers list (refer to Step 5). Choose the Add to Favorites command.

Sharing with the Print to Retail option

Unlike other options in this section, Print to Retail doesn't send a document or an image to a printer near you. Well, *near you* as in the same room or building. No, what the Print to Retail option does is send the document or image to a local photo developer, such as Costco.

After you choose the Print to Retail option from the Share command menu, the Droid 3 uses its GPS feature to locate nearby retail photo developers. You can choose one of them and then fill in the blanks to begin the printing process. Your pictures are eventually sent electronically to the developer and printed. They're available for pickup later.

Connect, Store, Share

In This Chapter

▶ Getting the phone and a computer to talk

▶ Mounting the phone as computer storage

▶ Synchronizing media

▶ Copying files between the phone and computer

▶ Understanding phone storage

▶ Connecting the Droid 3 to an HDMI monitor

▶ Sharing media with DNLA

*N*o gizmo is an island. Despite its completely mobile nature, there are times when the Droid 3 yearns for some wired companionship. That direct connection helps the phone quickly communicate with a computer. The purpose: to share, swap, and synchronize. Though that physical connection is a positive thing, the process is laden with technical traps and beset with confusion. Therefore, I present this chapter on the necessary and useful topic of connecting and sharing between your phone and your computer.

The USB Connection

The most direct way to mate a Droid 3 with a computer is to use a USB cable. Coincidentally, a USB cable comes with the phone. It's a match made in heaven, but like many matches, it often works less than smoothly. Rather than hire a counselor to get the phone and computer on speaking terms, I offer you some good USB connection advice in this section.

Connecting the phone to a computer

Communication between your computer and the Droid 3 works faster when both devices are physically connected. This connection happens by using the USB cable: The cable's A end plugs into the computer. The other end, known as the *micro-USB connector,* plugs into the Droid 3's left flank.

The connectors cannot be plugged in either backward or upside down. That's good.

 When the Droid 3 is connected via USB cable to a computer, you see the USB Connection notification icon appear. Refer to the next section to see what you can do with this notification to configure the USB connection.

- ✔ If you don't have a USB cable for your phone, you can buy one at any computer- or office-supply store. Get a USB-A-male-to-micro-USB cable.

 ✔ A flurry of activity takes place when you first connect the Droid 3 to a Windows PC. Notifications pop up about new software that's installed, or you may see the AutoPlay dialog box, prompting you to install software. Do so.

Configuring the USB connection

Upon successful connection of your Droid 3 to a computer, you have the option of configuring the USB connection. You have several choices, as shown in Figure 20-1.

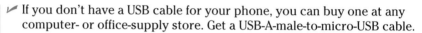

Figure 20-1: The USB Connection menu.

To see the USB Connection menu, pull down the notifications and choose USB Connection. Select an item from the menu, and touch the OK button. Here's what each of the items means:

PC Mode: Don't use this option.

Windows Media Sync: This option is used on a Windows PC to treat the phone as a media device, similar to a camera or a MP3 music player. It's ideal for synchronizing files.

USB Mass Storage: When this option is chosen, the computer treats the phone like a removable storage device, such as a USB thumb drive or a media card.

Charge Only: Use this option when you only want to charge the phone and not have it communicate with the computer.

When in doubt, choose the Charge Only option. I write elsewhere in this chapter about using the other options.

✔ When you're in doubt about which USB connection mode to choose, I recommend selecting the USB Mass Storage option.

✔ On a Macintosh, use either the Charge Only or USB Mass Storage option for connecting the phone. The Mac may not recognize the Droid 3 PC Mode or Windows Media Sync settings.

✔ After choosing the Windows Media Sync or USB Mass Storage options, you see one or two AutoPlay dialog boxes on your Windows PC. You can choose how to deal with the phone by using this dialog box to choose an item such as Open Folder to View Files or Windows Media Player. Or, just close the dialog box.

✔ The reason you may see two AutoPlay dialog boxes is that the Droid 3 features two storage locations: internal storage and the MicroSD card. One AutoPlay dialog box appears for each storage location. See the later section "Phone Storage Fun" for additional information on Droid 3 storage.

✔ When you're done accessing information on the Droid 3, you should properly unmount the phone from your computer system. See the next section.

✔ You cannot access the phone's storage while the Droid 3 is mounted into a computer storage system. Items such as your music and photos are unavailable until you disconnect the phone from the computer or choose the Charge Only setting for the USB connection.

✔ No matter which USB connection option you've chosen, the phone's battery charges when it's connected to a computer's USB port — as long as the computer is turned on, of course.

Disconnecting the phone from the computer

When you're using any USB connection option other than Charge Only, you must properly disconnect the phone from the computer. Never just yank out the USB cable. Never! Never! Never! Doing so can damage the phone's storage, which is a Bad Thing. Instead, follow these steps to do things properly:

1. **Close whichever programs or windows are accessing the Droid 3 from the computer.**

2. **Properly unmount the phone from the computer's storage system.**

   On a PC, locate the phone's icon in the Computer or My Computer window. Right-click the icon, and choose either the Eject or Safely Remove command.

   On a Macintosh, drag the phone's storage icon to the Trash.

3. **On the Droid 3, pull down the notifications.**

4. **Choose USB Connection.**

5. **Choose Charge Only.**

6. **Touch the OK button to confirm.**

   The phone's storage is unmounted and can no longer be accessed from your computer.

7. **If you like, unplug the USB cable.**

When you choose to keep the phone connected to the computer, the phone continues to charge. (Only when the computer is off does the phone not charge.) Otherwise, the computer and phone have ended their little *tête-à-tête,* and you and the phone are free again to wander the earth.

That Syncing Feeling

The synchronizing process involves hooking your Droid 3 to a computer and then swapping information back and forth. This process can be done automatically by using special software, or it can be done manually. The manual method isn't pleasant, though oftentimes it's necessary.

 ✔ See Chapter 15 for information on swapping pictures between your Droid 3 and your computer or the Internet.

 ✔ The topic of synchronizing music between your phone and computer is covered in Chapter 16.

Synchronizing with doubleTwist

One of the most popular ways to move information between your Android phone and a computer is to use the third-party utility doubleTwist. This amazing program is free, and it's available at www.doubletwist.com.

doubleTwist isn't an Android app. You use it on your computer, either a PC or a Macintosh. The app lets you easily synchronize pictures, music, videos, and web page subscriptions between your computer and its media libraries and any portable device, such as the Droid 3. Additionally, doubleTwist gives you the ability to search the Android Market and obtain new apps for your phone.

To use doubleTwist, connect your phone to your computer as described earlier in this chapter. Ensure that USB sharing is on; the MicroSD card is added to your computer's storage system as a USB mass storage device. Start up the doubleTwist program if it doesn't start by itself. The simple doubleTwist interface is illustrated in Figure 20-2.

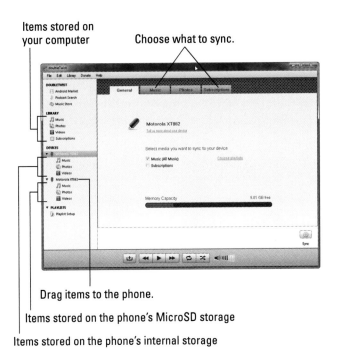

Items stored on your computer

Choose what to sync.

Drag items to the phone.

Items stored on the phone's MicroSD storage

Items stored on the phone's internal storage

Figure 20-2: The doubleTwist synchronization utility.

The way I use doubleTwist is to drag and drop media either from my computer to the Droid 3 or the other way around. Use the program's interface to browse for media, as shown in Figure 20-2.

- ✔ You cannot copy media purchased at the iTunes store from the Mac to the Droid 3. Apparently, you need to upgrade to iTunes Plus before the operation is allowed.

- ✔ doubleTwist doesn't synchronize contact information. The Droid 3 automatically synchronizes your phone's Contacts list with Google. For synchronizing vCards, see the next section.

- ✔ *Subscriptions* are podcasts or RSS feeds or other types of updated Internet content that can be delivered automatically to your computer.

Doing a manual sync

When you can't get software on your computer to synchronize automatically, you have to resort to doing the old manual connection. Yes, it can be complex. And bothersome. And tedious. But it's often the only way to get some information out of the Droid 3 and on to a computer, or vice versa.

Follow these steps to copy files between your computer and the Droid 3:

1. Connect the Droid 3 to the computer by using the USB cable.

2. Choose the USB Mass Storage option for the USB connection.

Specific directions are offered earlier in this chapter.

Your Droid 3 storage system *mounts* itself onto your computer's storage system. Because the Droid 3 can have two storage locations — internal and MicroSD card — two *volumes* may mount: MOT, which is the internal storage, and Removable Disk or NO NAME, which is the MicroSD card.

3a. On a PC, in the AutoPlay dialog box, choose the option Open Folder to View Files.

The option might instead read Open Device to View Files.

You see a folder window appear, which looks like any common folder in Windows. The difference is that the files and folders in this window are on the Droid 3, not on your computer.

If the Droid 3 has a MicroSD card installed, you use the second AutoPlay dialog box to mount it as well.

3b. On a Macintosh, open the removable drive icon(s) to access the phone's storage.

The Mac uses generic, removable drive icons to represent the Droid 3 storage. If two icons appear, one is named MOT, which is the phone's internal storage, and the second is named NO NAME, for the phone's MicroSD card or removable storage.

4. Open a folder window on your computer.

It's either the folder from which you're copying files to the Droid 3 or the folder that will receive files from the Droid 3 — for example, the Documents folder.

If you're copying files from the phone to your computer, use the Pictures folder for pictures and videos and the Documents folder for everything else.

5. Drag the file icons from one folder window to the other to copy them between the phone and computer.

Use Figure 20-3 as your guide.

Specific folders on the phone

Droid 3 MicroSD is Drive J on this PC.

Drag files to here to copy to the "root."

Droid 3 internal storage is Drive I on this PC.

Files on your computer

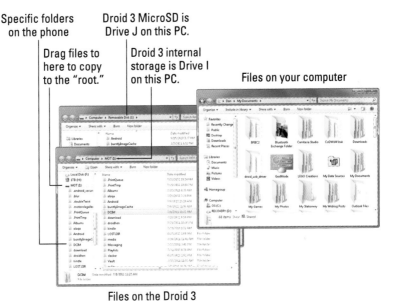

Files on the Droid 3

Figure 20-3: Copying files to the phone.

6. When you're done, properly unmount the Droid 3 storage from your computer's storage system and disconnect the USB cable.

You must eject the Droid 3 storage icon(s) from the Macintosh computer before you can turn off USB storage on the phone.

Any files you've copied to the phone are now stored on the Droid 3, either on the internal storage or on the MicroSD card. What you do with them next depends on the reasons you copied the files: to view pictures, use the Gallery, import vCards, use the Contacts app, listen to music, or use the Music Player, for example.

- It doesn't matter to which storage location you copy files — internal storage or MicroSD card (removable storage). I recommend using the MicroSD card because the phone seems to prioritize its internal storage and can fill up quickly.

- Files you've downloaded on the Droid 3 are stored in the `Download` folder.

- Pictures and videos on the Droid 3 are stored in the `dcim/Camera` folder.

- Music on the Droid 3 is stored in the `Music` folder, organized by artist.

- If you don't find the `Download`, `dcim/Camera`, or `Music` folder on the phone's internal storage, look for these folders on the MicroSD card (removable storage).

- Quite a few files can be found in the *root folder,* the main folder on the Droid 3's MicroSD card, which you see when the phone is mounted into your computer's storage system and you open its folder.

- A good understanding of basic file operations is necessary to get the most benefit from transferring files between your computer and the phone. These basic operations include copying, moving, renaming, and deleting. It also helps to be familiar with the concept of folders. A doctorate in entanglement theory is optional.

Phone Storage Fun

Information stored on your phone (pictures, videos, music) is kept in two places: on the removable MicroSD card and on the phone's internal storage. That's about all you need to know, though if you're willing to explore the concept further — including the scary proposition of file management on a cell phone — keep reading.

Generally speaking, you use specific apps to access the stuff stored on your phone — for example, the Gallery app to view pictures or the Music app to listen to tunes. Beyond that, you can employ some nerdy apps to see where stuff on the Droid 3 dwells.

The first app, which is the least scary, is the Downloads app. It displays the Downloads screen, which is used to review the files you've downloaded from the Internet (via the web or an e-mail attachment) to your phone.

The second app, which is scary because it's a file management app and these apps aren't that friendly, is the Files app. It works like this:

1. **Start the Files app.**

    It's found on the App menu.

2. **Choose which storage device to examine: internal phone storage or SD card.**

3. **Browse the files just as you would on a computer.**

   If you're familiar with computer file management, you'll be right at home amid the folder and file icons: Touch a folder icon to open it and see which subfolders and files dwell inside. Touch a file icon to preview it — if that's possible.

4. **To manage a file or folder, long-press it.**

   A menu appears, where you can perform typical file management operations: delete, rename, copy, or move, for example.

You can press the Home soft button when you're done being frightened by file management in the Files app.

 ✔ Every storage location on the phone is a *volume*. It's the same term used on a computer: If your PC has two hard drives, for example, each of them is a volume.

 ✔ You can also examine files and folders on your phone by mounting the phone's storage to a computer system. This method is easier to manage because you have access to a full-size screen and keyboard — plus, a computer mouse to move things around. See the preceding section.

 ✔ Another option available for browsing files is titled Shared Folders. Basically, this option lets you access file servers over the Internet or your local network to browse shared folders. If the preceding sentence makes any sense, give it a try! Otherwise, you can safely avoid choosing the Shared Folders option.

Viewing Your Media Elsewhere

The Droid 3 has the ability to project its media — pictures, video, and music — onto other devices. As you would expect, getting the phone to connect to other media devices isn't the simplest task in the universe.

Making the HDMI connection

It's possible to connect the Droid 3 to a large-screen monitor. This ability sates your big-screen desires for playing Angry Birds without totally losing the phone's ability to easily slip into your pocket. The trick is to connect the phone to an HDMI monitor or television set.

HDMI stands for High Definition Multimedia Interface.

To see your phone's display *really big,* follow these steps:

1. **Attach the HDMI cable to the HDMI monitor or TV set.**

   If it's an HDMI TV, make a note of the port number so that you can switch to that input channel for viewing the phone.

2. **Plug the HDMI cable into the Droid 3's HDMI jack.**

   The jack is right next to the micro-USB connector, and they look similar.

3. **Choose which option you want for HDMI viewing.**

   Three options are displayed on the Droid 3 screen:

   Gallery: The Gallery app opens. You can start a slideshow by choosing My Library and then pressing the Menu soft button and choosing the Slideshow command.

   Music: The Music app starts. Choose a playlist, an album, or an artist, and enjoy watching the Music app on the big screen. (The sound should play from the TV's speakers.)

   Mirror On Display: The Droid 3 screen output is duplicated on the HDMI TV or monitor.

4. **Disconnect the HDMI cable when you're done.**

   There's no need to give any commands or officially touch a button; just unplug the cable.

If you change your mind about your choice from Step 3, pull down the notifications and choose the item Connected to HDMI Cable. Choose another option from the menu.

Doing the DLNA thing

After wandering into the land of mysterious acronyms, you'll encounter one DNLA, which stands for Digital Living Networking Alliance. Your Droid 3 is a DNLA device, which means that it can easily share information — specifically, media files such as pictures, videos, and music — with other DNLA gizmos. The connection can be direct or over a Wi-Fi network.

The easiest way (if there is such a way) to do the DNLA thing is to configure your networked Windows computer for media sharing. Further, the Windows computer must have access to a wireless network before it can connect to the phone.

To play media from a computer on your phone, follow these steps:

1. **Ensure that the phone's Wi-Fi is turned on and that the phone is plugged in to a power source.**

2. **Start the DNLA app, found on the App menu.**

   The first time you run the app, you have to dismiss a few warnings or accept a few conditions.

3. **Touch the huge Play Media button.**

4. **Choose the Windows PC from the list that's displayed.**

   If you don't see the Windows PC listed, either you haven't configured it for media sharing or it's unavailable on the wireless network.

5. **Choose the type of media you want to play.**

   On my screen, I see folders for Music, Pictures, Playlists, and Videos.

6. **Browse to find the media; continue opening folders as necessary.**

7. **Touch a media item to watch or listen, or both.**

   At this point, the phone plays the media, which you can enjoy on the touchscreen.

Press the Back button to back out of a folder or category, or just keep pressing the Back button to return to the main DLNA screen.

- You can use the Share Media option to make the Droid 3's pictures, videos, and music accessible from a DNLA-enabled PC. You can use the PC to browse for the Droid 3, which it finds as a media server.

- The Copy Media options on the DNLA app's screen can be used to copy music, pictures, or video between your phone and a Windows PC. This operation works only when the computer has been properly configured to send and receive files.

- I cover turning on media sharing for a Windows computer in my book *PCs For Dummies* (John Wiley & Sons, Inc.). Buy several copies to ensure that you properly understand the information.

On the Road Again

In This Chapter

▶ Understanding roaming

▶ Disabling data-roaming features

▶ Entering Airplane mode

▶ Contacting friends abroad

▶ Using Skype Mobile

▶ Using the Droid 3 overseas

*B*ack when life was simple, all I had to do was leave the house with my wallet. Then I had to carry around some keys: car keys, house keys, keys to work. As I grew older, glasses were added to the list of items I had to carry with me. Now I have my Droid 3, another must-have accessory that I must tote everywhere I go. I'm just glad that clothes come with pockets.

You can not only carry the Droid 3 with you but also take it wherever you go — across town, across the state, or across the country. You can even take the Droid 3 overseas. Talk about exotic: It's *all* possible. My gentle words of advice in this chapter help make your, and your phone's, travels fruitful and fortuitous.

Where the Phone Roams

The word *roam* takes on an entirely new meaning when applied to a cell phone. It means that your phone receives a cell signal whenever you're outside your cell phone carrier's operating area. In that case, your phone is *roaming*.

Roaming sounds handy, but there's a catch: It almost always involves a surcharge for using another cellular service — an *unpleasant* surcharge.

The Droid 3 alerts you whenever you're roaming. You see the Roaming icon appear at the top of the screen, in the status area. The icon tells you that you're outside the regular signal area, possibly using another cellular provider's network.

There's little you can do to avoid incurring roaming surcharges when making or receiving phone calls. Well, yes: You can wait until you're back in an area serviced by your primary cellular provider. You can, however, altogether avoid using the other network's data services while roaming. Follow these steps:

1. **At the Home screen, press the Menu soft button.**

2. **Choose Settings, and then choose Battery & Data Manager.**

3. **Choose Data Delivery.**

4. **Ensure that the Data Roaming option isn't selected.**

   Remove the green check mark by Data Roaming.

The phone can still access the Internet over the Wi-Fi connection when you're roaming. Setting up a Wi-Fi connection doesn't make you incur extra charges, unless you have to pay to get on the wireless network. See Chapter 19 for more information about Wi-Fi.

Another network service you might want to disable while roaming has to do with multimedia, or *MMS,* text messages. To avoid surcharges from another cellular network for downloading an MMS message, follow these steps:

1. **Open the Text Messaging app.**

2. **If the screen shows a specific conversation, press the Back soft button to return to the main messaging screen.**

   (It's the screen that lists all your conversations.)

3. **Touch the Menu soft button.**

4. **Choose Messaging Settings.**

5. **Remove the green check mark by Auto-Retrieve.**

   Or, if the item isn't selected, you're good to go — literally.

For more information about multimedia text messages, refer to Chapter 9.

When the phone is roaming, you may see the text *Emergency Calls Only* displayed on the locked screen.

Airplane Mode

If you've been flying recently, you're already familiar with the cell phone airplane rules: Placing a call on your cell phone while on an airborne plane is strictly forbidden. That's because if you did, the navigation system would completely screw up, the plane would invert, and everyone onboard would die in a spectacular crash on the ground, in a massive fireball suitable for the 5 o'clock Eyewitness News. It would be breathtaking.

Seriously, you're not supposed to use a cell phone when flying. Specifically, you're not allowed you make calls in the air. You can, however, use your Droid 3 to listen to music or play games or do anything else that doesn't require a cellular connection. The secret is to place the phone in *Airplane mode.*

The most convenient way to put the Droid 3 in Airplane mode is to press and hold the Power button. From the menu, choose Airplane Mode. You don't even need to unlock the phone to perform this operation.

The most inconvenient way to put the Droid 3 into Airplane mode is to follow these steps:

1. **At the Home screen, press the Menu soft button.**
2. **Choose Settings, and then choose Wireless & Networks.**
3. **Touch the square by Airplane Mode to set the green check mark.**

   When the green check mark is visible, Airplane mode is active.

When the phone is in Airplane mode, a special icon appears in the status area, as shown in the margin. You might also see the text *No Service* appear on the phone's locked screen.

To exit Airplane mode, repeat the steps in this section. On the Wireless & Network Settings screen, remove the green check mark by touching the square next to Airplane Mode.

- ✔ Officially, the Droid 3 should be powered *off* when the plane is taking off or landing. See Chapter 2 for information on turning off the phone.

- ✔ Rather than power off the phone, you can place the Droid 3 into Sleep mode for the duration of a flight. It's faster for the phone to wake up from Sleep mode than it is to turn it on. See Chapter 2.

- ✔ Bluetooth networking is disabled when you activate the Droid 3 Airplane mode. See Chapter 19 for more information on Bluetooth.

- ✔ You can compose e-mail while the phone is in Airplane mode. The messages aren't sent until you disable Airplane mode and connect again with a data network. Unless:

TIP

✔ Many airlines now feature wireless networking onboard. You can turn on wireless networking for the Droid 3 and use a wireless network in the air: Simply activate the Droid 3 Wi-Fi feature, per the directions in Chapter 19, after placing the phone in Airplane mode — well, after the flight attendant tells you that it's okay to do so.

Droid 3 air-travel tips

I don't consider myself a frequent flyer, but I travel several times a year. I do it often enough that I wish the airports had separate lines for security: one for seasoned travelers, one for families, and one, of course, for frickin' idiots. The last category would have to be disguised by placing a Bonus Coupons sign or a Free Snacks banner over the metal detector. That would weed 'em out.

Here are some of my cell phone and airline travel tips:

✔ **Charge your phone before you leave.** This tip probably goes without saying, but you'll be happier with a full cell phone charge to start your journey.

✔ **Take a cell phone charger with you.** Many airports feature USB chargers, so you might need just a USB-to-micro–USB cable. Still, why risk it? Bring the entire charger with you.

✔ **At the security checkpoint, place your phone in a bin.** Add to the bin all your other electronic devices, keys, brass knuckles, razor blades, and so on. I know from experience that keeping your cell phone in your pocket most definitely sets off airport metal detectors.

✔ **When the flight crew asks you to *turn off* your cell phone for takeoff and landing, obey the command.** That's *turn off*, as in power off the phone or shut it down. It doesn't mean that you place the phone in Airplane mode. Turn it off.

✔ **Use the phone's Calendar app to keep track of flights.** The combination of airline and flight number can serve as the event title. For the event time, I insert take-off and landing schedules. For the location, I add the origin and destination airport codes. Remember to input the proper time zones. Referencing the phone from your airplane seat or in a busy terminal is much handier than fussing with travel papers. See Chapter 17 for more information on the Calendar.

✔ **Remember that some airlines may eventually feature Android apps you can use while traveling.** Rather than hang on to a boarding pass printed by your computer, for example, you just present your phone to the scanner.

✔ **Some apps you can use to organize your travel details are similar to, but more sophisticated than, using the Calendar app.** Visit the Android Market, and search for *travel* or *airline* to find a host of apps.

International Calling

You can use your cell phone to dial up folks who live in other countries. You can also take your cell phone overseas and use it in another country. Doing either task isn't as difficult as properly posing for a passport photo, but it can become frustrating and expensive when you don't know your way around.

Dialing an international number

A phone is a bell that anyone in the world can ring. To prove it, all you need is the phone number of anyone in the world. Dial that number using your Droid 3, and as long as you both speak the same language, you're talking!

To make an international call with the Droid 3, you merely need to know the foreign phone number. The number includes the international country-code prefix, followed by the number.

Before dialing the international country-code prefix, you must dial a plus sign (+) on the Droid 3. The + symbol is the *country exit code,* which must be dialed in order to flee the national phone system and access the international phone system. For example, to dial Finland on your Droid 3, you dial +358 and then the number in Finland. The +358 is the exit code (+) plus the international code for Finland (358).

To produce the + code in an international phone number, press and hold the 0 key on the Droid 3 dialpad. Then input the country prefix and the phone number. Touch the Dial button (the green Phone icon) to complete the call.

- ✔ You also pay a surcharge for sending text messages abroad. Presently Verizon charges 25 cents per international message sent, and you're charged 20 cents for every international message sent to your phone.

- ✔ In most cases, dialing an international number involves a time zone difference. Before you dial, be aware of what time it is in the country or location you're calling.

- ✔ Dialing internationally also involves surcharges, unless your cell phone plan already provides for international dialing.

- ✔ Verizon has the international calling feature I-Dial. It's an international calling feature you can add to your cell phone plan when you frequently dial outside the United States. For more information, dial (800) 922-0204.

✔ The + character is used on the Droid 3 to represent the country exit code, which must be dialed before you can access an international number. In the United States, the exit code is 011. (In the United Kingdom, it's 00.) So, if you're using a landline to dial Russia from the United States, you dial 011 to escape from the United States and then 7, the country code for Russia. Then dial the rest of the number. You don't have to do this on the Droid 3 because + is always the country exit code and replaces the 011 for U.S. users.

✔ The + character isn't a number separator. When you see an international number listed as 011+20+xxxxxxx, do not insert the + character in the number. Instead, dial +20 and then the rest of the international phone number.

✔ International calls fail for a number of reasons. One of the most common is that the recipient's phone company or service blocks incoming international calls.

✔ Another reason that international calls fail is the zero reason: Oftentimes, you must leave out any zero in the phone number that follows the country code. So, if the country code is 254 for Kenya and the phone number starts with 012, you dial +254 for Kenya and then 12 and the rest of the number. Omit the leading zero.

✔ You can also send text messages to international cell phones. It works the same way as making a traditional phone call: Input the international number into the Messaging app. See Chapter 9 for more information on text messaging.

✔ Know which type of phone you're calling internationally — cell phone or landline. The reason is that an international call to a cell phone often involves a surcharge that doesn't apply to a landline.

Making international calls with Skype Mobile

Your Droid 3 comes with the Skype Mobile app, which can be used to make inexpensive international calls. It's an excellent option, especially when your cellular contract doesn't provide for international calling.

If you don't yet have a Skype account, use your computer to create one. You need the account in order to use Skype Mobile. Set up the account by first obtaining the Skype program for your computer: Visit www.skype.com to get started. Further, you must have Skype Credit to make the international call. That credit can be purchased on the Skype website.

The Skype Mobile app is found on the App menu. After starting the app, log in with your Skype name and password.

You can't make an international call unless you've created a contact with an international number. The contact must be a Skype contact, shown on the Contacts tab on the Skype Mobile screen, illustrated in Figure 21-1.

Skype notification

Skype contacts | Touch to make international calls.

Dialpad   Press and hold to insert
a + sign in the number.

Figure 21-1: Calling internationally with Skype Mobile.

To make an international call, touch the Call Phones tab at the top of the screen. Punch in the number, including the + symbol for international access, as described earlier in this chapter and shown in Figure 21-1. Touch the Call button to make the call.

After the call is connected by Skype Mobile, the Droid 3 touchscreen looks similar to the way it looks when you regularly place calls. You can use the phone's dialpad, if necessary, mute the call, or put it on speaker, for example.

When you're finished with the call, touch the End button.

REMEMBER

- You're always signed in to Skype Mobile unless you sign out. Pressing the Home button to switch away from the app doesn't log you out of Skype.

- To log out of Skype Mobile, press the Menu soft button and then choose Sign Out. If the Sign Out command isn't visible at first, touch the More command to find it.

- The first time you use the Skype Mobile app, you're required to read various information and agree to the licensing terms. La-di-da.

- At the time this book went to press, Skype Mobile required a digital cellular signal; it doesn't work over a Wi-Fi connection.

- Check with your cellular provider to see whether you're charged connection minutes for using Skype Mobile. Even though the international call is free, you might still be dinged for the minutes you use on Skype to make the call.

Taking your Droid 3 abroad

Good news: Your Droid 3 is truly an international phone. It's designed to use cellular technology that's widely available all over the world. Bad news: Using this technology requires a modicum of setup, and you may incur fees if you don't have an international calling plan.

Before you leave for overseas, you need to activate your Droid 3. Call Verizon customer service by dialing *611 or (800) 922-0204. The rep will tell you how best to configure your phone for use abroad and give you specific directions that may be necessary to connect the phone to the proper service.

On the Droid 3, you can set a mobile network to use by following these steps:

1. **At the Home screen, press the Menu soft button.**

2. **Choose Wireless & Networks, and then choose Mobile Networks.**

3. **Choose the Network Mode command.**

   It has three settings: Global, CDMA, and GSM/UMTS.

4. **Choose the network that's specific to the country in which you're travelling.**

   Or, choose the Global option so that the phone can decide.

Upon returning to the United States, choose Global (Step 3) so that you can return the Droid 3 to using the Verizon network.

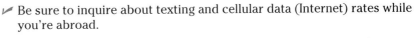

While you're abroad, you'll need to dial internationally. When calling the United States, you need to use a ten-digit number (phone number plus area code). You may also be required to type the country exit code when you dial; the friendly folks at Verizon can tell you the specifics, depending on which country you're visiting.

- Be sure to inquire about texting and cellular data (Internet) rates while you're abroad.

- Using the Droid 3 over a Wi-Fi network abroad incurs no extra fees (unless data roaming is on, as discussed earlier in this chapter). In fact, you can use the Skype Mobile app on your phone over a Wi-Fi network to call the United States or any International number at inexpensive rates.

- An alternative to taking the Droid 3 abroad is to rent or even buy a cell phone in the country where you plan to stay. I'm serious: Often, international roaming charges are so high that it's just cheaper to buy a throwaway cell phone wherever you go, especially if you plan to stay there for a while.

- While you're abroad, the name of the foreign country's compatible cellular service should show up at the top of the phone, where *Verizon Wireless* normally appears on the Droid 3 main screen. (Refer to Figure 2-1, in Chapter 2.)

- You receive calls on your cell phone internationally as long as the Droid 3 can access the network. Your friends need only dial your cell phone number as they normally do; the phone system automatically forwards your calls to wherever you are in the world.

- The person calling you doesn't pay extra when you're off romping the globe with your Droid 3. Nope — *you* pay extra for the call.

- Your Droid 3 can use both GSM and CDMA networks abroad. GSM, which stands for Global System for Mobile Communications, is probably the best standard for using a cell phone around the world. CDMA stands for Code Division Multiple Access. By using both standards, the Droid 3 is capable of communications just about anywhere on the planet.

Personalize Your Droid 3

In This Chapter

▶ Changing the Home screen background
▶ Working with icons and widgets on the Home screen
▶ Sticking an app on the Dock
▶ Adding security
▶ Silencing the phone's noise
▶ Enabling automatic answer and redial
▶ Modifying phone settings
▶ Setting accessibility options

Most advanced electronic gizmos have customization commands, designed so that you can make the device your own. You can choose backgrounds, colors, fonts, and similar appearance settings on your computer, for example, though most people choose not to. In fact, you can argue that having these types of options is intimidating. After all, you can customize your car, but few people bother doing that, either.

It's entirely possible to customize your Droid 3. You can make it look and sound the way you like. Even if you prefer not to have a superhero background or organize apps and widgets on the Home screen, the phone has other options and settings you may find useful, such as phone security and a smattering of other odds and ends, all described in this chapter.

It's Your Home Screen

The Droid 3 sports a roomy Home screen. It's really *five* Home screen panels. Of course, the phone comes preconfigured with lots of icons and widgets festooning every panel. You can customize the panels by removing widgets and icons, especially those you seldom use, and replacing them with icons and widgets you frequently use. You can also add folders to organize things, and you can even put a new wallpaper on the Home screen. Truly, you can make the Home screen look just the way you want.

For the most part, the key to changing the Home screen is the *long-press:* Press and hold your finger on a blank part of the Home screen (not on an icon). You see a pop-up menu appear, as shown in Figure 22-1. From the menu, you can begin your Home screen customization adventure, as discussed in this section.

Figure 22-1: The Add to Home Screen menu.

Changing wallpaper

The Home screen has two types of backgrounds, or *wallpapers:* traditional and live. *Live* wallpapers are animated. A not-so-live wallpaper can be any image, such as a picture from the Gallery.

To set a new wallpaper for the Home screen, obey these steps:

1. **Long-press the Home screen.**

   The Add to Home Screen menu appears, as shown in Figure 22-1.

2. **Choose Wallpapers.**

   Another menu appears, with three options.

3. **From the Select Wallpaper From menu, select an option based on the type of wallpaper.**

   Your choices are

   Gallery: Choose a still image stored in the Gallery app.

   Live Wallpapers: Choose an animated or interactive wallpaper from a list.

   Wallpapers: Choose a wallpaper from a range of stunning images (no nudity).

4. **Choose the wallpaper you want from the list.**

   For the Gallery option, you see a preview of the wallpaper where you can select and crop part of the image.

   For certain live wallpapers, the Settings button may appear. The settings let you customize certain aspects of the interactive wallpaper.

5. **Touch either the Save or Set Wallpaper button (whichever one you see) to confirm your selection.**

   The new wallpaper takes over the Home screen.

Live wallpaper is interactive, usually featuring some form of animation. Otherwise, the wallpaper image scrolls slightly as you swipe from one Home screen panel to another.

- ✔ To restore the Droid 3's original wallpaper, choose the Wallpapers option and touch the Reset to Default button at the bottom of the screen.

- ✔ You cannot long-press on a Home screen that's already full of icons and widgets. The reason? There's nothing else you can add to that screen.

- ✔ The Zedge app has some interesting wallpaper features. Check it out at the Android Market; see Chapter 18.

- ✔ See Chapter 15 for more information about the Gallery, including information on how cropping an image works.

Adding apps to the Home screen

You need not live with the unbearable proposition that you're stuck with only the apps supplied on the Home screen. Nope — you're free to add your own apps. Just follow these steps:

1. **Visit the Home screen panel on which you want to stick the app icon shortcut.**

   The screen must have room for the icon shortcut.

2. **Touch the Launcher button to display the App menu.**

3. **Long-press the icon of the app you want to add to the Home screen.**

4. **Choose the command Add to Home.**

   A copy of the app's icon is placed on the Home screen.

The app hasn't moved: What you see is a copy or, officially, a *shortcut.* You can still find the app on the App menu, but now the app is available — more conveniently — on the Home screen.

See the later section "Rearranging and removing icons and widgets" for information on moving the app around on the Home screen or from one panel to another or for removing an app shortcut.

Adding an app to the Dock

The *Dock* is the group of four icons sitting at the bottom of every Home screen panel. It's composed of three app icons plus the Launcher. The first is the Dialer app, and I don't recommend replacing it. You can, however, replace the other two icons by following these steps:

1. **Long-press the Dock icon you want to replace.**

   Long-press for only a brief moment and then release your finger.

2. **Choose the new icon from the list.**

   The new app icon is stuck to the Dock, replacing the app icon you long-pressed in Step 1.

It's not possible to remove a Dock icon and replace it with nothing; the Dock must always have three app icons and the Launcher.

The Droid 3 ships with the following three apps on the Dock: Dialer, Text Messaging, and Camera. The fourth icon is the Launcher, which cannot be removed or replaced.

Slapping down widgets

The Home screen is the place where you can find *widgets,* or tiny, interactive information windows. A widget often provides a gateway into another app or displays information such as status updates, the currently playing song, or the weather. To add a widget to the Home screen, heed these steps:

1. **Switch to a Home screen panel that has room enough for the new widget.**

   Unlike app icons, some widgets can occupy more than a postage-stamp-size piece of real estate on the Home screen.

2. **Long-press the Home screen, and choose Widgets.**

3. **From the list, choose the widget you want to add.**

   For example, choose the Power Control widget to get quick access to several popular phone features, such as Wi-Fi or Bluetooth or other settings you often turn on or off.

   The widget is plopped on the Home screen.

The variety of available widgets depends on the applications you have installed. Some applications come with widgets; some don't.

- ✔ More widgets are available at the Android Market. See Chapter 18.

- ✔ To remove, move, or rearrange a widget, see the later section "Rearranging and removing icons and widgets."

Creating shortcuts

Besides widgets, everything on the Home screen is a shortcut. The app icons? Shortcuts. But the variety of shortcuts doesn't end with apps. You can add shortcuts to the Home screen that help you get at a phone feature or display an informational tidbit without digging deep in the phone. That's why they're called *shortcuts.*

For example, I have a shortcut on my Home screen that uses the Maps app Navigation feature to help me return to my house. I don't use the app when I'm running from an irate mob, either.

To add a shortcut, long-press the Home screen and choose the Shortcuts command from the Add to Home Screen menu (refer to Figure 22-1). What happens next depends on which shortcut you choose.

For example, when you choose Bookmark from the Select Shortcut menu, you add a web page bookmark to the Home screen. Touch the shortcut to open the Browser app and visit that web page.

Choose the Contact shortcut to display contact information for a specific person. The Droid 3 has shortcuts for Music and the Maps app (Direction & Navigation), plus shortcuts for various apps are installed on your phone and shortcuts to common phone settings such as battery use, Wi-Fi, and more.

Rearranging and removing icons and widgets

Icons and widgets aren't fastened to the Home screen. If they are, it's day-old chewing gum that binds them, considering how easily you can rearrange and remove unwanted items from any Home screen panel.

Press and hold an icon on the Home screen to move it. Eventually, the icon seems to lift and break free, as shown in Figure 22-2.

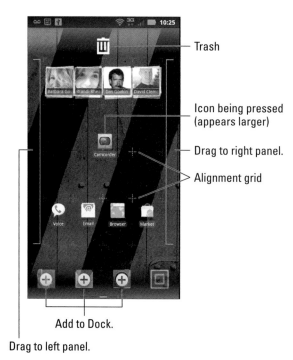

Trash

Icon being pressed (appears larger)

Drag to right panel.

Alignment grid

Add to Dock.

Drag to left panel.

Figure 22-2: Moving an icon.

You can drag a free icon to another position on the Home screen or to another Home screen panel, or you can drag it to the Trash icon that appears at the top of the Home screen, which deletes the shortcut (refer to Figure 22-2).

Widgets can also be moved or removed in the same manner as icons.

When you drag an icon to the bottom of the screen, where the Dock is shown in Figure 22-2, the icon replaces one of the three Dock items. The Dock items appear on all Home screen panels. (You cannot replace the Launcher icon on the Dock.)

- Dragging a Home screen icon or widget to the Trash removes the icon or widget from the Home screen. It doesn't uninstall the application or widget; the app can still be found on the App menu, and the widget can once again be added to the Home screen.

- You cannot drag an icon off the Dock. You can only replace a Dock icon with a new icon.

- When an icon hovers over the Trash, ready to be deleted, its color changes to red.

- See Chapter 18 for information on uninstalling applications.

Droid 3 Security

The Droid 3 comes with a *lock,* the simple touchscreen gizmo you slide to the right to unlock the phone and gain access to its information and features. For most folks, this lock is secure enough. For others, the lock is about as effective as lighting a candle to stop the wind.

You can add three additional types of security locks to your phone: pattern, PIN, or password. The details are provided in this section.

Finding the screen locks

The Droid 3 stores all its screen locks in the same location: on the Choose Screen Lock screen. Heed these steps to visit that screen:

1. **At the Home screen, press the Menu soft button.**

2. **Choose Settings.**

3. **Choose Location & Security.**

4. **If no additional lock is set, choose Set Up Screen Lock; otherwise, choose Change Screen Lock.**

If the screen lock is already set, you have to work the lock to proceed: Trace the pattern or type the PIN or password to continue. You then get access to the Choose Screen Lock screen, which contains four items: None, Pattern, PIN, and Password. Using those items is covered in the next few sections.

✔ The lock you apply affects the way you turn on and wake up your Droid 3. See Chapter 2 for details.

✔ The locks don't appear when you answer an incoming phone call. You are, however, prompted to unlock the phone if you want to use its features while you're on a call.

✔ See the sidebar "The lock doesn't show up!" for information on setting the Security Lock timer, which affects when the screen locks appear after you put the phone to sleep.

Removing the lock

To disable the pattern, PIN, or password screen lock on your Droid 3, choose the None option from the Screen Unlock Security screen. When None is chosen, the phone uses the standard slide lock, as described in Chapter 2.

Refer to the preceding section for information on finding the None option on your Droid 3.

Creating an unlock pattern

The unlock pattern is perhaps the most popular, and certainly the most unconventional, way to lock the Droid 3 screen. The pattern must be traced on the touchscreen to unlock the phone.

The lock doesn't show up!

The lock screen shows up whenever you turn on the phone or whenever you wake it up from Sleep mode. Whether the lock appears after the phone awakens depends on how long the phone has been sleeping. If you awaken the phone right away, for example, the lock may not even show up. The timing depends on the Security Lock Timer setting.

The Security Lock Timer setting specifies how long the phone waits after being put to sleep before the screen lock appears. Initially, the timer is set to 20 minutes. You can set it to a shorter interval, which is more secure: From the Home screen, press the Menu soft button and choose Settings. Choose Location & Security, and then choose Security Lock Timer. Choose a new time-out value from the list.

To set the unlock pattern, follow these steps:

1. **Summon the Screen Unlock Security screen.**

   Refer to the earlier section "Finding the screen locks."

2. **Choose Pattern.**

   If you haven't yet set a pattern, you may see a tutorial describing the process; touch the Next button to skip merrily through the dreary directions.

3. **Trace an unlock pattern.**

   Use Figure 22-3 as your guide. You can trace over the dots in any order, but you can trace over a dot only once. The pattern must cover at least four dots.

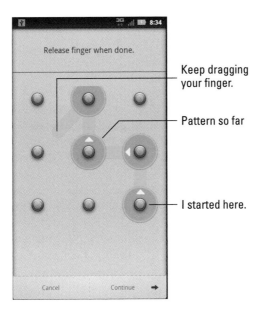

Figure 22-3: Setting the unlock pattern.

4. **Touch the Continue button.**

5. **Redraw the pattern again, just to confirm that you know it.**

6. **Touch the Confirm button.**

   The pattern lock is set.

Ensure that a check mark appears by the option Use Visible Pattern, found on the Location & Security Settings screen. That way, the pattern shows up when you need to unlock the phone. For even more security, you can disable this option, but you *must* remember how the pattern goes.

✔ To remove the pattern lock, set None as the lock type, as described in the preceding section.

✔ The pattern lock can start at any dot, not necessarily the lower right dot shown in Figure 22-3.

✔ The unlock pattern can be as simple or as complex as you like. I'm a big fan of simple.

✔ Wash your hands! Smudge marks on the display can betray your pattern.

Setting a PIN

A *PIN lock* is a code between 4 and 16 numbers long. It contains only numbers, 0 through 9. To set the PIN lock for your Droid 3, follow the directions in the earlier section "Finding the screen locks" to reach the Choose Screen Lock screen. Choose PIN from the list of locks.

Type your PIN twice to confirm to the doubting computer that you know it. The next time you need to unlock your phone, type the PIN on the keyboard and then touch the Enter button (shown in the margin) to proceed.

Refer to Figure 2-3 (in Chapter 2) for an image of what the PIN Unlock screen looks like.

Assigning your Droid 3 a password

Perhaps the most secure way to lock the Droid 3 screen is to apply a full-on password. Unlike a PIN (refer to the preceding section), a *password* contains a combination of numbers, symbols, and uppercase and lowercase letters.

Set the password by choosing Password from the Choose Screen Lock screen; refer to the earlier section "Finding the screen locks" for information on getting to that screen.

The password you create must be at least four characters long. Longer passwords are more secure but easier to mistype.

You type the password twice to set things up, which confirms to the Droid 3 that you do know the password and will, you hope, remember it in the future.

The phone prompts you to type the password whenever you unlock the screen, as described in Chapter 3. You also type the password whenever you change or remove the screen lock, as discussed in the section "Finding the screen locks," earlier in this chapter.

Various Phone Adjustments

The Droid 3 has many options and settings for you to adjust. You can fix things that annoy you or make things better to please your tastes. The whole idea is to make the phone more usable for you.

Stopping the noise!

The Droid 3 features a bag of tricks designed to silence the phone. These techniques can come in quite handy, especially when a cell phone's digital noise can be outright annoying.

Vibration mode: You can make the phone vibrate for all incoming calls, which works in addition to any ringtone you've set (and still works when you've silenced the phone). To activate Vibration all-the-time mode, follow these steps:

1. **At the Home screen, press the Menu soft button.**

2. **Choose Settings and then Sound.**

3. **Choose Vibrate.**

4. **Choose Always.**

Silent mode: Silent mode disables all sounds from the phone, except for music and YouTube and other types of media, as well as alarms that have been set by the Alarm & Timer and Calendar apps.

To enter Silent mode, follow Steps 1 and 2 in the previous set of steps and then place a check mark by the item Silent Mode.

Performing automatic phone tricks

Two phone settings on the Droid 3 might come in handy: Auto Answer and Auto Retry. Both options are found on the Call Settings screen: At the Home screen, press the Menu soft button, choose Settings, and then choose the Call Settings item.

By placing a check mark by Auto Retry, you direct the phone to automatically redial a number when the call doesn't go through. Obviously, this feature is ideal for radio show call-in contests.

The Auto Answer option directs the Droid 3 to automatically answer the phone whenever the headset is attached. It has three settings: 2, 5, and 10 seconds, which specify how long to wait before the call is answered. The fourth setting, Off, disables the Auto Answer feature.

Changing various settings

This section describes a smattering of settings you can adjust on the phone — all made from, logically, the Settings screen. To get there from the Home screen, press the Menu soft button and choose the Settings command.

You can also view the Settings screen by choosing the Settings app from the App menu.

Screen brightness: Choose Display and then choose Brightness. The Automatic Brightness setting uses the phone's magical light sensors to determine how bright it is where you are. If you disable this setting, you can move the slider on the screen to specify how bright the display appears.

Screen timeout: Choose Display and then choose Screen Timeout. Select a time-out value from the list. This duration specifies when the phone goes into Snooze mode.

Ringer volume: Choose Sound and then choose Volume. Use the sliders to specify how loud the phone rings for incoming calls (ringtones) and media and alarms. If you place a check mark by the Notifications item, the Ringtone setting also applies to notifications. Touch OK when you're done.

Call Connect: Choose Sound, and place a check mark by the option Call Connect. Whenever a new call comes in, you hear a sound, alerting you to the new call. This option is especially helpful when you use the Droid 3 to listen to music.

Network Lost Tone: Choose Sound and then place a check mark by the option Network Lost Tone. The Droid 3 plays a tone whenever a phone call is dropped because of a poor network connection.

Keep the phone awake when plugged in: Choose Applications and then choose Development. Place a check mark by the option Stay Awake.

Adjust the keyboards: Choose Language & Keyboard and then choose Multi-Touch Keyboard. A smattering of interesting options appears — options you can set when they please you or deactivate when they annoy you.

Settings for the sliding keyboard can be found on the Language & Keyboard screen: Choose the Built-in Keyboard menu item.

Disable automatic word correction and suggestions: To halt the keyboard's (often incorrect) spell checking and suggestions, choose Language & Keyboard and then Multi-Touch Keyboard. On the Multi-Touch Keyboard Settings screen, you find options for both the onscreen and sliding keyboards with regard to automatic word correction and suggestions: Remove the check marks by Show Suggestions in both the On-Screen Keyboard and Device Keyboard areas. Also, remove the check mark by the item Auto-Correct Errors in both areas, if that feature is vexing you.

Setting the Double Tap Home Launch soft button function

As master of your Droid 3, you can determine what happens when you press the Home soft button twice. It's the _Double Tap Home Launch_ function. As the Droid 3 comes out of the box (at least, as my Droid 3 did), pressing the Home soft button twice quickly does nothing. You can change this behavior so that pressing the Home button twice does a variety of interesting or useful things.

To modify the Double Tap Home Launch function, heed these steps:

1. **At the Home screen, press the Menu soft button.**

2. **Choose Settings and then Applications.**

3. **Choose Double Tap Home Launch.**

4. **Choose a new function or app from the menu.**

   For example, you can choose Dialer to summon the Phone app whenever you press the Home button twice. Choose None to disable the Double Tap Home Launch feature.

A handy option to choose for Double Tap Home Launch is the Camera. I find this setting extremely useful, even more so than having the Camera app's shortcut on the Home screen Dock.

Using accessibility settings

If you find the Droid 3 not meeting your needs or you notice that some features don't work well for you, consider taking advantage of some of the phone's accessibility features. Follow these steps:

1. **While at the Home screen, press the Menu soft button.**

2. **Choose Settings and then Accessibility.**

3. **Place a check mark by the Accessibility option.**

   Two options become available when accessibility is on:

   - *Zoom Mode:* A magnification window appears on the touchscreen, allowing you to better see teensy information.

   - *Voice Readouts:* Touching items on the screen directs the phone to read that text.

4. **Touch the OK button after reading the scary warning.**

   The Accessibility feature is active.

To disable any accessibility settings, repeat these steps and remove check marks in Step 3. Or, just deselect the Accessibility setting to disable them all. Touch OK to confirm.

When the Screen Reader is activated, you double-tap items on the touchscreen to activate them.

Maintenance and Troubleshooting

In This Chapter

▶ Checking the phone's battery usage

▶ Making the battery last

▶ Cleaning the phone

▶ Keeping the system up to date

▶ Dealing with problems

▶ Finding support

▶ Getting answers to common questions

*P*ray tell, what kind of maintenance can a cell phone need? It isn't like you need to winterize your Droid 3. It has no regular tune-up schedule. And thank goodness you never need to change its oil. For you, phone maintenance duties are rather light and with the pleasant side effect that they're relatively painless. Because of that, I've had to toss in the topic of troubleshooting just to make a full-length chapter.

.urs

End:

10:00pm

5:00am

Turn off data after:

15 minutes

Battery Care and Feeding

Perhaps the most important item you can monitor and maintain on your Droid 3 is its battery. The battery supplies the necessary electrical juice by which the phone operates. Without battery power, your phone is about as useful as a tin can and a string for communications. Keep an eye on the battery.

Peak hours

Turn off data after:

Always On

htness

Monitoring the battery

The Droid 3 displays the current battery status at the top of the screen, in the status area, next to the time. The icons used to display battery status are shown in Figure 23-1.

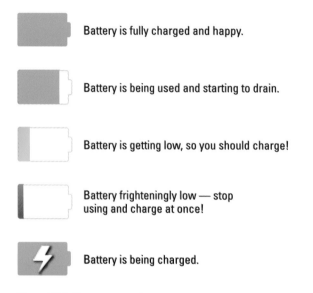

Battery is fully charged and happy.

Battery is being used and starting to drain.

Battery is getting low, so you should charge!

Battery frighteningly low — stop using and charge at once!

Battery is being charged.

Figure 23-1: Battery status icons.

You might also see the icon for a dead or missing battery, but for some reason I can't get my phone to turn on and display it.

You can check the specific battery level by following these steps:

1. **At the Home screen, press the Menu button.**
2. **Choose Settings.**
3. **Choose About Phone.**
4. **Choose Status.**

The top two items on the Status screen offer information about the battery:

Battery Status: This setting explains what's going on with the battery. It might say *Full* when the battery is full, *Discharging* when the battery is in use, or *Charging* when the battery is being charged. Other text may be displayed as well, depending on how desperate the phone is for power.

Battery Level: This setting reveals a percentage value describing how much of the battery is charged. A value of 100 percent indicates a fully charged battery. A value of 110 percent means that someone can't do math.

Later sections in this chapter describe activities that consume battery power and tell you how to deal with battery issues.

- Heed those low-battery warnings! The phone sounds a notification whenever the battery power gets low. (See the orange Battery icon shown earlier, in Figure 23-1.) The phone sounds another notification when the battery gets *very* low. (See the red Battery icon in Figure 23-1.)

- When the battery is too low, the phone shuts itself off.

- In addition to the status icons, the Droid 3 notification light turns a scary shade of red when battery juice is dreadfully low.

- The best way to deal with a low battery is to connect the phone to a power source: Either plug the phone into a wall socket or connect the phone to a computer by using a USB cable. The phone charges itself immediately — plus, you can use the phone while it's charging.

- The phone charges more efficiently when it's plugged into a wall socket rather than a computer.

- You don't have to fully charge the phone to use it. If you have only 20 minutes to charge and the power level returns to only 70 percent, that's great. Well, it's not great, but it's far better than a 20 percent battery level.

- Battery percentage values are best-guess estimates. Just because you talked for two hours and the battery shows 50 percent doesn't mean that you're guaranteed two more hours of talking. Odds are good that you have much less than two hours. In fact, as the percentage value gets low, the battery appears to drain faster.

Determining what is sucking up power

A nifty screen on the Droid 3 reviews which activities have been consuming power when the phone is operating from its battery. The informative screen is shown in Figure 23-2.

To get to this screen, follow these steps:

1. **At the Home screen, press the Menu soft button.**

2. **Choose Settings and then Battery & Data Manager.**

   You see a wonderfully big graphical battery meter. It's pretty, but it's not your final destination.

3. **Touch the big Battery icon.**

   You see a screen similar to the one shown in Figure 23-2.

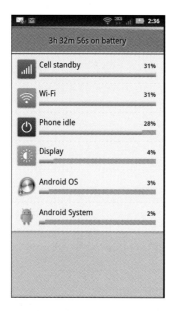

Figure 23-2: Things that drain the battery.

The number and variety of items listed on the Battery Use screen depend on what you've been doing with your phone between charges and how many different programs you're using.

Managing battery performance

The Droid 3 features Battery mode settings to help you manage the phone's power consumption. Similar to managing power on a computer, you can configure your phone to use one of four power modes:

Maximum Battery Saver: In this most restrictive mode, the phone dims the display and disables automatic synchronization after 15 minutes of inactivity.

Nighttime Saver: In this mode, the phone uses Performance mode (no battery savings) during daytime hours but switches to Maximum Battery Saver mode between 10 p.m. and 5 a.m.

Performance Mode: In this mode, nothing is held back and no time-outs are set. It is, essentially, *no* power management.

Custom Battery Saver: This mode allows you to configure timeout, brightness, and peak usage times yourself.

To set a battery profile on your Droid 3, follow these steps:

1. **At the Home screen, press the Menu soft button.**

2. **Choose Settings and then Battery & Data Manager.**

3. **Choose Battery Mode.**

4. **Choose a battery profile from the list.**

5. **Read the warning message, and touch the OK button.**

 Configure Custom Battery Saver mode by touching the icon to the right of that option. You can then use the screen that appears, shown in Figure 23-3, to configure its options, time-outs, and other settings.

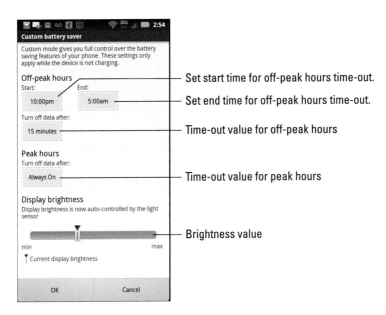

Figure 23-3: Battery settings for Custom Battery Saver mode.

Saving battery life

Here's a smattering of things you can do to help prolong battery life in your Droid 3:

Turn off vibration options: The phone's vibration is caused by a teensy motor. Though you don't see much battery savings by disabling the vibration options, it's better than no savings. To turn off vibration, follow these steps:

1. **At the Home screen, press the Menu soft button.**

2. **Choose Settings, and then choose Sound.**

3. **Choose Vibrate.**

4. **Choose Never.**

5. **Also on the Sound Settings screen: Remove the check mark by Haptic Feedback.**

   The Haptic Feedback option is what causes the phone to vibrate when you touch the soft buttons.

Additionally, consider lowering the volume of notifications by choosing the Volume option. This option also saves a modicum of battery life, though in my travels, I've missed important notifications by setting the volume too low.

Dim the screen: The display is capable of drawing down quite a lot of battery power. Though a dim screen can be more difficult to see, especially outdoors, it definitely saves on battery life.

You set the screen brightness from the Settings app: Choose Display and then choose Brightness.

Turn off Bluetooth: When you're not using Bluetooth, turn it off. Or, when you *really* need that cyborg Bluetooth ear thing, try to keep your phone plugged in. See Chapter 19 for information on turning off Bluetooth.

Turn off Wi-Fi: Wi-Fi networking on the Droid 3 keeps you on the Internet at top speeds but drains the battery. Because I tend to use Wi-Fi when I'm in one place, I keep my phone plugged in. Otherwise, the battery drains like my bank account at Christmas. Refer to Chapter 19 for information on turning off the phone's Wi-Fi.

Disable automatic syncing: The Droid 3 syncs quite often. In fact, it surprises me when I update something on the Internet and find the phone updated almost instantly. When you need to save battery power and frequent updates aren't urgent (such as when you're spending a day traveling), disable automatic syncing by following these steps:

1. **At the Home screen, press the Menu soft button.**

2. **Choose Settings, and then choose Accounts.**

3. **Choose your Google account.**

4. Remove the green check mark by each item.

When saving battery juice isn't important, remember to repeat these steps to reenable background and automatic synchronization.

Deactivate global roaming: As a global phone, your Droid 3 has been preconfigured to search for overseas cell phone signals even when you're not overseas. This feature can reduce battery life. To disable it, follow these steps:

1. At the Home screen, press the Menu soft button.

2. Choose Wireless & Networks, and then choose Mobile Networks.

3. Choose Network Mode.

4. Choose CDMA.

Turn on the Data Saver: A solid way to conserve battery power is to activate the Droid 3 Data Saver feature, which reduces the phone's cellular data usage. Obey these steps:

1. At the Home screen, press the Menu soft button.

2. Choose Battery & Data Manager, and then choose Data Saver.

3. Place a green check mark by the Data Saver option.

The Data Saver restricts the Internet access of the Browser, Gallery, Email, and Market apps to Wi-Fi networks only, which not only saves battery life but can also help you avoid overcharges for accessing the digital cellular network.

Battery replacement

Unlike on some cell phones, you can easily replace the battery in the Droid 3. Chapter 1 discusses how to install and remove the battery. It's cinchy! But the real questions come when you need to replace the battery and have to decide what to replace it with.

Under normal usage, the battery in the Droid 3 should last at least as long as the typical two-year cellular contract. The battery is probably good for about four years, if you treat it properly. Even so, at some point, the battery will fail: The battery charge decreases, and eventually the battery doesn't even hold a charge.

Ensure that any replacement battery you buy is compatible with the Droid 3. A BF5X battery from Motorola (the phone's manufacturer) works best. Otherwise, ensure that it's a 3.7V battery, designed for the Droid 3. Avoid buying batteries for your electronics at swap meets or from the back of pickup trucks in grocery store parking lots.

Regular Phone Maintenance

The Droid 3 gives you only two tasks that you can do for regular maintenance on the phone: Keep it clean, which is probably something you're doing already, and keep important information backed up.

Keeping it clean

You probably already keep your phone clean. I must use my sleeve to wipe the touchscreen at least a dozen times a day. Of course, better than your sleeve is something called a *microfiber cloth*. This item can be found at any computer- or office-supply store.

 ✔ Never use any liquid to clean the touchscreen — especially ammonia or alcohol. These substances damage the touchscreen.

 ✔ If the screen continually gets dirty, consider adding a *screen protector.* This specially designed cover prevents the screen from getting scratched or dirty but also lets you use your finger on the touchscreen. Be sure that the screen protector is designed for use with the Droid 3.

 ✔ You can also find customized Droid 3 cell phone cases, belt clips, and protectors, though I've found that these add-on items are purely for decorative or fashion purposes and don't even prevent serious damage if you drop the phone.

Backing it up

A *backup* is a safety copy of the information on your Droid 3. It includes any contact information, music, photos, videos, and apps you've recorded, downloaded, or installed, plus any settings you've made to customize your phone. Copying this information to another source is one way to keep the information safe, in case anything happens to the phone.

On your Google account, information is backed up automatically. This information includes your Contacts list, Gmail messages, and Calendar app appointments. Because the Droid 3 automatically syncs this information with the Internet, a backup is always present.

To confirm that your Google account information is being backed up, heed these steps:

1. **From the Home screen, touch the Launcher button.**

2. **Choose My Accounts.**

3. **Choose your Google account.**

4. **Ensure that a green check mark appears by every option.**

   When no check mark is there, touch the gray square to add one.

If you have more than one Google account synchronized with the Droid 3, repeat these steps for every account.

I'm required by my Verizon cellular contract to mention the Verizon app Backup Assistant. Let me say this: You don't have to use Backup Assistant. It doesn't do anything that's necessary, and it's a pain in the butt to set up. There. I've completed my contractual obligation.

Updating the system

Every so often, a new version of your phone's operating system becomes available. It's an *Android update* because *Android* is the name of the Droid 3 operating system, not because your phone thinks that it's some type of robot.

Whenever an automatic update occurs, you see an alert or a message appear on the phone, indicating that a system upgrade is available. You have three choices:

- ✔ Install Now
- ✔ Install Later
- ✔ More Info

Where to find phone information

Who knows what evil lurks inside the heart of your phone? Well, the phone itself knows. You can view information about the battery, phone number, mobile network, and uptime, plus other information. To see this collection of trivia, summon the Settings app and choose About Phone and then Status.

For specific information about your account, such as minutes used and data transmitted,

you have to visit the cellular service's website. In the United States, the Droid 3 is supported by the Verizon Wireless network at the time this book goes to press. The website is `www.verizonwireless.com`. You set up or access your account, which then leads you to information about your phone usage and billing and other trivia.

My advice is to choose Install Now and get it over with — unless you have something (a call, a message, or another urgent item) pending on the phone, in which case you can choose Install Later and be bothered by the message again.

You can manually check for updates: From the Settings screen, choose About Phone and then choose System Updates. When your system is up to date, the screen tells you so. Otherwise, you find directions for updating the system.

Help and Troubleshooting

Things aren't as bad as they were in the old days. Back then, you could try two sources for help: the atrocious manual that came with your electronic device or a phone call to the guy who wrote the atrocious manual. It was unpleasant. Today, things are better. You have many resources for solving issues with your gizmos, including the Droid 3.

Getting help

The Droid 3 comes with a modicum of assistance for your weary times of woe. Granted, its advice and delivery method aren't as informative or entertaining as the book you hold in your hands. But it's something!

Two apps can help you with your Droid 3: Guided Tours and Help Center. Both apps are found on the App menu.

Guided Tours: The Guided Tours app lists a clutch of video tutorials you can view. Choose a category and then select a video.

Help Center: The Help Center app lists Videos (coincidentally borrowed from the Guided Tours app), along with an online guide, list of tips, and support information.

Some of the information presented is good but basic. It's also, at its core, simply what would have once been printed and bundled with the Droid 3: the dratted manual.

Of course, none of the information found in the Guided Tours or Help Center apps helps you when you can't get turn on the phone. That's why books such as the one you're reading right now will probably never go out of style.

Fixing random and annoying problems

Aren't all problems annoying? There isn't really such a thing as a welcome problem, unless the problem is welcome because it diverts attention from another, preexisting problem. And random problems? If problems were predictable, they would serve in office. Or maybe they already are?

Here are some typical problems and my suggestions for a solution:

Your phone has general trouble. For just about any problem or minor quirk, consider restarting the phone: Turn off the phone and then turn it on again. This procedure will most likely fix a majority of the annoying and quirky problems you encounter on the Droid 3.

When restarting doesn't work, consider turning off the Droid 3 and removing its battery. Wait about 15 seconds, and then return the battery to the phone and turn on the phone again.

You need to check the data connection. Sometimes, the data connection drops but the phone connection stays active. Check the status bar. If you see bars, you have a phone signal. When you don't see the 3G, 1X, or Wi-Fi icon, the phone has no data signal.

Sometimes, the data signal suddenly drops for a minute or two. Wait, and it comes back around. If it doesn't, the cellular data network might be down, or you may simply be in an area with lousy service. Consider changing your location.

For wireless connections, you have to ensure that the Wi-Fi is set up properly and working. Setup usually involves pestering the person who configured the Wi-Fi signal or made it available, such as the cheerful person in the green apron who serves you coffee.

Music begins to play while you're on the phone: I find this quirk most annoying. For some reason, you start to hear music playing while you're in a conversation on the phone. I wonder why the phone's software doesn't disable music from even being able to play while the phone is in use.

Anyway, it might seem to you that stopping the music is impossible. It's not: Press the Home soft button to go to the Home screen. (You might have to unlock the phone.) Pull down the notifications, and choose the Music Playing notification. Press the Pause button to pause the music.

The phone's storage is busy: Most often, the storage — internal or MicroSD card — is busy because you've connected the Droid 3 to a computer and the computer is accessing the phone's storage system. To "unbusy" the storage, unmount the phone or stop the USB storage. See Chapter 20.

When the phone's storage remains busy, consider restarting the phone, as described earlier in this section.

An app has run amok: Sometimes, apps that misbehave let you know. You see a warning on the screen announcing the app's stubborn disposition. Touch the Force Close button to shut down the errant app.

When you see no warning or an app appears to be unduly obstinate, you can shut 'er down the manual way, by following these steps:

1. **At the Home screen, press the Menu soft button.**
2. **Choose Settings, and then choose Applications.**
3. **Choose Manage Applications.**
4. **Touch the Running tab at the top of the Manage Applications screen.**
5. **Choose the application that's causing you distress.**

   An example is a program that doesn't start or that says it's busy or has another issue.

6. **Touch either the Stop or Force Stop button.**

   The program stops.

After stopping the program, try opening it again to see whether it works. If the program continues to run amok, contact its developer: Open the Market app, press the Menu soft button, and choose My Apps. Open the app you're having trouble with, and choose the option Send Email. Send the developer a message describing the problem.

You need to reset the phone's software (a drastic measure). When all else fails, you can do the drastic thing and reset all the phone's software, essentially returning it to the state it was in when it first arrived. Obviously, you need not perform this step lightly. In fact, consider finding support (see the next section) before you start:

1. **At the Home screen, press the Menu soft button.**
2. **Choose Settings, and then choose Privacy.**
3. **Choose Factory Data Reset.**

By itself, the Factory Data Reset option merely resets the phone's software. The information you have on the phone's storage (internal and MicroSD card) remains. That way, the pictures, videos, music, and other information saved on the phone's storage aren't erased. That is, unless you:

4. **Optionally, place green check marks by the Erase options for the phone's internal storage and MicroSD card.**

   Erasing these options isn't required in order to fix phone problems. The only time I've used them is when I've sold a phone or traded it in.

5. **Touch the Reset Phone button.**

6. **Touch the Erase Everything button to confirm.**

   All the information you've set or stored on the phone is purged.

Again, *do not* follow these steps unless you're certain that they will fix the problem or you're under orders to do so from someone in tech support.

Getting support

The easiest way to find support for the Droid 3 is to dial 611. You're greeted by a cheerful Verizon employee, or an automated robot system, who will gladly help you with various phone issues.

On the Internet, you can find support at these websites:

```
www.motorola.com
http://market.android.com/support
http://support.vzw.com/clc
```

Droid 3 Q&A

I love Q&A! That's because not only is it an effective way to express certain problems and solutions but some of the questions might also cover things I've been wanting to ask.

"The touchscreen doesn't work!"

The touchscreen, such as the one used on the Droid 3, requires a human finger for proper interaction. The phone interprets complicated electromagnetic physics between the human finger and the phone to determine where the touchscreen is being touched.

You cannot use the touchscreen when you're wearing gloves, unless they're specially designed gloves that claim to work on touchscreens. Batman wears this type of glove, so it probably exists in real life.

The touchscreen might also fail when the battery power is low or when the phone has been physically damaged.

"The battery doesn't charge"

Start from the source: Is the wall socket providing power? Is the cord plugged in? The cable may be damaged, so try another cable.

When charging from a USB port on a computer, ensure that the computer is turned on. Most computers don't provide USB power when they're turned off.

"The phone gets so hot that it turns itself off!"

Yikes! An overheating phone can be a nasty problem. Judge how hot the phone is by seeing whether you can hold it in your hand: When the phone is too hot to hold, it's too hot. If you're using the phone to warm up your coffee, the phone is too hot.

Turn off the phone. Take out the battery and let it cool.

If the overheating problem continues, have the phone looked at for potential repair. The battery might need to be replaced.

"The phone doesn't do Landscape mode!"

Not every app takes advantage of the Droid 3's ability to orient itself in Landscape mode. For example, the Home screen doesn't "do landscape" unless you extend the sliding keyboard. One program that definitely does Landscape mode is Browser, described in Chapter 11. So just because an app doesn't enter Landscape mode doesn't mean that it *can* enter Landscape mode.

The Droid 3 has a setting you can check to confirm that landscape orientation is active: From the App menu, choose Settings and then Display. Ensure that a check mark appears by the Auto-Rotate Screen option. If not, touch the square to put a green check mark there.

Part VI
The Part of Tens

The 5th Wave By Rich Tennant

"Well, here's what happened–I forgot to put it on my AK Notepad."

In this part . . .

Because of a translation error, the final part of the original *Droid For Dummies* book was titled the *Part of Tense* in German. This error resulted in a schnitzel full of e-mail comments regarding how the information failed to make anyone tense. Worse was *The Part of Tins* from the Dutch translation, followed by *The Part of Tents* for the Hungarian translation. Things began to go downhill, until it was explained that the final part of the book contained afterthoughts, leftovers, tips, tricks, hints, and other good information all organized into chapters with ten items each. That left just about everyone satisfied, although the Germans remained tense.

 Apps
 Blockbuster
 Books
 Browser

 Calculator
 Calendar
 Camcorder
 Camera

 Citrix
 City ID
 Contacts
 Dialer

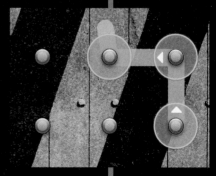

Ten Tips, Tricks, and Shortcuts

In This Chapter

▸ Using Quick Launch

▸ Using sliding-keyboard menu shortcuts

▸ Activating In-Pocket Detection

▸ Taking advantage of Contact Quick Actions

▸ Unlocking dirty words on voice input

▸ Putting a new word in the dictionary

▸ Adding a direct-dial screen shortcut

▸ Adding a direct-text screen shortcut

▸ Finding a lost phone

▸ Nerding out with Task Manager

1'd like to think that everything I mention in this book is a tip, trick, or shortcut for using your Droid 3. Given that this is a Part of Tens chapter, however, I have the freedom to simply list what I feel are ten tips, tricks, and shortcuts. These are some of the things I know about from using the Droid 3 and from overcoming some of its more frustrating aspects.

…d on page

Menu+f

Save page

Menu+v

Select text

…nu+e

Quick Launch

The sliding keyboard has 36 keys to which you can assign app shortcuts. That's 1 shortcut for every letter key, A through Z, plus 10 for the numbers 1 through 9 and 0. The keyboard shortcuts make up the Quick Launch function. Setting them up works like this:

1. **At the Home screen, press the Menu soft button.**

2. **Choose Settings, and then choose Applications.**

3. **Choose Quick Launch.**

   You see various entries titled Assign Application, followed by the 36 keys from the keyboard, A through Z, and then 0 through 9. If an app is already assigned to a key, you see the app listed. Otherwise, you see the text *No Shortcut.*

4. **Choose a letter to assign an app to that key.**

   For example, choose the C key.

5. **Select an app to assign to the Quick Launch key.**

   Pluck an app from the scrolling menu, such as the Calculator.

6. **Repeat Steps 4 and 5 to assign more apps to Quick Launch keys.**

To use a Quick Launch shortcut, press and hold the Search key on the sliding keyboard, and then touch the Quick Launch key shortcut, such as Search+C to launch the app associated with the C key.

To reassign an app to a key, repeat the steps in this section and choose a new app in Step 5.

To remove an app from a key, long-press its entry on the Quick Launch screen. Touch the OK button to confirm that that you're clearing the key.

Sliding-Keyboard Menu Shortcuts

A quick way to access menu commands is to use the sliding keyboard. After pressing the Menu soft key, you can press certain keys on the keyboard to quickly access the commands that are displayed.

For example, pressing the Menu key while using the Maps app displays the onscreen menu. Pressing the C key at this point chooses the Clear Map command, which is the only command on the menu that begins with the letter *C.* Though this trick works, it doesn't work all the time.

Some menus feature the shortcut keys on the menu itself, as shown in Figure 24-1. In that case, you can access any command by pressing the Menu soft button (to display the menu) and then pressing the corresponding key on the sliding keyboard.

Add bookmark
Menu+a

Find on page
Menu+f

Save page
Menu+v

Select text
Menu+e

Page info
Menu+g

Share page
Menu+s

Downloads
Menu+d

Settings
Menu+p

Figure 24-1: Sliding-keyboard menu shortcuts.

For example, in Figure 24-1, the sliding keyboard shortcut for the Downloads command is Menu+D. Press the Menu soft button and then press the D key on the sliding keyboard to display the Downloads window. You don't even have to touch the More command to see the additional menu items; simply press the Menu soft button, and then touch the shortcut key on the sliding keyboard.

When no keyboard shortcuts are apparent, you use the sliding keyboard's arrow keys to navigate the menus. Press the OK key to choose a command.

In-Pocket Detection

I'm a big fan of wearing earphones with my Droid 3. I enjoy talking hands-free, probably because of my Italian background. So I answer the call, insert the earphones, lock the phone, and thrust it into my pocket. With the phone locked, you don't need to worry about the call being accidentally muted or disconnected.

Actually, locking the phone is an extra step. That's because you can have the phone locked automatically whenever you thrust it into your pocket, thanks to the Droid 3's In-Pocket Detection feature. Obey these steps to activate it:

1. **At the Home screen, press the Menu soft button.**
2. **Choose Settings and then Display.**
3. **Place a green check mark by the option In-Pocket Detection.**

Now, whenever you thrust your phone into your pocket, it locks automatically.

Contact Quick Actions

You may have noticed that a contact's picture contains three dots beneath the image. These three dots are there whether the image is a photo or the stock Android icon. They hold significance in that they can be used to summon the Quick Actions menu for that contact, as shown in Figure 24-2.

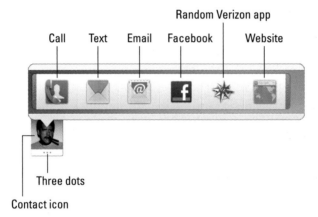

Figure 24-2: Quick Actions for a contact.

Summon the Quick Actions menu by long-pressing the contact's image.

The number and variety of icons on the Quick Actions menu depend on how much information is available for the contact. But no matter where the contact's icon is found, as long as you see those three dots, you see the Quick Actions menu.

Add Spice to Dictation

I feel that too few people use dictation, despite how handy it can be — especially for text messaging. Anyway, if you've used dictation, you might have noticed that it occasionally censors some of the words you utter. Perhaps you're the kind of person who won't put up with that kind of s***.

Relax. You can lift the vocal censorship ban by following these steps:

1. **At the Home screen, press the Menu soft button.**

2. **Choose Settings, and then choose Voice Input and Output.**

3. **Choose Voice Recognizer Settings.**

4. **Remove the check mark by the option Block Offensive Words.**

And just what are offensive words? I would think that *censorship* is an offensive word. But no, apparently only a few choice words fall into this category. I won't print them here, because the Droid 3 censor retains the initial letter and generally makes the foul language easy to guess. D***.

Add a Word to the Dictionary

Betcha didn't know that the Droid 3 has a dictionary. The dictionary is used to keep track of words you type — words that may not be recognized as being spelled properly.

Words unknown to the Droid 3 appear with a red-dashed underline onscreen. To add one of these words to the dictionary, follow these steps:

1. **Long-press a red-underlined word.**

2. **From the Edit Text menu, choose the command Add *Word* to Dictionary, where *Word* is the word you long-pressed.**

3. **Use the Edit Word dialog box to modify the word, if you need to.**

    For example, remove the *S* if you want to add the root of a plural word.

4. **Touch the OK button.**

    The word is added to the Droid 3 dictionary and is no longer flagged as misspelled.

To review the contents of the dictionary, open the Settings app and choose Language & Keyboard and then User Dictionary. You see a list of words you've added. Touch a word to edit it or to delete it from the dictionary. You can manually add words to the dictionary by pressing the Menu soft key and choosing the Add command.

Create a Direct-Dial Shortcut

For the numbers you dial most frequently, you can create Home screen contact shortcuts. Here's how:

1. **Long-press the Home screen.**

2. **Choose Shortcuts.**

3. **Choose Direct Dial.**

4. **Choose the contact you want to direct-dial.**

   Contacts with multiple phone numbers have more than one listing.

A shortcut to that contact's phone number (with the contact's picture, if they have one) appears on the Home screen. Touching the shortcut instantly dials the contact's phone number.

Create a Direct Text-Message Shortcut

Just as you can create a direct-dial shortcut (shown in the preceding section), you can create an icon to directly text-message a contact. The difference is that you choose Direct Message in Step 5 rather than Direct Dial.

The widget that appears on the Home screen can be used to instantly send that contact a text message. Simply touch the icon and start typing with your thumbs.

See Chapter 9 for more information about text messaging.

Find Your Lost Cell Phone

Someday, you may lose your Droid 3. It might be for a few panic-filled seconds, or it might be for forever. The hardware solution is to weld a heavy object to the phone, such as an anvil or a school bus, yet that kind of defeats the entire mobile/wireless paradigm. The software solution is to use a cell phone locator service.

Cell phone locator services employ apps that use a phone's cellular signal as well as its GPS to help locate the missing gizmo. These types of apps are available on the Android Market. I've not tried them all, and many of them require a subscription service or registration at a website to complete the process.

Here are some suggestions for cell phone locator apps:

✔ Wheres My Droid
✔ Lookout Mobile Security
✔ Mobile Phone Locator

The Task Manager

If you want to get your hands dirty with some behind-the-scenes stuff on your Droid 3, Task Manager is the app for you. It's not for everyone, so feel free to skip this section if you want to use your phone without acquiring any computer nerd sickness that you have otherwise successfully avoided.

The Task Manager app is found on the App menu. It's main interface is shown in Figure 24-3. You see all the phone's currently running apps displayed, along with trivial information about each one: The CPU item shows how much processor power the app is consuming, and the RAM item shows how much storage the app occupies.

Selected apps

Figure 24-3: Managing your tasks.

You can use Task Manager to kill off tasks that are hogging too much CPU time or memory or that just bug the stuffing from your couch. As illustrated in Figure 24-3, touch items you want to kill off, and then touch the End Apps button. The apps are silently snuffed out.

A nifty feature in Task Manager is the Auto-End list. When apps have been assigned to this list, they automatically exit two minutes after the display times out. To add apps to the list, select them from the main screen (refer to Figure 24-3) and touch the Add to Auto-End button at the bottom of the screen.

  ✔ There's no need to kill off an app flagged as "not running."

  ✔ Task Manager doesn't delete apps; it merely stops them from running. To delete an app, use the Android Market, as discussed in Chapter 18.

  ✔ Also see Chapter 23 on using the Force Stop button to kill an app run amok.

  ✔ The Android operating system does an excellent job of managing apps. If resources are needed for another app, Android automatically closes any open apps as needed. There's no need to futz with Task Manager, unless you just enjoy messing with such a thing.

Ten Things to Remember

In This Chapter

▷ Locking the phone
▷ Using landscape orientation
▷ Taking advantage of the arrow keys
▷ Saving typing time
▷ Minding activities that consume battery power
▷ Checking for phone roaming
▷ Using the + key to dial international calls
▷ Mounting and unmounting phone storage
▷ Taking a picture of your contacts
▷ Using the Search command

*I*t's difficult to narrow to ten items the list of all the things I want you to remember when using your Droid 3. So even though you'll find ten good things not to forget in this chapter, don't think for a moment that there are *only* ten. In fact, as I remember more, I'll put them on my website, at www.wambooli.com. Check it for updates about the Droid 3 and perhaps even more things to remember.

Lock the Phone on a Call

Whether you dialed out or someone dialed in, after you start talking, you should lock your phone: Press the Power Lock button atop the Droid 3. By doing so, you ensure that the touchscreen is disabled and the call isn't unintentionally disconnected.

Of course, the call can still be disconnected by a dropped signal or the other party getting all huffy and hanging up on you, but by locking the phone, you prevent a stray finger or your pocket from disconnecting (or muting) the phone.

Also see the tip in Chapter 24 about the Droid 3's In-Pocket Detection feature.

Landscape Orientation

The natural orientation of the Droid 3 is vertical — the so-called *portrait* orientation. Sure, you can slide out the keyboard and use apps in the landscape orientation, but sometimes you don't need the keyboard, so you don't slide it out. Even so, that doesn't mean you have to use the app in portrait orientation.

Turning the phone to its side — even when you don't need to use the sliding keyboard — makes many apps appear wider, such as the Browser app and the Maps app. That's often a better way to see things, to see more available items on certain menus, and if you're using the onscreen keyboard, it gives you larger key caps on which to type.

Not every app supports landscape orientation.

Use the Arrow Keys

The Droid 3 sliding keyboard has something every cell phone can envy: arrow keys. You can use them to edit text better than you can stab your finger on the screen to move the cursor.

The best use of the arrow keys is for hopping between links on a web page: Use the keys to move between links or left, right, up, or down. Press the OK key to "click" a link.

The arrow keys might also be used in certain games to move around your little man and shoot his various weapons.

Use the Keyboard Suggestions

Don't forget to take advantage of the suggestions that appear above the keyboard when you're typing text. In fact, you don't even need to touch a suggestion: To replace your text with the highlighted suggestion, simply touch the Space key. Zap! The word appears.

The setting that directs the keyboard to make suggestions work is Show Suggestions. To ensure that this setting is active, open the Settings app and choose Language & Keyboard and then Multi-Touch Keyboard.

Things That Consume Lots of Battery Juice

Three items on the Droid 3 suck down battery power faster than a former girlfriend updates her Facebook status to Single:

✔ Navigation

✔ Bluetooth

✔ Wi-Fi networking

Navigation is certainly handy, but because the phone's touchscreen is on the entire time and dictating text to you, the battery drains rapidly. If possible, try to plug the phone into the car's power socket when you're navigating. If you can't, keep an eye on the battery meter.

Both Bluetooth and Wi-Fi networking require extra power for their wireless radios. When you need that speed or connectivity, they're great! I try to plug my phone into a power source when I'm accessing Wi-Fi or using Bluetooth. Otherwise, I disconnect from those networks as soon as I'm done, to save power.

✔ Technically speaking, using Wi-Fi doesn't drain the battery as drastically as you would think. In fact, the Wi-Fi signal times itself out after about 15 minutes of non-use. So it's perfectly okay to leave Wi-Fi on all day — you experience only a modicum of battery loss because of it. Even so, I'm a stickler for turning off Wi-Fi when I don't use it.

✔ See Chapter 23 for more information on managing the Droid 3 battery.

Check for Roaming

Roaming can be expensive. The last non-smartphone (dumbphone?) I owned racked up $180 in roaming charges the month before I switched to a better cellular plan. Even though you too may have a good cell plan, keep an eye on the phone's status bar. Ensure that when you're making a call, you don't see the Roaming status icon on the status bar atop the touchscreen.

Well, yes, it's okay to make a call when your phone is roaming. My advice is to remember to *check* for the icon, not to avoid it. If possible, try to make your phone calls when you're back in your cellular service's coverage area. If you can't, make the phone call, but keep in mind that you will be charged roaming fees. They ain't cheap.

Use + When Dialing Internationally

I suppose most folks are careful when dialing an international number. On the Droid 3, you can use the + key to replace the country's exit code. In the United States, the code is 011. So, whenever you see an international number listed as 011-xxx-xxxxxxx, you can instead dial +xxx-xxxxxx, where the x characters represent the number to dial.

See Chapter 21 for more information on international dialing.

Properly Access Phone Storage

To access the Droid 3 storage area from your computer, you must properly mount the phone's storage. For the Droid 3, it's the phone's internal storage as well as the MicroSD card.

After the storage is mounted, you can use your computer to access files — music, videos, still pictures, contacts, and other types of information — stored on your phone.

When the phone's storage is mounted on a computer storage system, you cannot access phone storage by using the phone. If you try, you see a message explaining that the storage is busy.

When you're done accessing the phone's storage from your computer, be sure to stop USB storage: Pull down the USB notification, and choose Charge Only. Touch the OK button. (See Chapter 20 for more details.)

Do not simply unplug the phone from the USB cable when the computer is accessing the phone's storage. If you do, you can damage the phone's storage and lose all information stored there.

Snap a Pic of That Contact

Here's something I always forget: Whenever you're near one of your contacts, take the person's picture. Sure, some people are bashful, but most folks are flattered. The idea is to build up your Contacts list so that all contacts have photos. That makes receiving a call much more interesting when you see the caller's picture displayed, especially a silly or embarrassing picture.

When taking the picture, be sure to show it to the person before you assign it to the contact. Let them decide whether it's good enough. Or, if you just want to be rude, assign a crummy-looking picture. Heck, you don't even have to do that: Just take a random picture of anything, and assign it to a contact: A plant. A rock. Your cat. But seriously, the next time you meet up with a contact, keep in mind that the phone can take the person's picture.

See Chapter 14 for more information on using the Droid 3 camera and assigning a picture to a contact.

The Search Command

Google is known worldwide for its searching abilities. By gum, the word *google* is now synonymous for searching. So please don't forget that the Droid 3, which uses the Google Android operating system, has a powerful Search command.

The Search command is not only powerful but also available all over. The Search soft button can be pressed at any time, in just about any program to search for information, locations, people — you name it. It's handy. It's everywhere. Use it.

Ten Worthy Apps

In This Chapter

▷ AK Notepad

▷ CardStar

▷ Dolphin Browser

▷ Gesture Search

▷ Google Finance

▷ Google Sky Map

▷ Movies

▷ SportsTap

▷ Voice Recorder

▷ Zedge

*W*elcome to the most controversial chapter of this book! It's an almost impossible task to narrow the list of more than 200,000 Android apps for the Droid 3 into the ten most worthy. I know for certain that I haven't tried all the apps. Still, I feel that I should pass along some suggestions and ideas for what I've found to be my favorites. The only restriction I put on my decision-making process is that the apps must be free. You can find them at the Android Market. See Chapter 18.

..tepad

.tch.com

★★★★☆ 19,724

Angry Birds Seasons

Rovio Mobile Ltd.

★★★★☆ 78,226

Barcode Scanner

ZXing Team

★★★★☆ 82,958

Facebook for Android

.cebook

630,054

Get thee a bar code scanner app

Many apps from the Android Market can be quickly accessed by scanning their bar code information. Scanning with what? Why, your Droid 3, of course!

By using a bar code scanner app, you can instantly read in and translate bar codes into links to that app at the Android Market.

Plenty of bar code apps are out there, though I use one called Barcode Scanner. It's easy:

Run the app. Point the phone's camera at a bar code, and in a few moments you see a link or an option for what to do next. To get an app, choose the Open Browser option, which opens the Android Market on your phone.

You can use the Barcode Scanner app to take advantage of the various QR Code icons that appear in this chapter, as well as throughout this book. To install an app, choose the option Open Browser.

AK Notepad

 One program that the Droid 3 is missing out of the box is a notepad. A good choice for an app to fill that void is AK Notepad: You can type or dictate short messages and memos, which I find handy.

For example, before a recent visit to the hardware store, I made (dictated) a list of items I needed by using AK Notepad. I also keep some important items as notes — things that I often forget or don't care to remember, such as frequent flyer numbers, my dress shirt and suit size (like I ever need that info), and other important notes I might need handy but not cluttering my brain.

 Perhaps the most important note you can make is one containing your contact information. A note labeled *In Case You Find This Phone* on my Droid 3 contains information about me in case I ever lose my phone and someone is decent enough to search it for my information. (Also see Chapter 24 for information on finding lost phones.)

CardStar

 The handy CardStar app answers the question, "Why do I have all these store-rewards cards?" They aren't credit cards — they're marketing cards designed for customer loyalty programs. Rather than tote those cards around in your wallet or on your keychain, you can scan a card's bar code using your Droid 3 and save the "card" on the phone.

After you store your loyalty cards in the Droid 3, you simply run the CardStar app to summon the appropriate merchant. Show the checkout person your phone, or scan the bar code yourself. CardStar makes it easy.

Dolphin Browser

 Though I don't mind using the Browser app that comes with the Droid 3, it's universally despised by many Android phone owners. A better and more popular alternative is Dolphin Browser.

Like many popular computer browsers, Dolphin Browser features a tabbed interface, which works much better than the silly multiple-window interface of the standard Browser app on the Droid 3.

Dolphin Browser also sports many handy tools, which you can access by pressing the Menu soft button. Unlike other Android apps, the tools pop up on a menu you can see on the screen.

Gesture Search

 The Gesture Search app provides a new way to find information on your Droid 3. Rather than use a keyboard or dictate, you simply draw on the touchscreen the first letter of whatever you're searching for.

Start the Google Search app to begin a search. Use your finger to draw a big letter on the screen. After you draw a letter, search results appear on the screen. You can continue drawing more letters to refine the search or touch a search result.

Gesture Search can find contacts, music, apps, and bookmarks in the Browser app.

Google Finance

 The Google Finance app is an excellent market-tracking tool for folks who are obsessed with the stock market or want to keep an eye on their portfolios. The app offers you an overview of the market and updates to your stocks, as well as links to financial news.

To get the most from this app, configure Google Finance on the web, using your computer. You can create lists of stocks to watch, which are then instantly synchronized with your Droid 3. You can visit Google Finance on the web at

```
www.google.com/finance
```

As with other Google services, Google Finance is provided to you for free, as part of your Google account.

Google Sky Map

Ever look up into the sky and say, "What the heck is that?" Unless it's a bird, an airplane, a satellite, a UFO, or a superhero, Google Sky Map helps you find what it is. You may learn that a particularly bright star in the sky is, in fact, the planet Jupiter.

The Google Sky Map app is elegant. It basically turns the Droid 3 into a window you can look through to identify objects in the night sky. Just start the app, and hold the phone up to the sky. Pan the phone to identify planets, stars, and constellations.

Google Sky Map promotes using the Droid 3 without touching the screen. For this reason, the screen goes blank after a spell, which is merely the phone's power-saving mode. If you plan extensive stargazing with Google Sky Map, consider resetting the screen time-out. Refer to Chapter 2 for details.

Movies

The Movies app is the Droid 3 gateway to Hollywood. It lists currently running films and films that are opening, and it has links to your local theaters with showtimes and other information. It's also tied into the popular Rotten Tomatoes website for reviews and feedback. If you enjoy going to the movies, you'll find the Movies app a valuable addition to your Droid 3.

SportsTap

I admit to not being a sports nut, so it's difficult for me to identify with the craving to have the latest scores, news, and schedules. The sports nuts in my life, however, tell me that the very best app for that purpose is a handy thing named SportsTap.

Rather than blather on about something I'm not into, I'll just ask that you take my advice and obtain SportsTap. I believe you'll be thrilled.

Voice Recorder

 The Droid 3 can record your voice or other sounds, and Voice Recorder is a good app for performing this task. It has an elegant and simple interface: Touch the big Record button to start recording. Make a note for yourself or record a friend doing his Daffy Duck impression.

Previous recordings are stored in a list on the Voice Recorder main screen. Every recording is shown with its title, the date and time of the recording, and the recording duration.

Zedge

 The Zedge app is a helpful resource for finding wallpapers and ringtones for the Droid 3. It's a sharing app, so you can access wallpapers and ringtones created by other Android phone users as well as share your own.

Zedge features an easy-to-use interface, plus lots of helpful information on what it does and how it works.

Avoiding Android viruses

How can you tell which apps are legitimate and which might be viruses or evil apps that do odd things to your phone? Well, you can't. In fact, most people can't, because most evil apps don't advertise themselves as such.

The key to knowing whether an app is evil is to look at what it does, as described in Chapter 18. If a simple grocery-list app uses the phone's text messaging service and the app doesn't need to send text messages, it's suspect.

In the history of the Android operating system, only a handful of malicious apps have been distributed, and most of them were found in Asia. Google routinely removes these apps from the Android Market, and a feature of the Android operating system even lets Google remove apps from your phone. So you're pretty safe.

Generally speaking, avoid "hacker" apps and porn, and apps that use social engineering to make you do things on your phone that you wouldn't otherwise do, such as text an overseas number to see racy pictures of politicians or celebrities.

Also, I highly recommend that you abstain from obtaining apps from anything but the official Android Market. The Amazon Market is okay, but some other markets are basically distribution points for illegal or infected software. Avoid them.

Index

• Numerics & Symbols •

+ character
  in international phone numbers, 276
  replacing country code with, 276, 322
#BAL, 102
#DATA, 102
#MIN, 102
#PMT, 102
#Warranty Center, 102
1X network, 248
3G (third generation) network
  about, 248
  mobile hotspots in, 252
8-megapixel camera, 16

• A •

abbreviations (texting), 120
accelerometer, 37
accessibility settings, 294
activate
  Bluetooth, 69, 254
  locations, 171
  new phones, 22
  voice input, 52
  Wi-Fi, 249
add
  address book contacts, 103–107
  apps to Dock, 284
  apps to Home screen, 284
  bookmarks, 146, 147
  contacts, 80, 103–107
  contacts to group, 112
  e-mail attachments, 139
  events, 221–223
  layers to Maps, 169–170
  music, 209–213
  phone to Google Voice, 95–96
  shortcut, 285–286
  social networking accounts, 156–157
  Wi-Fi network, 251
  widgets, 285
  words to dictionary, 315–316

Add Wi-Fi Network command, 251
address
  e-mail, 109, 119
  street, 171, 174
address book. See also contact(s)
  adding contact images, 108–109
  adding contacts, 103–107
  contact groups, 111–112
  Contacts app, 100–103
  default phone number and e-mail
    address, 109
  editing contacts, 107–108
  Favorites, 110–111
  overview, 99
  removing contacts, 112–113
  searching contacts, 103
  sharing contacts, 112
  sorting Contacts list, 102–103
Address box (web page), 144–145
Airplane mode
  and making phone calls, 71
  using, 273–274
AK Notepad app, 326
Alarm & Timer app, 224–225
Albums option (music library), 206
Aldiko, 226
alerts
  about, 25
  setting, 223
Alt key
  accessing symbol characters with, 55
  locking symbol characters with, 56
Alt Lock light, 16
Alternative characters key (sliding
    keyboard), 53
Alternative keyboard (Multi-Touch
    keyboard), 52
Amazon Kindle, 226–228
Amazon MP3 app, 211–213
Amazon.com, 227
Android Market
  buying apps, 237–238
  creating app groups, 242–243
  finding apps, 235

Android Market *(continued)*
  free apps, 236–237, 325
  games, 231
  managing apps, 238–243
  removing downloaded apps, 240–241
  renting movies, 230
  reviewing downloaded apps, 238–239,
    241–242
  sharing apps, 239–240
  shopping, 233–238
  updating apps, 240
  visiting, 234–235
Android operating system
  overview, 26
  sharing information, 149–150
  task management, 318
  updating, 303
  viruses, 329
Android phones, upgrading to Droid 3
    from, 12
animated wallpaper
  changing Home screen to, 282
  touching Home screen with, 40
  traditional versus, 282–283
App menu
  defined, 45
  reviewing most recently used, 47
  starting apps from, 45–46
App menu groups, 242–243
appearance (web pages), 153
application icon, 39
appointments
  adding events, 221–223
  browsing dates, 218–220
  Google Calendar, 218
  overview, 217–218
  reviewing schedule, 220–221
apps (applications). *See also* Android
    Market; *specific apps*
  bar code for installing, 3
  defined, 4
  e-mail, 128
  locating, 46
  number of, 217
  paying for, 237
  preinstalled, 241
  ratings, 235
  recommended, 325–329

  starting, 44–46
  troubleshooting, 306
  web browsing versus, 144
apps groups, 242
arrow keys, 320
Artist option (music library), 206
attachments
  e-mail, 138–139
  Gmail indicator for, 132
  media files, 203
  multimedia messages, 123, 125
AutoAnswer, 291–292
AutoPlay dialog boxes, 261
AutoRetry, 291–292

• *B* •

Back button (web browsing), 146
Backspace key
  on Multi-Touch keyboard, 51
  on sliding keyboard, 53
backup, 302–303
Backup Assistant
  in setup process, 23
  using, 303
bar codes, 3
bar codes scanner apps, 326
battery
  charging, 13–14
  determining power-consuming activities,
    297–298
  importance of, 295
  installing, 12–13
  largest power consumers, 321
  managing power consumption, 298–299
  monitoring, 296–297
  in original package, 10
  prolonging life of, 299–301
  replacing, 301
  status, 297–298
  troubleshooting, 308
  turning on phone, 22
battery cover, 16
Blockbuster app, 231
Bluetooth
  activating, 69, 254
  in Airplane mode, 273
  defined, 253

headset, 18, 71, 76
  overview, 253–255
  power consumed by, 321
  turning off, 300
  using headset, 254–255
Bluetooth printer, 256–257
bookmark(s)
  for Google account page, 27
  opening, 148
  web browsing, 146–148
Bookmark button, 145
Books app
  in Android Market, 234
  using, 226–227
brightness, changing, 292
Browser app, 144. *See also* web browsing
Browsing history (web browsing)
  in Browser program, 147
  clearing, 146
businesses, finding, 174–175

 C

Calculator app, 223
Calendar app
  adding events, 221–223
  browsing dates, 218–220
  colors and event categories, 220
  reviewing schedule, 220–221
Calendar widget, 218
call(s). *See also specific topics*
  conference, 69, 84–85
  dialing, 72–73
  to displayed contacts, 101
  Favorites list, 74
  forwarding, 85–86
  incoming signal volume, 77–78
  missed, 78
  placing, 68–71
  receiving, 74–76, 83–84
  Recent Calls list, 73–74
  reviewing, 79–80
  ringtones, 87–89
  sending to voice mail, 86–87
  signal strength, 72
  Switch Calls, 84
  Text Message Reply, 76–77
  Voice command for, 63

Call Connect, 292
Call duration, 69
call forwarding
  overview, 85–86
  to voice mail, 86–87
Call in Progress notification
  in Dialer app, 69
  function of, 71
Call Voice Mail button, 92
Camcorder app
  overview, 187
  recording video, 188
  video quality, 189
Camera app
  on Dock, 284
  taking pictures with, 182–186
Camera Roll
  function of, 194
  viewing, 195
cameras
  adjusting, 187
  changing resolution, 184–185
  deleting images, 183–184
  front-facing, 190
  location of, 15–16
  panorama shots, 185–185
  recording video, 187–189
  self-portrait, 185
  setting flash, 184
  setting image location, 186–187
  setting video quality, 189–190
  taking pictures, 182–183
  Video Message mode, 190–191
  zoom function, 17
capital letters (sliding keyboard), 55
Caps Lock, 55
Caps Lock light, 51
car cell phone charger
  as accessory, 19
  using, 14
Car Home screen, 41–42
CardStar app, 326–327
carrier voice mail
  overview, 91–92
  retrieving messages, 92–93
  setting up, 92
carrying cases, 20
carrying the phone, 19–20

CDMA (Code Division Multiple Access), 279
cell phone locator services, 317
cellular data network, 248
cellular service
  provider of, 3
  and text messaging charges, 118
censor feature
  disabling, 315
  for voice commands, 64
Charge Only option (USB connection), 261
charger/data cable, 10
charger head, 10
charging battery
  procedure, 13–14
  storing phone while, 20
  from wall socket vs. computer, 297
checkbox icon
  and disabling/enabling options, 301
  for phone options, 3
cleaning phone, 302
Clear Form Data, 154
Code Division Multiple Access (CDMA), 279
commands, voice, 63–64
Compass app, 170
Compass Pointer (Maps app)
  and Perspective view, 169
  and phone's direction, 170
computer
  adding music from, 209–211
  connecting phone with, 259–260
  importing contacts from, 105–106
conference calls
  Add call button for, 69
  procedure for making, 84–85
Connected screen
  components of, 69
  returning to, 70
connection. *See also* wireless connection
  checking, 305
  to other media devices, 267–269
  USB, 259–262
  Wi-Fi, 251
contact(s)
  adding, 80, 103–107
  adding images, 108–109
  adding in Maps app, 106–107, 175
  dialing, 72–73
  editing, 107–108
  favorite, 110–111

grouping, 111–112
locating with Maps app, 176
removing, 112–113
setting image for, 201–202
setting ringtones for, 88
sharing, 112
sorting, 102–103
sources of information on, 102
starting new e-mail message from, 137
taking pictures of, 322–323
contact groups, 111–112
Contact tag, 199
Contacts app, 100–103
Contacts list, 102–103
cookies, clearing, 154
Copy Media, 269
copying text, 61–62
cropping images, 200
cursor
  moving, to edit text, 58
  and Shift key, 55
  and typing on Droid 3, 54
Custom Saver mode, 299
customer service (Verizon), 278
customization. *See also* personalization
  e-mail, 139–141
  phone, 281
cutting text, 61–62

• *D* •

Data Saver, 301
dates, browsing, 218–220
Day view (Calendar), 218–220
default
  e-mail account, 141
  phone number and e-mail address, 109
Default Ringtone, 88
Del key, 54
delete. *See also* remove
  alarms, 225
  bookmarks, 147
  contacts from group, 112
  e-mail, 134, 140–141
  images, 183–184, 202
  music, 215
  pictures, 183–184
  songs from playlist, 215
  text messages, 125

Dialer app
  on Dock, 284
  location on Home screen, 39
  using, 68
dialing calls
  international, 71, 275–276, 279
  overview, 72–73
  from Recent Calls list, 73–74
  speed dial, 82
dialpad, 22
Dictate address (web browsing), 145
dictating to phone
  censor feature, 64
  overview, 62–63
  steps for, 315
  text messages, 119
  voice commands, 63–64
Dictation key, 53
dictionary, adding words to, 315–316
DIF setting (video quality), 189
Digital Living Networking Alliance (DNLA)
      devices, 268–269
digital network, 248
digital zoom, 183
direct-dial shortcuts, 316
direction keys
  moving cursor with, 58
  on sliding keyboard, 53
direction of phone. *See* orientation
directions (Maps app), 175–177
disconnection
  audio alert for, 71
  from computer, 262
Display symbols palette, 53
DNLA (Digital Living Networking Alliance)
      devices, 268–269
Dock
  adding apps to, 284
  dragging icons, 287
  on Home screen, 39
Dolphin Browser, 327
Done key
  function, 52
  on Multi-Touch keyboard, 51
  in setup process, 23
Double Tap Home Launch function
  and double-tap method, 35
  setting, 293

double-tap technique, 35
doubleTwist
  function of, 211
  using, 263–264
Download Complete icon, 151
downloading
  from Android Market, 234–236
  from web, 150–152, 212
Downloads app, 266
Downloads screen, 152
dropped calls, alert for, 71
DVD setting (video quality), 189

• **E** •

e-book, 225
e-book reader apps
  Amazon Kindle, 226–228
  Google Books, 226–227
  overview, 225–226
e-mail
  in Airplane mode, 273
  apps for, 128
  attachments, 138–139, 191
  checking Gmail inbox, 131–132
  composing, 135–137
  to displayed contacts, 101
  getting messages, 131
  importing contacts from, 105
  manual delete option, 140–141
  overview, 127
  reading messages, 133–135
  replying, 134–135
  signature, 54, 139–140
  text messages versus, 122
  universal inbox, 132–133
e-mail account. *See also* Gmail
  ISP, 129–130
  setting default, 141
  web-based, 128–129
e-mail address
  default, 109
  in text message, 119
earbud-style earphones
  storing, 18
  using, 17–18
earphones, 17–18
  Bluetooth, 255
  locking phone when using, 70

Edit Text menu, 60
editing. *See also* text editing
  contacts, 107–108
  images, 200–202
Effects adjustment (camera), 187
8-megapixel camera, 16
Email app. *See also* Gmail
  customizing, 139–141
  getting messages, 131
  reading messages, 133–135
  replying, 134–135
  setting up accounts, 128–130
  universal inbox, 132–133
Emergency Call button, 26
emergency calls, 26
End Block marker, 59
End Call button
  function of, 70
  and juggling two phone calls, 84
  location of, 69
Enter key
  on Multi-Touch keyboard, 51
  on sliding keyboard, 53
Erase key
  on Multi-Touch keyboard, 51
  on sliding keyboard, 53
events
  adding, 221–223
  details of, 220–221
external speaker, 16

• F •

face tag, 199
Facebook, 158–162
Facebook for Android app
  on menu for sharing, 203
  using, 161–162
Favorites list
  address book, 110–111
  calls, 74
  wireless printer, 257
FBReader, 226
features, 14–17
files, downloading, 151
Files app, 266–267

flash
  location of, 16
  for recording video, 191
  setting, 184
Force Stop button, 241
Forward button (web browsing), 146
forwarding
  calls, 85–87
  e-mail, 134
  text messages, 121–122
free apps
  from Android Market, 236–237
  Internet radio, 215–216
  recommended, 325–329
front-facing camera
  location of, 15
  videotaping with, 190

• G •

Gallery app
  creating new album, 196–197
  deleting images, 202
  finding image location on map, 199
  HDMI option, 268
  overview, 194–195
  picture editing, 200–202
  for pictures, 183
  printing pictures, 200
  tagging images, 197–198
  uploading images, 160, 162–163
  for video, 189
  viewing albums in library, 195–196
games, 231
Genres option (music library), 206
Geo-Tag, 186
Gesture Search app, 327
global positioning system (GPS)
  finding your location with, 171
  and Maps app, 168
Global System for Mobile Communications
    (GSM), 279
gloves, 36
Gmail
  checking inbox, 131–132
  contacts removed from, 113
  creating new contacts with, 105
  deleting mail, 141

overview, 128
Save Draft button, 137
Sent messages, 137
signature for, 139
voice mail transcripts, 97
Go button (web browsing), 145
Go key
function of, 52
on Multi-Touch keyboard, 51
Google, 26
Google account
advantages of, 4, 27
backup, 302–303
coordinating phone with, 22
creating, 27
setting up, 28–29
storing contacts in, 104
syncing with, 27
Google Books, 226–227
Google Buzz, 163
Google Calendar, 218
Google Checkout, 238
Google Finance app, 327–328
Google Labs, 170
Google location services, 171
Google Mobile search page, 153
Google Search widget, 148–149
Google Sky Map app, 328
Google Talk, 126
Google Voice
adding phone to, 95–96
and call forwarding, 86
overview, 94–95
retrieving messages, 96–97
setting up, 95
GPS (global positioning system)
finding your location with, 171
and Maps app, 168
groups
apps, 242
contact, 111–112
GSM (Global System for Mobile
Communications), 279
Guided Tours
getting help from, 304
and setup process, 23

• H •

hands-free headset, 17–18
HD+ setting (video quality), 189
HDMI cable
as accessory, 19
location, 15
and projecting media, 267–268
HDMI viewing options, 268
headphone jack, 15
headset, 17–18
Bluetooth, 18, 69, 71, 76, 254–255
hands-free, 17–18
heat, 20
help, 304
Help Center app, 304
hibernation (Sleep mode)
about, 26
activating, 30–31
high definition setting (video quality), 189
History list (web browsing)
in Browser program, 147
clearing, 146
Home button, 70
home page
blank, 153
Google, 145
web browsing, 144–145, 152–153
Home screen
adding apps, 284
apps shortcuts, 237
bookmarked websites on, 147
Car Home, 41–42
creating shortcuts, 285–286
defined, 25
features, 38–40
navigation shortcut on, 178–179
personalizing, 282–287
rearranging/removing icons and widgets,
286–287
reviewing notifications, 42–44
starting applications, 44
using widgets, 45
viewing all panels, 40–41
wallpaper, 282–283
widgets, 285
hotspot, mobile wireless, 252
human engineering, 153

• I •

I-Dial, 275
icons, rearranging and removing, 286–287
images. *See also* photo album; picture(s)
    for contacts, 108–109
    downloading from web, 151
    editing, 200–201
    finding location on map, 199
    sharing, 202–203
    storage locations, 183
    tagging, 197–198
In-Pocket Detection, 313–314
information about phone, 303
installing battery, 12–13
instructions, 10
international calling
    dialing international numbers,
        71, 275–276
    from overseas, 278–279
    with Skype Mobile, 276–279
    using + key in, 276, 322
Internet connection, tethering, 253
Internet radio, 215–216
Internet service provider (ISP), 129
ISP e-mail accounts, 129–130
iTunes Agent, 211

• J •

JPEG images, 183

• K •

keyboard(s), 57. *See also* sliding keyboard
    adjusting, 293
    arrow keys, 320
    Multi-Touch, 50–56, 58, 293
    onscreen, 22–23, 50
    suggestions, 293, 320–321
    Swype, 50
    types, 50
Keyword tag, 199
Kobo, 226

• L •

labels (Gmail), 132
landscape orientation
    activating, with sliding keyboard, 38, 40
    advantages of, 320
    changing from portrait to, 37
    changing Home screen to, 40
    and sliding keyboard, 17
    troubleshooting for, 308
Laputa, 226
Launcher
    on Dock, 284
    location on Home screen, 39
    replacing, 287
layers (Maps app), 169–170
library
    Kindle, 228
    music, 206–207
    photo albums, 195–196
license agreement, 236
Light On, 191
LinkedIn, 163
links
    in other open windows, 148
    selecting on web pages, 145
    in text messages, 119
    YouTube, 204
Linux operating system, 26
List view (bookmarks), 148
live wallpaper
    changing Home screen to, 282
    touching Home screen with, 40
    traditional versus, 282–283
location. *See also* Maps app
    activating, 171
    of contacts, 101, 176
    disabling location services, 154
    finding where you are, 171–173
    of images, 199
    in Maps app, 168, 170
    of pictures, 183, 186–187
    sending to others, 173
Location Consent screen, 23
locks, 287–288. *See also* Power Lock button

long-press technique
  activating Swype with, 50
  on Home screen, 282
  manipulating touchscreen with, 35
lost phone, finding, 317

• *M* •

main microphone, 15
maintenance
  backup, 302–303
  battery, 295–301
  cleaning, 302
  updating system, 303–304
manual delete (e-mail), 140–141
manual sync, 264–266
Maps app
  activating locations, 171
  adding contacts, 106–107, 175
  adding layers, 169–170
  businesses, restaurants, or points of
      interest, 174–175
  directions, 176–177
  finding out where you are, 171–173
  locating contacts, 176
  locating displayed contacts, 101
  navigating, 177–178
  navigation shortcut on Home screen,
      178–179
  overview, 167
  Places command, 175–176
  sending location to others, 173
  specific addresses, 174
  using, 168–169
Market app, 234
Maximum Battery Saver mode, 298
Me (preset in Contact list), 102
Me button (social networking), 158
Me tag, 199
media devices, connecting to, 267–269
Meebo, 163
megapixel (MP), 185
message subject (Gmail), 132
Messaging app
  deleting messages with, 141
  as universal message inbox, 132–133
micro-USB connector
  about, 260
  mini-USB versus, 14

microfiber cloth, 302
microphone
  on earphones, 17
  headset, 18
  main, 15, 17
  noise-canceling, 16
  turning off, 69
Microphone key, 63
MicroSD (memory storage) card
  capacities of, 12
  defined, 11
  images stored on, 183
  installing, 11–12
  recommendation for, 3, 266
Microsoft Live mail, 128
Microsoft Office document
      attachments, 138
Mirror On Display app, 268
missed calls
  dealing with, 78
  and voice mail, 91
MMS. *See* multimedia message
mobile wireless hotspot, 252
Month view (Calendar), 218–220
Most Visited tab (web browsing), 147
MOTOPRINT, 257
Motorola, 50, 301
Motorola Terms of Service agreement, 22
Move to Media Area button, 241
Move to Phone button, 241
movies
  renting, 230–231
  viewing, 228–229
Movies app, 328
moving cursor, 58
MP (megapixel), 185
Multi-Touch keyboard
  special characters, 56
  suggestions, 58, 293
  on touchscreen, 50
  typing, 51–55
multimedia message (MMS)
  composing, 123–124
  overview, 122–123
  receiving, 125, 203
  video for, 189
Multimedia Station
  as accessory, 18
  storing phone in, 20

multiple windows (web browsing), 148
music
  adding from a computer, 209–211
  adding from Amazon MP3 store, 211–213
  browsing music library, 206–207
  creating playlists, 209, 214–215
  deleting, 215
  Internet radio, 215–216
  organizing, 213–215
  overview, 205
  playing, 207–209
  reviewing playlists, 213–214
  as ringtone, 88–89
  in Sleep mode, 26
  troubleshooting, 305
Music app, 268
Music Headquarters app, 206
music library, 206–207
mute
  doodle button as, 17
  and Mute icon, 70
  for phone calls, 69–70
  for video recording, 188
MyBookmarks app, 148
MySpace, 163

• N •

Name Card option, 124
navigation
  Calendar app, 220
  shortcut on Home screen, 178–179
Navigation (Maps app)
  and battery performance, 321
  using, 177–178
network
  digital, 248
  Wi-Fi, 248–251
Network icon, 72
Network Lost Tone, 292
New Window, 148
News Feed (Facebook), 162
Next key
  function of, 52
  on Multi-Touch keyboard, 51
Nighttime Saver mode, 298
noise-canceling microphone, 16
Normal Video, 190

notification light, 15
notifications
  of alarms set, 225
  dismissing, 44
  Download, 151
  e-mail, 131
  event, 223
  Google Voice, 96–97
  Home screen, 38
  hotspot, 252
  icons for, 42, 44
  low battery, 297
  missed calls, 78
  of music playing, 208
  New Text Message, 121
  reviewing, 42–44
  social networking, 158–159
  when turning on phone, 25
Nova game app, 231
Now Playing option (music library), 207
number keys
  on alternative keyboard, 52
  on Multi-Touch keyboard, 51

• O •

offensive words
  disabling censorship of, 315
  and voice censor, 64
online photo album, 197
onscreen keyboard
  Done key, 23
  in setup process, 22
operating system
  Android, 26, 149–150, 303, 318, 329
  Linux, 26
  updating, 303–304
optical zoom, 183
opting out (texting), 124
orientation, 37–38
  camera, 183
  landscape, 17, 37–38, 40, 308, 320
  options for, 37
  of pictures, 200–201
  portrait, 37–38
  troubleshooting, 308
  for web pages, 153
overheating, 308

• P •

packaging contents, 10–11
pan (Maps app), 169
Pandora Radio app
  function of, 215
  StreamFurious versus, 216
panel indicator, 40
Paperclip icon (e-mail), 138
password
  appearance of, 23
  assigning, 290–291
  e-mail, 130
  Gmail, 128
  Google account, 29
  social networking sites, 157
  typing, 54
  Wi-Fi network, 250
password unlock screen, 25
pasting text, 61–62
pattern lock
  as security feature, 23
  unlocking, 24
  using, 288–290
pause, adding (to phone number), 71
paying for apps, 237
PC mode (USB connection), 261
Performance mode (battery), 298
personalization
  accessibility settings, 294
  adding apps to Dock, 284
  adding apps to Home screen, 284
  assigning password, 290–291
  AutoAnswer, 291–292
  AutoRetry, 291–292
  creating shortcuts, 285–286
  creating unlock pattern, 288–290
  Double Tap Home Launch function, 293
  Home screen, 282–287
  icons and widgets, 286–287
  overview, 281
  ringtone, 89
  screen locks, 287–288
  security, 287–291
  setting changes, 292–293
  setting PIN, 290
  silencing features, 291
  wallpaper, 282–283
  widgets, 285
Perspective view (Maps app), 169
phone information, finding, 303
phone numbers
  adding for exiting contacts, 104
  adding pause prompt to, 71
  default, 109
  international, 275–276
  sending text messages to, 121
  in text message, 119
phone status, 38
photo album
  Camera Roll, 194–195
  creating, 196–197
  cropping images, 200
  deleting images, 202
  editing pictures, 200–202
  Facebook, 162
  finding image location on map, 199
  Gallery app, 194
  overview, 193
  printing pictures, 200
  rotating pictures, 200–201
  setting images for contacts or as
    wallpaper, 201–202
  sharing, 202–204
  tagging images, 197–199
  uploading video to YouTube, 204
  viewing albums, 195–196
photo-editing software, 200
Photos (Facebook), 162
Picasa photo-sharing site, 203
picture(s). *See also* photo album
  adjusting camera, 187
  changing resolution, 184–185
  of contacts, 109, 322–323
  deleting, 183–184
  in e-mail messages, 138
  with Facebook app, 162
  image location, 183, 186–187
  panorama shots, 185–185
  printing, 200
  self-portrait, 185
  sharing, 202–204
  for social networking sites, 160–161
  taking, 182–183

PIN
  setting a, 290
  unlocking phone with, 25
PIN lock
  defined, 290
  disabling, 288
pinch technique, 35
Places command (Maps app), 175–176
placing calls, 68–71
  conference calls, 84–85
  direct-dial shortcuts, 316
  overview, 68–71
  speed dial, 82
plastic cling sheets, 10
playing music, 207–209
playlist
  creating, 209, 214–215
  defined, 213
  removing/deleting songs, 215
  reviewing, 213–214
Playlists option (music library), 206
+ (plus) character
  in international phone numbers, 276
  replacing country code with, 276, 322
points of interest, finding, 174–175
POP mail server, 130
pop-up blocking, 153
portrait orientation
  applications fixed in, 38
  changing from landscape to, 37–38
Postcard icon, 176
power connector, 15
power consumption
  determining, 297–298
  largest sources of, 321
  managing, 298–299
  Navigation mode, 178
Power Control widget
  activating Wi-Fi radio with, 249
  turning on Bluetooth with, 254
Power Lock button
  location of, 15–16, 21
  overview, 21
  for Silent mode, 36
  snooze mode, 29
  touchscreen enabled by, 20
  turning off phone, 31

  turning on phone, 21, 23–24
  waking phone with, 26
  while on a call, 319–320
preinstalled software, 241
press-and-hold, 57
primary unlock screen, 23
Print to Retail
  function of, 203
  sharing documents with, 258
printing
  pictures, 200
  wireless, 255–258
privacy options
  location technology, 170
  web browsing, 153–154
Profile (Facebook), 162
program. *See* apps (applications)
proximity sensor
  and making phone calls, 70
  and touchscreen, 20
punctuation marks, dictating, 63

• Q •

Quick Actions, 314
Quick Launch, 311–312
QVGA setting (video quality), 189
QWERTY keyboard, 50

• R •

radio
  Internet, 215–216
  Wi-Fi, 249
ratings (apps), 235
reading e-mail messages, 133–135
rearranging icons and widgets, 286–287
receiving calls
  overview, 74–76
  in Sleep mode, 26, 31
  when on another call, 83–84
receiving text messages, 121
Recent Calls list
  adding contacts from, 103–104
  adding speed-dial number from, 82
  dialing numbers from, 73–74
  using, 79–80

recently used apps, 47
recording video, 187–189
refunds for apps, 238
Remember Form Data, 154
reminder icon, 5
reminders, setting or dismissing, 222
remove
  apps, 240–241
  contacts, 112–113
  contacts from group, 112
  events, 222–223
  icons and widgets, 286–287
  lock, 288
  navigation route, 178
  social networking account, 157
  songs from playlist, 215
renting movies, 230–231
Repeat button (music)
  icons for, 208
  and playing music, 207
replacing battery, 301
reply
  e-mail, 122, 134–135
  text message, 76–77
Reply All (e-mail), 134
resolution
  pictures, 184
  video, 188–189
restaurants, finding, 174–175
retrieving messages
  carrier voice mail, 92–93
  e-mail, 131
  Google Voice, 96–97
  visual voice mail, 94
Return key
  on Multi-Touch keyboard, 51
  on sliding keyboard, 53
review
  calls, 79–80
  downloaded apps, 238–239, 241–242
  downloaded information, 152
  most recently used apps, 47
  notifications, 42–44
  playlists, 213–214
  schedule, 220–221
ringer volume, 292

ringtone
  choosing, 87–88
  creating, 89
  defined, 76
  music as, 88–89
  setting, 88
roaming
  checking for, 321
  deactivating, 301
  icon for, 72
  surcharges for, 271–272
roaming surcharges, 272
root folder, 266
rooting, 241
rotate
  image, 200–201
  Maps app, 169
  on touchscreen, 35
Route Info (Maps app), 178

• *S* •

Satellite view (Maps app), 169
Scenes adjustment (camera), 187
schedule, 220–221. *See also* Calendar app
screen locks, 287–288
Screen Timeout, 292
scrolling
  in Contacts list, 100
  in Maps app, 169
search
  Android Market, 234
  contacts, 103
  Gmail messages, 132
  Maps app, 173–175
  web, 148–149
  YouTube videos, 228
Search command, 323
Search key, 53
security
  assigning password, 290–291
  creating unlock pattern, 288–290
  customizing, 287–291
  screen locks, 287–288
  setting PIN, 290
  web browsing options, 153–154

Security Lock Timer, 288
selecting text, 59–61
self-portraits, 185
self-video recordings, 190
sender (Gmail), 132
setting status (social networking), 159–160
settings, changing, 292–293
setup, phone, 21–23
share
  apps, 239–240
  contacts, 112
  media items, 124
  pictures and video, 160, 197, 202–204
  with Print to Retail, 258
  web pages, 149–150
  wireless connection, 251–253
Share button
  on application's info screen, 242
  location of, in Browser app, 145
  using, for photos and videos, 202
Share Media, 269
Shared Folders, 267
Shift key
  and appearance of cursor, 55
  on Multi-Touch keyboard, 51
  on sliding keyboard, 53
Shift Lock light, 16
shortcuts
  for apps, 47, 237
  to bookmarks, 147
  creating, 285–286
  direct-dial, 316
  navigation, 178–179
  with sliding keyboard, 312–313
  for test messaging, 316
Show alphabetic keyboard, 52
Show alternative keyboard, 52
Show numbers or symbols keyboard, 51
Shuffle button (music)
  icons for, 208
  and playing music, 207
Sign In button, 23
signal strength
  icon for, 72
  and making phone calls, 71
  of Wi-Fi network, 251
signature, e-mail
  creating, 139–140
  reason for including, 54

silencing phone
  methods of, 36
  with Silent mode, 291
Silent mode
  activating, 36
  entering, 291
SIM card
  location of, 12
  using, 13
Skype Mobile
  about, 126
  making international calls with, 276–279
  text messages versus, 118
sleep, 26
  options, 29
  Sleep mode, 26, 30–31
  snooze mode, 29–30
Sleep mode
  about, 26
  activating, 30–31
Slideshow option, 124
sliding keyboard
  arrow keys, 320
  features, 53
  location, 15
  menu shortcuts, 312–313
  overview, 15–17
  and soft buttons, 35
  special characters, 57
  suggestions, 58
  text selection, 60
  typing, 54–57
snooze mode, 29–30
social networking
  adding accounts, 156
  with displayed contacts, 101
  Facebook app, 161–162
  managing accounts, 157
  overview, 155
  popular sites, 163
  setting status, 159–160
  Social Networking app, 155–161
  status updates, 156–157, 160
  Twitter app, 162–163
  uploading picture, 160–161
Social Networking app
  adding accounts, 156
  managing accounts, 157
  overview, 155

setting status, 159–160
status updates, 158–159
uploading picture, 160
Social Networking widget, 160
soft buttons
  functions of, 17
  location of, 15, 17
  using, 34–35
software, resetting, 306–307. *See also* apps
  (applications)
Songs option (music library), 206
Space key
  and automatic placement of period, 54
  on Multi-Touch keyboard, 51
spam, 124
speaker(s), 16
Speaker button
  function of, 70
  location, 15
  location of, 69
  for phone calls, 69–70
  in setup process, 22
special characters, accessing, 56–57
speed dial, 82
SportsTap app, 328
spread technique, 35
SSID, 251
Star icon (Gmail)
  on e-mail message, 134
  in Gmail inbox, 132
Start Block marker, 59
starting apps. *See also individual apps*
  from App menu, 45–46
  from Home screen, 44
status
  battery, 297–298
  social networking, 159–160, 162
status bar, 38
status updates (social networking),
  158–159
Stay Awake, 292
Stop button (web browsing), 145
storage (information)
  accessing, 322
  of apps, 242
  apps for, 266–267
  images, 151, 183
  music, 207, 211

places for, 266
troubleshooting, 306
video recordings, 189
storing phone, 18–20
streamed video, 230
StreamFurious app, 216
StreamFurious Pro, 216
street addresses
  finding, for your location, 171
  looking for, 174
Street View (Maps app), 173
suggestions
  activating setting for, 320–321
  choosing, while typing, 58
sunlight, 20
swipe technique, 35
Switch Calls button, 84
Swype keyboard, 50
symbols
  accessing, 55–57
  on Multi-Touch keyboard, 52
  on sliding keyboard, 53
Symbols keyboard, 52
syncing (synchronizing)
  automatic, 300
  with doubleTwist, 211, 263–264
  with Google account, 27
  Google Books, 226–227
  manual, 264–266
  music, 209–211
  with other accounts, 29
  overview, 262

Tab key, 53
tag, 197
tagging images, 197–198
Talk app, 126
Task Manager, 317–318
tech support (Verizon), 307
technical information icon, 5
Terms of Service agreement, 22
Terrain view (Maps app), 169
tethering feature
  about, 251
  using, 253

text
  adjusting size of, 153
  e-mail, 136
  finding on web pages, 149
  selecting, 59–61
text editing
  copy and paste, 61–62
  cutting, 61–62
  moving cursor, 58
  selecting text, 59–61
  of voice-input text, 63
Text Message Reply, 76–77
text messages (texting)
  abbreviations for, 120
  alternatives to, 126
  attaching media, 203
  attaching video, 191
  composing, 118–119
  creating shortcut for, 316
  deleting, 125
  to displayed contacts, 101
  e-mail versus, 122
  forwarding, 121–122
  international, 274
  multimedia, 122–125
  opting out, 124
  overview, 117–118
  receiving, 121
  sending to phone numbers, 121
Text Messaging app, 284
3G (third generation) network
  about, 248
  mobile hotspots in, 252
Thumbnail view (bookmarks), 148
timer, 224–225
tips icon, 5
touch technique, 35
touchscreen
  cleaning, 302
  defined, 2
  disabling, 20
  incoming call info on, 74–75
  keyboards on, 50
  location of, 15
  manipulating, 35–36
  overview, 17
  in Sleep mode, 26

text selection on, 59
  troubleshooting, 307–308
troubleshooting, 304–308
turning off, 31
turning on
  after first time, 23–25
  and battery, 22
  for first time, 14, 22–23
  Power Lock button, 21
tweet, 163
Twitter
  posting messages, 163
  purpose of, 162
  signing in, 163
  status, 159
  updates, 158
Twitter app
  on menu for sharing, 203
  using, 162–163
typing
  accessing special characters, 56–57
  guidelines, 54–56
  Multi-Touch keyboard, 54–56
  phone numbers to call, 68–69
  sliding keyboard, 54–57
  suggestions, 58, 320–321
  Swype keyboard, 50
  text messages, 118–119

• U •

Uninstall button, 241
uninstalling apps, 241
Universal Inbox, 132–133
unlock pattern, 288–290
unlocking screen(s)
  password, 25
  pattern lock, 23–24
  primary, 23
unread message indication (Gmail), 132
update
  apps, 240
  operating system, 303–304
  password, 157
  social networking, 156–157, 160
upgrading, from Android phones, 12

upload, 151
  images, 160, 162–163
  video to YouTube, 204, 229
USB cable
  configuring, 260–261
  connecting phone to computer, 260
  disconnecting phone from computer, 262
  overview, 259
USB Connection, 260–261
USB connector, 15
USB Mass Storage option (USB
    connection), 261
username, 130

• V •

vCard files
  importing contacts with, 105–106
  in multimedia text messages, 124
Verizon
  Backup Assistant app, 303
  cellular service from, 3
  customer service, 278
  international calling, 275
  location services, 171
  tech support, 307
  voice mail, 91–93
  voice mail phone number, 92
  voice-mail system commands, 93
VGA setting (video quality), 189
Vibration mode
  activating, 36
  adjusting, 291
  and battery performance, 300
video. *See also* photo album
  playing back, 194
  recording, 187–189
  renting movies, 230–231
  setting quality, 189–190
  sharing, 202–204
  uploading to YouTube, 204
  Video Message mode, 190–191
  viewing, 228–229
Video Message, 190–191
Videos app, 230

viruses
  avoiding, 329
  and text messaging, 124
Visual Voice Mail, 92–94
Voice app, 96
voice input
  activating, 52
  censor feature, 64
  commands, 63–64
  dictating to phone, 62–63
voice mail
  carrier, 91–93
  Google Voice, 94–97
  retrieving messages, 92–94, 96–97
  sending calls to, 84, 86–87
  Visual, 93–94
voice navigation, 177–178
Voice Recorder app, 329
volume
  incoming call signal, 77–78
  ringer, 292
  setting, 18, 36
volume (storage), 267
volume control
  location of, 15, 17
  music, 209

• W •

waking phone
  methods of, 26
  with sliding keyboard, 17
wallpaper
  from Android Market, 235
  changing, 282–283
  live wallpaper feature, 40
  setting image for, 201–202
Warhol, Andy, 228
warning icon, 5
warranty, 10
web-based e-mail accounts, 128–129
web browsing
  bookmarks, 146–148
  changing appearance, 153
  downloading, 150–152

web browsing *(continued)*
  getting to web pages, 144–145
  managing multiple windows, 148
  moving back and forward, 146
  overview, 143–144
  privacy and security options, 153–154
  searching, 148–149
  selecting links, 145
web pages
  changing appearance, 153
  getting to, 144–145
  home, 144–145, 152–153
  reloading, 145
  selecting links, 145
  sharing, 149–150
  stop loading, 145
  switching between, 148
  text selection on, 61
  viewing, 144
Week view (Calendar), 218–220
What's Nearby command (Maps app), 173
Wi-Fi
  accessing, 250–251
  activating, 249
  Android Market downloading, 234
  location information, 171
  power consumed by, 321
  turning off, 300
  understanding, 248
  for web browsing, 143
  when roaming, 272
Wi-Fi radio, 249
widgets. *See also specific widgets*
  adding, 285
  from Android Market, 235
  Home screen, 39
  rearranging and removing, 286–287
  using, 45
window mount, 19

Windows Media Player
  synchronizing music with, 209–211
  and Windows Media Sync USB option, 261
Windows Media Sync option (USB
    connection), 261
wireless connection. *See also* Bluetooth;
    Wi-Fi
  in airplanes, 274
  creating mobile hotspot, 252
  digital network, 248
  overview, 247
  printing, 255–258
  sharing, 251–253
  tethering feature, 251, 253

Yahoo! Mail
  and Email app, 128
  New Mail notification icon, 131
YouTube
  sharing option, 203
  uploading video to, 204
  viewing videos on, 228–229
YouTube app
  sharing option for, 204
  viewing videos with, 228–229

Zedge app
  about, 329
  ringtones from, 89
  wallpaper features of, 283
zoom function, 17
  Camera app, 183
  Maps app, 169, 175
  video recording, 188

Apple & Macs

iPad For Dummies
978-0-470-58027-1

iPhone For Dummies,
4th Edition
978-0-470-87870-5

MacBook For Dummies, 3rd
Edition
978-0-470-76918-8

Mac OS X Snow Leopard For
Dummies
978-0-470-43543-4

Business

Bookkeeping For Dummies
978-0-7645-9848-7

Job Interviews
For Dummies,
3rd Edition
978-0-470-17748-8

Resumes For Dummies,
5th Edition
978-0-470-08037-5

Starting an
Online Business
For Dummies,
6th Edition
978-0-470-60210-2

Stock Investing
For Dummies,
3rd Edition
978-0-470-40114-9

Successful
Time Management
For Dummies
978-0-470-29034-7

Computer Hardware

BlackBerry
For Dummies,
4th Edition
978-0-470-60700-8

Computers For Seniors
For Dummies,
2nd Edition
978-0-470-53483-0

PCs For Dummies, Windows
7 Edition
978-0-470-46542-4

Laptops For Dummies,
4th Edition
978-0-470-57829-2

Cooking & Entertaining

Cooking Basics
For Dummies,
3rd Edition
978-0-7645-7206-7

Wine For Dummies,
4th Edition
978-0-470-04579-4

Diet & Nutrition

Dieting For Dummies,
2nd Edition
978-0-7645-4149-0

Nutrition For Dummies,
4th Edition
978-0-471-79868-2

Weight Training
For Dummies,
3rd Edition
978-0-471-76845-6

Digital Photography

Digital SLR Cameras &
Photography For Dummies,
3rd Edition
978-0-470-46606-3

Photoshop Elements 8
For Dummies
978-0-470-52967-6

Gardening

Gardening Basics
For Dummies
978-0-470-03749-2

Organic Gardening
For Dummies,
2nd Edition
978-0-470-43067-5

Green/Sustainable

Raising Chickens
For Dummies
978-0-470-46544-8

Green Cleaning
For Dummies
978-0-470-39106-8

Health

Diabetes For Dummies,
3rd Edition
978-0-470-27086-8

Food Allergies
For Dummies
978-0-470-09584-3

Living Gluten-Free
For Dummies,
2nd Edition
978-0-470-58589-4

Hobbies/General

Chess For Dummies,
2nd Edition
978-0-7645-8404-6

Drawing
Cartoons & Comics
For Dummies
978-0-470-42683-8

Knitting For Dummies,
2nd Edition
978-0-470-28747-7

Organizing
For Dummies
978-0-7645-5300-4

Su Doku For Dummies
978-0-470-01892-7

Home Improvement

Home Maintenance
For Dummies,
2nd Edition
978-0-470-43063-7

Home Theater
For Dummies,
3rd Edition
978-0-470-41189-6

Living the
Country Lifestyle
All-in-One
For Dummies
978-0-470-43061-3

Solar Power Your Home
For Dummies,
2nd Edition
978-0-470-59678-4

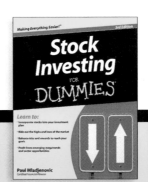

Available wherever books are sold. For more information or to order direct: U.S. customers visit www.dummies.com or call 1-877-762-2974.
U.K. customers visit www.wileyeurope.com or call (0) 1243 843291. Canadian customers visit www.wiley.ca or call 1-800-567-4797.

Internet

Blogging For Dummies,
3rd Edition
978-0-470-61996-4

eBay For Dummies,
6th Edition
978-0-470-49741-8

Facebook For Dummies, 3rd
Edition
978-0-470-87804-0

Web Marketing
For Dummies,
2nd Edition
978-0-470-37181-7

WordPress
For Dummies,
3rd Edition
978-0-470-59274-8

Language & Foreign
Language

French For Dummies
978-0-7645-5193-2

Italian Phrases
For Dummies
978-0-7645-7203-6

Spanish For Dummies,
2nd Edition
978-0-470-87855-2

Spanish For Dummies,
Audio Set
978-0-470-09585-0

Math & Science

Algebra I For Dummies,
2nd Edition
978-0-470-55964-2

Biology For Dummies,
2nd Edition
978-0-470-59875-7

Calculus For Dummies
978-0-7645-2498-1

Chemistry For Dummies
978-0-7645-5430-8

Microsoft Office

Excel 2010 For Dummies
978-0-470-48953-6

Office 2010 All-in-One
For Dummies
978-0-470-49748-7

Office 2010 For Dummies,
Book + DVD Bundle
978-0-470-62698-6

Word 2010 For Dummies
978-0-470-48772-3

Music

Guitar For Dummies,
2nd Edition
978-0-7645-9904-0

iPod & iTunes
For Dummies,
8th Edition
978-0-470-87871-2

Piano Exercises
For Dummies
978-0-470-38765-8

Parenting & Education

Parenting For Dummies,
2nd Edition
978-0-7645-5418-6

Type 1 Diabetes
For Dummies
978-0-470-17811-9

Pets

Cats For Dummies,
2nd Edition
978-0-7645-5275-5

Dog Training For Dummies,
3rd Edition
978-0-470-60029-0

Puppies For Dummies,
2nd Edition
978-0-470-03717-1

Religion & Inspiration

The Bible For Dummies
978-0-7645-5296-0

Catholicism For Dummies
978-0-7645-5391-2

Women in the Bible
For Dummies
978-0-7645-8475-6

Self-Help & Relationship

Anger Management
For Dummies
978-0-470-03715-7

Overcoming Anxiety
For Dummies,
2nd Edition
978-0-470-57441-6

Sports

Baseball
For Dummies,
3rd Edition
978-0-7645-7537-2

Basketball
For Dummies,
2nd Edition
978-0-7645-5248-9

Golf For Dummies,
3rd Edition
978-0-471-76871-5

Web Development

Web Design
All-in-One
For Dummies
978-0-470-41796-6

Web Sites
Do-It-Yourself
For Dummies,
2nd Edition
978-0-470-56520-9

Windows 7

Windows 7
For Dummies
978-0-470-49743-2

Windows 7
For Dummies,
Book + DVD Bundle
978-0-470-52398-8

Windows 7 All-in-One
For Dummies
978-0-470-48763-1

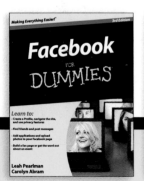
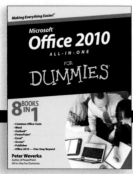
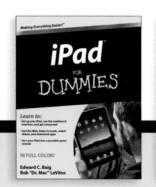
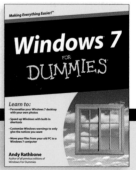

Available wherever books are sold. For more information or to order direct: U.S. customers visit www.dummies.com or call 1-877-762-2974.
U.K. customers visit www.wileyeurope.com or call (0) 1243 843291. Canadian customers visit www.wiley.ca or call 1-800-567-4797.